REGGIE

REGGIE

THE AUTOBIOGRAPHY

Reggie Jackson

with Mike Lupica

VILLARD BOOKS　NEW YORK　1984

LIBRARY OF CONGRESS CATALOGING IN PUBLICATION DATA
Jackson, Reggie.
  Reggie.
  1. Jackson, Reggie. 2. Baseball players—United
States—Biography. I. Lupica, Mike. II. Title.
GV865.J32A36 1984   796.357′092′4 [B]   83-50863
ISBN 0-394-53243-0

Manufactured in the United States of America
Designed by Beth Tondreau
9 8 7 6 5 4 3 2
First Edition

To My Dad
Martinez Clarence Jackson

I'd also like to dedicate this book to
Gary Walker, Everett Moss,
Matt Merola and Steven Kay.

And my biggest supporter of all . . . God.

I'd like to thank and acknowledge, for all their help, Mike Lupica and Peter Gethers. I'd also like to thank Gary Walker, Steven Kay and Bill Bertucio.

CONTENTS

REGGIE

PROLOGUE

I t was April 27, 1982, and to tell you the truth, I didn't feel much like Mr. October.

After five years with the New York Yankees, after all the home runs, the fighting with George, the fighting with Billy, after the whole crazy story with me right in the middle of it all the time, I was coming back to Yankee Stadium and No. 44 was on the back of an Angels uniform. The problem was I needed a home run, and I didn't know if I could hit one. After all the nights I had come to the Stadium carrying my black bat like it was a .44 magnum, it felt like a cap pistol now. A pea shooter. All in all, I figured it was a hell of a situation for Reginald Martinez Jackson to be in.

There was one thing I was always supposed to be able to do: Rise to the occasion. Rise to it, and rise above it. And I've always done that, maybe better than anyone, at least during my generation in the big leagues. I'll admit that I've always had trouble in meaningless situations. Maybe I should have been a better ballplayer than I was, and maybe that was the reason. But if you put the meat in the seats and made the game count, if you put me in a situation where the money was on the table, then I wanted to play.

People knocked me down, and I got up and hit home runs. I got beaned one year in Baltimore, took one right in the face. That's one thing you never get used to, getting hit like that. The lights go out; there's always that terrible moment, the terrible sound of ball hitting helmet and skull. But you've got to put it out of your mind and come back. I sat out five days that time in Baltimore, and my first time up when I came back, I hit a home run. When I came back to the dugout after the home run, Terry Crowley was waiting for me. He was an Oriole teammate that season. Crowley just put out his hand and said, "That's why you are who you are."

That's who I always thought Reggie was, too.

I hit four home runs on four consecutive swings in the World Series in 1977, three in that last game. Billy Martin benched me for the fifth and deciding game of the '77 playoffs against the Royals in Kansas City. I got into the game late anyway and pinchhit a single. We won the game. George Steinbrenner and Bob Lemon kept me out of the third game of the '81 World Series. The Yankees had won the first two games without me. I'm fairly certain Steinbrenner had already made up his mind to let me go, so he wanted to sweep the Dodgers without me. The Yankees lost the third game. When they finally let me play on Saturday and Sunday, I went three for three—a home run and two singles—and walked twice. Getting on base five times in a row in one game set a Series record. But I also dropped a fly ball for an error. The sun was blinding and, to tell the truth, I don't think the official scorer would have charged me with an error if my name didn't happen to be Reggie Jackson.

Things like that have happened a lot, especially in October.

I never really said I was "the straw that stirs the drink." That became a famous quote from a famous story about me in *Sport* magazine. I'll tell you about the story and the writer later. But the nickname stuck. Reggie, the straw that stirs the drink. I never did like it, but I have to admit there was some validity to the idea I was trying to get across to the writer. If the other ingredients were there for a good drink and if the mix was just about right, I could make the difference if I could hit enough dingers.

That's what I call home runs. Dingers. I've hit a bunch of them when it mattered, in Oakland and Baltimore and New York and now in California. I guess that's why the late Thurman Munson started calling me Mr. October. That was a nickname I liked.

I have to admit, my mind does wander when the big situation isn't there. I lose interest in lopsided games and meaningless situations. I don't like to be hassled, and I don't like to be quiet or diplomatic or to play the social games. Most of the controversial stuff that happened in New York I wish had never happened. I could have done so much more for the Yankees—on the field—if it hadn't. No excuse. Just fact. But when a game or a season hangs in the balance and I understand the task, I will get with the program. 1 won't pick up my bats and glove and go home. Or run and hide. I'll do what Cool Hand Luke said: I'll get my mind right. I call those times *Reggie Situations.* Those are the ones that have always stoked my fire. When the money's there and everyone is watching, I want to run the table.

Now it was April 1982. I had signed with the Angels as a free agent after George Steinbrenner didn't think I could play anymore. I was happy to be back home in California. I always wanted to wind up my career in California. But after the first month or so of the season, I was making Steinbrenner look pretty smart. I was hitting .173 when I came into Yankee Stadium. I had no home runs. On the plane to New York, I sat next to Rick Burleson, our shortstop and a hell of a player. I once told Rick that I would like to think of myself as the type of player I think he is—an all-out, hard-nosed SOB. Anyway, on the plane, I was joking around with Burleson. I told him that I was really glad finally to be playing on the same team with him after all those years when he was with the Red Sox and I was with the Yankees. Burleson asked why.

I said, "'Cause you're the only player on this team with a lower batting average than mine." Burleson was hitting a cool .161 at the time.

It had been an April of cap pistols and pea shooters.

I was coming back to the Stadium. For five years, we had put on the greatest baseball show on earth there. Perhaps the greatest sports show, period. There had been two world championships, three pennants, four divisional titles. Some of it had been good, some of it had been bad, a lot of it had been just plain ludicrous. There had never been a show quite like it, and I had been the catalyst somehow, the lightning rod, the center of the storms. Now I was coming back, and one more time I had a lot to prove. To my ex-teammates, who'd be looking at me from the dugout across the way. To the Yankee fans in the stands. To the owner up in his private box. To my own teammates, who were probably starting to wonder what this Reggie fuss was all about.

Mostly to myself. It had always been this way, no matter what I've done and where I've gone. One more battle. One more war. One more swing. Can he still do it? Can Reggie still produce? Funny thing—I was asking myself those very same questions. I figured that if I couldn't hit one out in this type of situation—a Reggie Situation if there ever was one—then maybe I couldn't do it anymore.

I had been pointing to April 27 for a long time, practically since I signed with the Angels. In February, I was working as a commentator for ABC Sports on their "Superstars" show in Key Biscayne, Florida. A writer from New York, Phil Pepe of the *Daily News,* came down and asked me if I'd thought about my first time back to New York as an Angel.

I said, "Not really." But I had. I'd been playing it down, not saying very much about it. But I'd thought about it a great deal. In a way, my season was going to be starting there, one way or another. For better or worse. Richer or poorer. And I really was ambivalent. My emotions were all mixed up. I didn't know whether to be scared or happy or joyous or uncomfortable. I had left on a bad note. We'd lost the World Series to the Dodgers. Steinbrenner said I couldn't play, that I'd asked him for a long-term contract and he couldn't commit to one because I was getting old. I was supposed to be a negative.

A cancer.

I always thought his views about my contract demands were sort of amusing since we never had one contract talk in all the months leading up to my free agency, or even after that. He would say he offered me three years and I asked for four. Well, he never made me an offer of any kind, so I had nothing at all against which to make a counteroffer. Maybe he is a mind reader.

So I wanted to go back and play against the Yankees, and I didn't want to. As we got closer and closer to the trip East, that was all anyone wanted to ask me about. Have you thought about going back? What do you think it will be like? I kept playing it down. But you're damn right I was thinking about it. And trying to be like Cool Hand Luke. Getting my mind right. Because on top of everything else, Ron Guidry was going to be pitching against us.

I'd always been proud to play with Guidry. I've called him the truest Yankee, because he was one of the few who had come all the way up through their system and seemed to *belong* in pinstripes. Guidry never bitched. He always just said, "Gimme the ball." Now he was on the other side. He'd come after me with left-handed sliders and fastballs, and I wanted to take him deep.

I thought: It would have to be Guidry.

The afternoon before the game was hectic. Two press conferences. One was for the Pony shoe company. There was another one later at the Stadium to make it easier for the writers since everyone was going to want to talk to me. I didn't mind doing the press conferences. I could always deal with the press. But throughout the whole day, what I mostly was was afraid. I was at .173. I was struggling. I wasn't Reggie. Those were the thoughts I couldn't get out of my mind.

I finally got out to the Stadium about two o'clock in the afternoon and hit for about forty-five minutes. In the middle of it, I started to feel decent. Not great. Decent. I was going to be in the other clubhouse and the other dugout, but I was in a familiar ballpark. It will always be The House That Ruth Built, but I had my times there. Ruth may have built it, but I managed to put some jazz in there. I began to hit some shots into the right-center-field bleachers. Then I hit some into the black—the seats they don't sell, the ones in dead center that they paint black to give the hitter a better background. I felt comfortable. Bobby Knoop, one of our coaches, was pitching to me. Unfortunately, I was aware that hitting against Bobby Knoop was not hitting against Ron Guidry.

Gene Mauch was our manager. Gene liked to play all right-handed hitters against Guidry. He played things by the book, too much sometimes. But he came over to me after I finished hitting and just said, "I know you have to be in there tonight."

I said, "Gene, I don't have any business in the world being in there tonight against Guidry the way I've been going. But, yeah, I got to be there."

After that afternoon practice it was idle time. I was sitting in the clubhouse around three-thirty, basically alone. The players don't have to arrive until five-thirty or six for a night game. While I was sitting and thinking—mostly about Guidry—Maury Allen, a writer from the *New York Post,* came by for a chat. Allen said, "Reggie, I was just over in the Yankee clubhouse. Everybody is talking about what it's like for you to be back in Yankee Stadium, what it's going to be like for the Yankees to be facing you."

I told him that was natural, considering the history of everything.

Then Allen told me he'd asked Guidry about facing me and that Guidry had said, "Go ask Reggie what it's going to be like facing *me.*"

I took that comment to be a bit condescending. Granted, I was defensive, probably looking for something to give me an extra edge. So I felt a little slighted because I'd always been such a Guidry fan. I consider him a friend to this day. Later on, I was sure Allen misrepresented Guidry a little because after the game, after I'd done what I did, Guidry got into trouble with Steinbrenner for saying, "It was the only fun I had all night." But I was glad Allen came by. I was able to get mad at Guidry for a couple of hours.

When I got back onto the field for batting practice, I still felt good at the plate. I hit more balls into the seats and got a nice reaction from the crowd that had showed up early, and the media and my old teammates. I needed that support. I was still insecure —I couldn't get .173 out of my mind—but I was starting to relax. Willie Randolph, the tough little second baseman who I feel Steinbrenner turned sullen because he never showed him enough appreciation, came over and shook my hand. And Dave Winfield, the Twenty-five Million Dollar Man—a big man, big smile— Steinbrenner's stud apparent, who was supposed to take my place but wouldn't, couldn't ever quite take my place. He was, however, carving out Dave Winfield's place. And Rick Cerone, the feisty catcher. How feisty? He told George to fuck off to his face one time. Is that feisty enough for you? And Tommy John came by, a friend who'd been a classy Christian gentleman every day of his career. I was on the wrong side of the field, but they seemed glad to see me. Which is the way it should have been. We'd been through wars together. In a way it was like a little reunion.

Right before the game, I was running in the outfield, and Guidry came out of the bullpen like he always does, walking slowly, his left arm in his jacket. I thought, "Uh-oh. Here comes that SOB with his slider and his fastball, and I ain't got my guns loaded."

When I came to the plate the first time, there was a lot of noise, the old symphony of cheers and applause and some boos. But most of it was warm. Suddenly they were chanting, "REG-gie! REG-gie," just like always. I heard it, and I felt glad that they remembered, but all I was thinking was, "How am I going to hit this man's slider?"

He threw me a slider that first time up, and I popped out. Still I felt I made a pretty good pass at it. I got back to the dugout, and Gene Mauch said, "You just missed that one, you know." I knew I had a good pass. Next time up I pulled off a little bit, but managed to get a single up the middle. As I stood there on first base, I could feel the blood pumping. I was off and running.

I walked after that. By the time I got up in the seventh, it was drizzling steadily. The score was 2–1 in our favor. I felt ready. I was comfortable, and the fans were making me feel more welcome every time I came to the plate. I could feel them rooting for me. Rooting for a dinger. Guidry hung a slider and I just exploded all over it. I mean, it was *kissed*. The ball ended up hitting the facing of the upper deck and damn near bounced back to Randolph at second base. As I rounded the bases, I remember watching Ken Griffey picking the ball up in short right and throwing it back in. The Stadium went crazy. I felt like a dam at Niagara Falls had burst —for me, for the fans, even for the Yankees. I knew the Yankees felt good for me. They had seen me do it before. Now they were seeing me do it at a time when they knew I needed to do it.

Now the chant really went up.

"REG-gie! REG-gie!"

This was a sound, a stadium, I knew. I had been here before.

I got back into the dugout, and the Angels mobbed me. And then it happened.

All the fans in the lower part of the stands turned and looked up at Steinbrenner's box near the press box, and they all started pointing. And chanting.

"Steinbrenner sucks! Steinbrenner sucks!"

They were telling him, finally, what they thought about him letting me go away. It went on and on, and after a while even I felt uncomfortable for him. I sat there and wondered how many people would have been in his ballpark shouting at him that way if it wasn't raining. There were 35,000 as it was.

"Steinbrenner sucks! Steinbrenner sucks!"

It was like a celebration for me, a funeral dirge for him. It stopped finally, and our half-inning ended. Mauch told me he was going to replace me in the outfield. That disappointed me a little bit. I was so full of energy. I had delivered, run the table and helped get us a win on a night when I so desperately needed to do those things. I think Gene took me out because he was afraid that if I showed up on the field again, the chant about Steinbrenner would start up again. Gene is the type of man who is embarrassed by that sort of thing. He's extremely decent. So I stayed in the dugout. Before Bobby Grich went back on the field, he grabbed my hand and said, "Only Reggie."

Only Reggie. I was in no mood to disagree with him. I wasn't scared anymore.

After the game, it was like a World Series in our clubhouse. The press was everyplace. One of the clubhouse men fought his way through the crowd in front of my locker and told me that Gene Autry, our owner, was calling from California. The Cowboy does things like that.

"I knew you'd hit one out when you got back there, big guy," Autry said. "The only thing I'm mad about is that I couldn't see it here on television."

I thanked him for calling and told him not to worry. He was going to see a lot more home runs before the year was out. And he would. There'd be thirty-nine in all and a share of the American League home-run title with Gorman Thomas.

The call from the Cowboy meant a lot. Let's just say that I hadn't exactly been in the habit of getting calls like that from my owner, at least not in my last years with the New York Yankees.

I was one of the last people to leave our clubhouse. Somebody told me it was still raining pretty hard, and I really wasn't in too big a hurry to let the night end. I'd go over to the Yankee clubhouse the next day for a real visit, but this one was mine. A few hours before I'd felt like a junkyard dog hunting for a bone, and now it was like old times at the Stadium, sitting around with writers and talking about a big dinger.

When I'd showered and dressed, I walked through the tunnel toward the front gate. Matt Merola, my agent, was with me, and Bill Bertucio, who's one of my best friends. The lobby was full of people waiting for me, and through the door I could see people still lined up against the police barricades, waiting in the rain, chanting REG-gie.

Something odd happened then. Something I would think was sad when I thought about it afterward. Bill Bertucio saw it.

We were still in the lobby, and I was talking to some of the security cops. Behind me, the elevator door opened, and there was Steinbrenner.

Only he wouldn't come out of the elevator.

He just let the door shut and let the elevator go back up.

I didn't think anything of it. I mean, he could have forgotten something and had to go back and get it. I was still in no hurry. It was raining harder now, so I kept chatting, shaking hands.

After a few minutes, the elevator door opened again. Steinbrenner saw that I was still there. He let it close again.

Amazing.

After all we'd been through, whether we were together or at odds, he couldn't come over and say, "Hi, big guy, how you doing? Hey, Jack, sorry it didn't work out between us. But you got me again, you sonofabitch, didn't you? Figured you'd do something like this, hit a home run on me tonight." He couldn't come over and shake my hand. I would've respected him more if he just walked by me with his head up and ignored me.

I'd done all that crashing and bashing for the man. I'd given him all that publicity. Back page of the *Daily News*. Front page of the *Post*. There's this radio station in New York, WINS, an all-news channel. Their slogan is "You give us twenty-two minutes, we'll give you the world." Well, there was a time in New York City, New York, when every twenty-two minutes they'd be talking about George and Reggie and the Yankees.

Reggie did this last night. George said that. I'm talking about *every day*. We had notoriety. I used to have a piece of adhesive tape over my locker, and on it I'd written "Badlands Territory," and not without good reason. But the bottom line on the publicity was pluses for everybody involved, all the way up and down the damn organization. I might add right here that George and I also made a whole lot of money in the process.

Here was the night when the process seemed to come full circle: the last chapter for the two of us was an elevator door opening and George not being able to say a word to me.

After all the noise we'd made, it ended with that strange silence. I thought that was a shame. I always thought things could have been so much better for us.

It was something while it lasted, though, even when it wasn't all fun and games. There was always some ugly soap opera going on behind the scenes. There were too many times when I would want to turn my back on all the craziness and jump the first flight to California. Somehow I never did. I kept coming back to center stage. There were the three home runs against the Dodgers. There was that World Series game the next year when I stuck out a hip and got hit by a throw to help win a game against the Dodgers; they said it was the first Sacrifice Thigh in the history of the Series. There was that scene with Billy in the dugout at Fenway Park. It was on national television, of course. There was the night I got suspended for bunting against the Royals when I wasn't supposed to bunt. I wanted them to send me away from the Yankees for good on that one, and they nearly did.

There were candy bars and champagne.

They chanted "REG-gie!" for me. They booed me hard. Someone fired a shot at me one night on Third Avenue. Graig Nettles threw a punch at me at a party in Oakland after we won the pennant in '81. That was my fault, or so I heard. Steinbrenner told me I was disgracing the Yankees again.

Why this book? Why now? The reasons are—like most things in my life—both complicated and simple. When I walk down the street, people talk to me. When I pass through a hotel lobby, I'll hear men, women and children call my name. Wherever I go, strangers ask me questions, make fairly personal comments. The thing about all these public and fleeting "friendships" is that these people assume some sort of intimacy. They think they know me.

They *think* they know me.

They don't, of course. They know *parts* of me, the parts I've revealed publicly or the parts that have been revealed by others. They assume things, sometimes correctly, usually incorrectly. I think it's sad actually, this false intimacy. Why people insist on it, I really don't know. Perhaps it's simply a logical extension of all the media hype that's part of being a twentieth-century celebrity. Television brings me into people's living rooms; maybe some of these people think I've actually *been* in their living rooms. It's something I have to deal with all the time. Now, with this book, I can reveal a bit of myself as I feel it should be revealed—truthfully, in depth, in context. It's time to set the story straight, to clear up some of the illusions, to show the stranger in the hotel lobby that I am not just an autograph-signing machine or a distant image on a TV screen.

Recently, I was in the lobby of a Miami hotel, the Fountainbleu, taping a "Superstar" show. As I was heading for the elevator, a teenager asked for my autograph. I gave it to him, then as I was walking away, he reached for one of those *intimate* moments. "I hate Steinbrenner, too," he said.

As I rode up the elevator, I thought, There's someone who thinks he knows me, who certainly thinks he knows how I feel, how I think. Of course, he was wrong. I don't hate George Steinbrenner. There were a few years when we were pretty close friends. There was a stretch when I was bitter about some of the things he did. Our relationship soured, sure, but *hate?* Uh-uh. I don't really hate anyone. I hated some of the things Billy Martin *did,* especially to me, but that's different from hating the man. Anyway, I hope that teenage kid reads this book.

I am going to tell about all of it as best I can remember. I am going to tell about the Oakland years, about Charlie Finley, about playing a season for Earl Weaver. I have never lacked interesting costars. Steinbrenner and Martin. Finley and Weaver. I even played football for Frank Kush.

There was even a night when I flew in a plane that Thurmon Munson was piloting, a night that probably should have given me a hint as to the tragic way he would die.

It has not been dull. There has been more winning than losing. Since 1968, I have not been on a ballclub that has finished lower than second in its division, except for the '79 Yankees and the '83 Angels. Teams on which I've played have been in the playoffs eleven times. There have been six World Series teams. We won three in Oakland and two in New York. I will always think we could have won another one in New York if Steinbrenner and Lemon hadn't kept me on the bench against Fernando Valenzuela in Game Three in '81. It is sort of interesting, as someone once said, how good teams have this way of following Reggie around.

It has been some ride from Wyncote, Pennsylvania, where it all started. I have been grateful for my celebrity, and celebrity has embraced me most of my adult life, but I have never returned the embrace with quite the same feeling. I can be completely comfortable in front of 50,000 screaming people with a baseball game that needs to be won. But I've never been at my ease in any crowd away from a baseball stadium. I'm a loner. I've always been apart. Because of that, some people think I'm cold and rude or even mean. Some have chosen to idolize me without knowing me at all.

I'm not just a baseball player. I'm a person. I'm a businessman, and I think a pretty good one. I take a great deal of satisfaction in the fact that I can hold my own in a business conversation with such giants as Marvin Davis and Edward Bennett Williams. I'm a collector of cars; if the truth be known, cars are probably my single greatest passion in life. (No, not true. My greatest passion is my desire for a successful and loving family. But as far as possessions go, I put great value on my car collection.) I'm confident of my abilities as a television commentator. I can be comfortable talking to the president of the United States and equally comfortable gabbing with a bunch of rednecks. I've known some women. I've had some unsuccessful relationships, but some great ones as well.

They call me Mr. October, but I've got to tell you something: The other months of the year have not exactly been uneventful.

If people want to think of me as the straw that has stirred the drinks, that's fine. But they ought to know that somebody was always buying another round wherever I've been.

1
WYNCOTE: MARTINEZ'S SON

I wasn't exactly brought up in one of those Norman Rockwell paintings you used to see on the cover of the *Saturday Evening Post.*

I was a black kid with Spanish, Indian, and Irish blood who lived in a white, Jewish suburb of Philadelphia called Wyncote. I was the product of a broken home—my mom and dad separated when I was six. She took three of her own four children with her.

I was the one who stayed behind.

I grew up poor, living upstairs over my dad's dry cleaning and tailor shop. My father was incarcerated for bootlegging corn liquor he made in our basement when I was a senior in high school, leaving me to run the shop, go to school, and get about the business of being a good enough athlete so that I could get a scholarship to college and just *be* somebody. My brother James helped me quite a bit my senior year, giving me money when I really needed it and lending me some of his clothes.

I was pretty hot as an athlete, playing baseball, basketball, football and track. Running the shop was the tough part.

However to this day, if I had to put a pocket on a pair of slacks, or put cuffs on them, I could do it. And make a pretty good living at it.

I learned a lot about dry cleaning, sewing and mending at 149 Greenwood Avenue, a two-story house set in between an Atlantic gas station on one side and the Glicklers' house on the other. I learned more about taking care of myself, showing initiative, being a man as well as a boy.

See, Martinez Clarence Jackson wouldn't have it any other way.

I remember a time when I was eight years old and my dad sent me out to the drugstore to buy him some Neapolitan ice cream. He always loved Neapolitan. Gave me a quarter, just like always, because that's what a pint of Neapolitan cost in the early '50s.

I took the quarter and ran. I ran everywhere as a kid, especially when I was running an errand for my dad. I got to the drugstore and found they were out of Neapolitan. I was eight, remember. All of a sudden, the ice cream was the most important thing in the world, because I hated ever telling Dad I couldn't get a job done for him.

I did something fairly sharp for an eight-year-old then.

I ran across the street to the Mobil gas station on the corner of Greenwood and Glenside avenues. A friend of my dad's, Bob Bradshaw, owned it. I went into his office, out of breath, and asked if I could borrow fifty cents.

"What's the emergency, Reggie?" he asked.

I babbled something quickly about the ice cream, and how I had to buy more for my dad than I thought, and how I'd pay him back.

Bob Bradshaw gave me the money. I went back to the drugstore. I used the extra fifty cents to buy a pint of vanilla, a pint of chocolate, and a pint of strawberry.

The free enterprise system at work (I've always had a flair for good business): Instant Neapolitan.

I hustled back home with the three pints of ice cream and set them on the kitchen table. My dad just smiled this great smile— an understanding smile—and asked me how I'd managed.

"You owe Bob Bradshaw fifty cents," I said, chest still pounding pretty good.

He reached into his pocket, gave me the money and said,

"Now git." I did, running back to the Mobile station, feeling like a million bucks instead of fifty cents every step of the way. I'd learned how to get the job done—which became something of a trademark with me later on.

When you achieve any kind of fame, you get asked this question a lot: "Did you know as a kid you were special?"

With me, they mean as a baseball player. Well, first of all, I always thought of myself as being a better football player than baseball player, right up until the time I got a football scholarship to Arizona State. So I never thought of myself as being blessed in any way as a baseball player growing up in Wyncote.

I just thought I was special because I was my dad's son.

To this day, my father is almost a mythical figure to me. Throughout my life, I've picked up bits and pieces about what a colorful character he was long before I was born. But I'm sure I'll never know all of it. He told the stories and I listened, but I never asked for them. I was just grateful when the stories came along. In my growing up years, I always had the sense that I could live to be 200 and never lead a life quite as interesting as my dad's. Maybe it happens that way a lot. Maybe you're lucky if you've got a father who always seemed tougher and quicker on his feet than you could ever be. Or would have to be.

He was a smiling, banty rooster of a man whose limp (because of a war injury) always reminded me more of a strut. He's a light-skinned black man who never showed any embarrassment or bitterness about being black. He almost looks Italian.

Martinez, the son of a black father and a Spanish mother, grew up in New Jersey. He did a little bit of everything as a kid, working as a tailor's apprentice and delivering groceries. He was a pretty fair ballplayer himself and even played for the Newark Eagles, one of the barnstorming Negro teams in the '20s and '30s. I can remember stories he used to tell about all the great players of those days, guys like Josh Gibson, Satchel Paige and Zach Clayton, and how romantic he made the life sound, how they all just got along by moving in an old bus from place to place, taking games wherever they could find them. He made five dollars a game. He also made some extra money driving the team bus.

"You've always got to show initiative, Reggie," he'd tell me.

"You've got to have ambition. Or you won't amount to a hill of beans."

To this day I'm an early riser. That comes from Dad always saying, "Off and on," meaning: "Off your ass and on the deck." He didn't like us lying around; we had to be productive.

I'd find out later that one of the ways he got by when things were desperate in the '30s was making bootleg whiskey. Even by the time I came around, he had that still in the basement.

Martinez made *fine* corn liquor. When I wasn't picking up spending money with the cleaning and the sewing, I was earning ten dollars a day helping to operate that old still downstairs.

During World War II, he flew with the Air Force, coming back home with a Purple Heart—having been injured over North Africa—and a hip that wouldn't be right the rest of his life (I finally convinced him to have an artificial hip put in in his early seventies). My father would walk with pain after the war, but I never heard him complain, and I never saw that it slowed him down any. Wasn't his way. Wasn't his idea of how a man should act.

Later on in my life, much later on, when things would look dark with either Charles O. Finley or George M. Steinbrenner or Alfred Manuel Martin, it was always my dad who said, "You don't whine and you don't complain. You just go out and play the best you can. Do your job. Earn the money they're paying you." When I would be feeling sorry for myself, it was my dad who could snap me out of it. Because I believed in his wisdom and experience.

After the war, he and my mom got their life savings together and bought the two-story house on Greenwood Avenue. He did his tailoring and cleaning downstairs. She took care of the family, which lived upstairs. There was a dining room, a small kitchen, three bedrooms, a living room and a bathroom. That all served seven of us. There was my dad and my mom, Clara. My brother Clarence, who we called Joe, and my sister Dolores were from my dad's earlier marriage. Then there were the children my parents had together: Beverly, James (known as Slug), me, and my youngest sister, Tina. Before my parents split up, Tina lived with one of my aunts. There just wasn't room for one more at 149 Greenwood Avenue.

Other than the floor we lived on and the shop, the greatest possessions of the Jackson family were a 1948 Ford truck and a brand new 1950 Buick. The truck was for business. When my father bought it, it had "Bond Bakery" written on the side. He painted it green and had "Greenwood Avenue Cleaners" written on the side instead. It was in that truck that he made his deliveries every day of his life except Sundays, taking me with him a lot of the time. I think that my love of cars was born in that truck; my greatest thrills as a kid were sitting with my dad and riding around Wyncote. I couldn't imagine a more wonderful way to get around.

I remember spending a lot of time on our front porch, watching cars zoom by and trying to tell the year and the make of each one. I got pretty good. My dad loved cars. He always wanted a red Cadillac (eventually he got one). We always had five or six cars, worth fifty to a hundred bucks apiece, sitting around. They were usually broken and we'd have to fix one before we could use it. That really rubbed off because even today I like to fix cars and make them work right. Often, once it's fixed I'll lose interest in it. I like muscle cars, cars with power and speed. I also appreciate fine lines—a BMW, a Corvette, a Porsche, a Rolls-Royce. But my favorite cars are the 1955–1970 Chevrolet muscle cars. They lost their popularity—mostly due to the oil crunch and the rising cost of gasoline—but they still excite me, turn me on.

The thing about growing up poor is that you really don't have any sense that you are in fact growing up poor. It was just the way things *were*. I didn't know anything else. I was a Jackson, and my father worked real hard, and there were always meals on the table. Never any food in the fridge, though. There was no such thing as eating between meals, but we did always eat. What was brought home at night was what we had for dinner, and then I went to bed. We never ate breakfast except for special Saturdays and Sundays when Dad cooked. That experience was the only experience. Like with haircuts. My father had these old military clippers, and when my hair would get too long, he'd run those clippers over my head three or four times and that would be that until the next time. He didn't worry about it looking funny or weird. He just cut it to the scalp so he wouldn't have to be cutting it all the time.

For the longest time in my life, I didn't think it was any big deal to wear matching socks. I just wore any socks I could get hold of. If I found two that were clean, I wore them. Clean was the thing; Dad always demanded clean. I had three shirts that I wore to grade school on alternate days during the week. Had two pairs of slacks to go with them. One pair of shoes for the school year. I'd come home from school and hang up the school clothes the first thing. Biggest sin in the world was to get the school clothes dirty. If I did, there was no discussion, nothing to argue about. If there were any problems with the clothes, there was always an excellent chance that Martinez Jackson would be looking to give a lickin'.

Allowance? There was none. But if I helped downstairs with the cleaning and pressing, I could get up to a dollar a week.

The only way I could blow that money was if I got up late for school. That might not sound like the world's most exciting challenge, getting up on time and getting dressed and getting to grade school, but it was exciting around the Jackson home, especially after Mom left. There was no alarm clock. Alarm clock? What was that? The Hope Diamond? And there was no tug on the shoulder from Dad; he was already downstairs working by eight o'clock in the morning. You just *woke . . . up.* On time. Every day.

Or else!

I have no bitterness about those years. I suppose that's because my father so dominated my life and there simply was never a place for bitterness in his heart. That kind of attitude rubs off; it sticks. At least it did to me. I've had a lot of things happen to me in my time. I've put up with a lot of, well, shit. But I don't think I have any bitterness. Or anger. There's no point in anger or bitterness— that's the way I've always felt. That's the Martinez Jackson in me.

My dad could be tough; Lord, he was tough when he had to be. But he could always smile, no matter how hard the times were. There is a charm about my father he was just born with, a way he can smile at people and make them think they are the most important people he's ever met. He hasn't gone through life by the numbers, not by a long shot, but he has a gift for living I admire to this day.

Martinez: "Getting by is the trick, Reggie. Fun is something you have to earn."

What I mostly remember about the house on Greenwood was being cold. The Wyncote winters were so hard on us. You woke up in the morning, and the first thing you saw was your breath in front of your face. I'm not talking about ice *outside* the windows; I'm talking *inside.* We'd go into the kitchen when we got up, and the first thing we'd do was turn the oven on. Then we'd hang an Army blanket across the doorway to the kitchen, to close it off and not let any of the heat escape. I dressed in there. That was after I went through the morning ritual of heating water on the stove, then taking it into the bathroom, pouring it into the basin, and washing my face and hands.

A cooked breakfast? I didn't know anything at all about a cooked breakfast. To this day, if someone gets up and cooks me breakfast, I just feel like that's *high* cotton.

Again, there was nothing remarkable about this if you were growing up black in the 1950s in this country. My experience is no different from that of millions of others, and I'm sure it was a lot better than most. The lessons I took away from the upbringing I had were to appreciate what you had, value them, take care of them, *nurture* them. Later on, I'd wonder what a George Steinbrenner might have been like if he'd grown up the way I did. But I also never hated him because he was the first man to give me the kind of money for playing baseball that I never could have dreamt about when I was cold as hell in Wyncote.

I struck out in the first big World Series of my life.

I was thirteen at the time.

My team was the Greater Glenside Youth Club—GGYC— and every year the GGYC would play this big all-star series against a team from Fort Lauderdale, Florida. The Dixie Series. It was a big deal in Wyncote and Glenside. I was already the best baseball player in my neighborhood, hell, in *all* the neighborhoods in the area. I was also the only black player on the Greater Glenside Youth Club team.

The coach wouldn't let me play against the Florida kids in the Dixie Series because of my color.

It was the first time I'd ever come up against anything like that; the first time I ever realized that black was different, that black could be a problem. Then, it wasn't even called black . . . I was colored. In the '60s I was a Negro, and now in the '70s and '80s, I'm black. I bet you can't say you've been three types of people in one lifetime.

I'd grown up with white kids, I'd gone to school with them my whole life. I felt like they'd accepted me. I had black friends, but they lived in the black neighborhood in Wyncote, on Hilltop Lane. White kids were my experience. Dad had situated us in a predominantly white neighborhood because he did most of his cleaning business with white families whose fathers—doctors and lawyers mostly—went to work in Philadelphia proper every morning.

Again, that's the way things were. I didn't want them changed. I didn't know they *could* be changed.

All I knew was I couldn't play in the Dixie Series. It wasn't explained very well to me by the coach. An explanation wouldn't have made it any easier anyway. I was No. 18, and I was the best player on the team, but I sat. Dad tried to cushion it for me, explaining that this was something I was going to come up against in my world; that even though it had been worse in *his* world, it was never going to be perfect, not ever.

I didn't want to hear that.

I just didn't get it at all at age thirteen.

In the last game, the coach let me go up and pinchhit, and I wanted to hit a home run so bad I couldn't see straight. I just wanted to hit one over the wall so far and so high that it would never come down. I didn't want them to ever *find* that ball. It was the first time I had an emotion quite like that in a game; it was an emotion that would become my stock in trade in the big leagues.

I struck out on three pitches. Never swung the bat. So much for emotion.

Dad was there, and I just felt so ashamed after the game, ashamed that I had gotten that one chance and failed me, failed him, failed everybody. He asked me if I wanted to ride home with him in the truck. I told him I wanted to walk.

It was about three miles back to the house. You can't wear spikes to walk around on pavement so, as usual, I'd brought slippers to the game to wear home afterward. I took off my spikes and put on the slippers, tying the laces of the spikes together and slinging them over my shoulder. I carried my glove in my hand.

And I walked. Crying.

I walked on Glenside Avenue to Waverly Road, past a stream called the Creek, along a big bend on Waverly that we called Dead Man's Curve. Finally to Greenwood and home.

And every time I put a foot down, I'd say the same thing.

"I'm gonna be a major leaguer."

Left foot.

"Gonna be a major leaguer."

Right foot.

"Gonna be a major leaguer."

Three miles.

It may sound overly dramatic now, and silly. It may not have been important later on in my life. But it was awfully dramatic to me that day.

You don't forget days like that one.

Until the Dixie Series, being black hadn't been a problem in my life. In fact, it hadn't been something I'd thought much about at all. It wasn't a force—positive or negative. I didn't know anything about an expression like "token." I knew that the Jacksons were the only black family on Greenwood, but as far as I could see, we were treated well there. By people like the Glicklers and by Bob Bradshaw; the time he lent me the fifty cents wasn't the only time he loaned or gave me money. To us, he was Uncle Bob. A man named Bob Kelso ran the Wyncote Market across the street, and we had a charge account there—for up to $20—so that's where we bought the groceries. We felt as though we were part of the neighborhood, felt accepted.

Dad made sure we didn't violate any of our privileges with the neighbors, particularly the shopkeepers. One time when I was five or six, I went with my dad on his cleaning route. We finished delivering all the clothes around eight-thirty at night and then stopped into the Penn Fruit Store to buy groceries for that night's dinner. When the clerk wasn't looking, I stuck a candy bar—a Clark Bar—in my pocket, then, as casually as possible, followed my dad out of the store. Back in the truck, I pulled out the Clark Bar and started to bite into it. But as soon as I saw the expression on my dad's face, I knew I'd made a *big* mistake.

"Where'd you get that?" he asked.

I knew I'd already done one thing wrong by stealing the candy bar. I also knew my father. I instantly made a wise decision not to compound my stupidity, so I threw myself on the mercy of my father's court.

I confessed.

He grabbed me by the scruff of my neck and marched me right back into the store, with candy bar. I remember there were a lot of people there and they all seemed to be staring at us. Martinez didn't care. In front of everybody, he made me tell the storekeeper what I'd done. He made me apologize. They even went so far as to pretend that I'd be locked up in jail. Finally, of course, I was taken home.

I spent a lot of time working quietly in the shop that weekend. I was embarrassed and angry at myself, humiliated. I felt like I'd disgraced my dad, and that was something I'd hoped I'd never do. He never mentioned it again, maybe today he doesn't even remember this incident. But I still remember the look of disappointment in his eyes. I never stole another *anything*.

Stealing wasn't my dad's idea of showing initiative. He himself tap-danced around the law occasionally to make extra money for us—the still in the basement—but I didn't know there was anything wrong with having the still. Even if I had, I knew that his philosophy was "Do as I say, not as I do."

All kids have heard that one. But it really was that way around 149 Greenwood. For instance, the Jackson kids were taught to be well-spoken at all times. We were to be *ar-ti-cu-late.* Always. From as far back as I can remember, I worked hard on my diction so as to impress my dad. Because when I would slip, he'd be right there.

He'd ask a question and maybe I'd answer it with a "yeah."

"What did you say, boy?" he'd snap.

I knew what the answer was supposed to be.

"Yes sir."

I wouldn't make a "yeah" slip anytime soon after that.

Thinking back on all that is amusing now. The phrase "articulate black" makes me laugh; it has become something of a racist cliché. I'll be watching a football game or something on television, and the announcer will go to great lengths to describe what a "very . . . (pause, pause) . . . *articulate* young man" one of the black kids is. Funny. I never hear announcers describe white players as being articulate. The implication is clear: Gee, how refreshing to meet a black kid who *is* articulate.

I think Dad saw it all coming. His kids would be able to use the language and use it properly. He knew it would pay off eventually.

No *sir.* There was no jive around the Jackson household.

The family broke up when I was around six. As far back as memory takes me, I remember my mom and dad fighting at times. It didn't strike me as odd but, again, you go with your own experience. It was just the way things were at 149 Greenwood.

And then things changed.

One day, toward the end of the familiar delivery route, I noticed there were tears in my dad's eyes. Confused, I asked if anything was wrong. Something was. "Your mom and I are splitting up," he told me. "She's leaving today."

You always expect to see your parents able to handle any situation. You always expect them to be strong. It was strange to see my dad with tears in his eyes, to see weakness rather than strength. It shook me up. It's hard for a kid to understand how heroes can cry.

The next thing I knew, my mother was just kind of gone. Her other three natural children went with her. I stayed with my dad. I was never aware of any conscious decision. It was more as if I just found myself with my dad. And with Joe and Dolores, Dad's kids from his previous marriage, who also stayed at 149 Greenwood.

I was sorry to see them all go, though I was happy to stay with Dad. In a sense I was better off; at least the arguments were over, the tension was gone. But still, suddenly I was without a mother and I didn't really understand why or how.

There are things that happen to you in your life that you don't question, maybe because you're afraid of what the answer will be. My mom leaving me behind is one of those things. I never asked her why. Nor did I ask my dad. I assumed it was just one of those things, one of those unsolvable problems. Once again, I didn't know any different. Maybe I didn't want to hear the real answer.

I know I will carry the scars of that breakup with me as long as I live. I have thought about it a lot in the years since. I went through a long painful period when I could not even bring myself to say the word "mom." Just couldn't do it. Dropped the word from my vocabulary.

As I've gotten older and more mature, a lot of my fear and bitterness has melted away. I've learned there are two sides to every story and I've come to realize, to accept the fact, that my father was not an angel and that my parents' divorce was due to problems on *both* sides. As an adult, I've become able to say, "This woman is my mother, I want the world to know it, and I want to *treat* her as my mother." I don't even view this as a reconciliation; I see it simply as maturation on my part.

So basically, from the age of six on, it was me and Dad and Joe. Joe would eventually go off and join the Air Force, but before he did he taught me a lot about discipline—washing the dishes, cleaning the floors, making beds. He really helped mold me in those years when it was needed. He mothered me quite a bit.

I think there has been a part of me, since the breakup of my parents, that has made me leery of women in some basic and fundamental way. I feel I'm close to my mom now—I have patched things up with her and I see her a lot—but being the product of a broken home has made me wary and suspicious in my relationships with women. In any serious relationship I've ever had, that suspicious, *scared* part of me has always been present.

Maybe it all goes back to when I was six, but I would like to take the time to explain something. Looking back, I can see that of the five or six serious romances I've had, including my marriage to a Mexican-American girl named Jennie Campos who I met and fell in love with at Arizona State, most of them have been with white women. Why? It could possibly be tied to the fact that I was separated from my mother. Maybe it was just the way I was raised —comfortable with white people in a basically white neighborhood. Like so many things in my life, that's simply the way things have been and I accept it.

To this moment, even in a serious relationship, I'm not entirely comfortable sleeping with my lady at *her* place. I'm talking about staying the whole night, waking up there. I can never feel quite right there; I've only done it a few times in my life. It's as though that's the first step toward a real commitment, a commitment I've been unable to make, including in that brief and unsuccessful marriage to Jennie. When it is my house, *my* place, I somehow feel I have at least some control over the matter.

I don't think I was ready to be a husband when I got married. I have always held back. That frightened kid of six has always had a remarkable ability to pull up the stakes in a relationship and head for the hills.

Sports became my release. Dad saw my promise as an athlete, particularly in football, but he never thought of my talent as a means to the end of becoming a professional. He just wanted me to get a scholarship so I would be assured of getting a college education.

"One way or another," he'd tell me, "you're going to get a degree. That's the ticket, Reggie. If football can get it for you, then use football that way."

I went to Cheltenham Township High School, which had about 1,500 kids, and I was on the football team, basketball team, baseball team and track team. I can remember baseball scouts coming to watch from the time I was a junior. It turned my head a little, sure. I liked the attention. One of the scouts was from the San Francisco Giants, a man named Hans Lobert, and that was a big thrill for me because Willie Mays had always been my idol. The scouts were nice and very flattering, but it was going to be football for me because I could run over people, run around them and run away from them, and I knew that was going to give me my chance to run to college.

Football was good for me because it was a place where I could use up a lot of the bitterness and hostility that had been quietly building in me since my home had broken up. I didn't understand all of the bitterness in those years, but I remember being an angry kid in high school. I tried not to act up in class—I sat in the front row for all my classes, setting world records for taking notes while never saying anything—but every so often my temper would get the better of me.

One time in high school, a kid accidentally took my lunch. I had him up against the wall before he knew what happened. The temper would just *escape* like that from time to time.

Later that day, my girlfriend Sandy was in her home economics class, and a teacher made an offhand remark to her that her "boyfriend Reggie" had thrown another tantrum in the lunchroom.

Sandy left the class crying. She told me about it after school.

The next day I made a point to go into the home ec class and confront the teacher in front of everyone.

High school was such a strange time for me. I was one of the most well-known athletes in the Philadelphia area—the baseball scouts were always around and the football recruiters were starting to frequent *all* the Cheltenham games—but I wasn't a particularly happy kid. The games didn't give me the joy they should have. I just kept getting tougher and tougher, building up walls, then running right through them. I remember one Cheltenham game when I got hit hard going through the line and chipped a tooth. I was furious about that. I came back to the huddle, spitting blood, and told the quarterback to give me the ball.

"Run the same play again," I snapped at him.

He said, "Reggie, maybe you want to get that tooth looked at."

I said, "Just run the damn play."

He did. I ran right at the kid who'd chipped my tooth, ran over him, made sure I stepped right in his face mask on the way.

It was the way I played then. The way I *was* then.

One thing that sports couldn't do for me in the early '60s was make it socially acceptable for me to have so many white friends, particularly girls. I did, but it was never easy.

I was dating one girl, Sandy, whose parents went out of their way to make things as hard for us as was humanly possible.

My dad had helped me buy my first car by then—a '55 Chevy —and my (white) friend George Beck had one just like it. When I'd want to take Sandy out, I'd keep my Chevy down the street from her house, and George would pick up Sandy, then he'd drive to where I was, she'd switch cars, and we'd all go out somewhere.

When it came time to drop her off, same switch.

To me it felt like a cheap and hypocritical way of life, but I wanted to go out with her and she wanted to go out with me, so that was the system all the time we dated.

In the late fall of my senior year I drove into the driveway at 149 Greenwood and saw police cars in front of the house.

I went inside. Dad wasn't in the shop. The next series of events is still extremely vague in my mind. I was dazed.

One of the policemen got out of his car just as I burst through the door. He told me that my father had been arrested.

I stood there, seventeen years old, and listened to the words, but could not believe what I was hearing. By then, I knew what the *still* meant, and I knew my father had had some problems in the past driving with a suspended license—he wasn't a stickler for details like that—but I never dreamt that he could ever be sent to jail. The corn liquor was just a way for him to make things a little easier financially for the family. They didn't send you to jail for that, did they?

Yes, they did.

They got him for another suspended license and for having bootleg liquor in the car. He was held at the jail across the street from the courthouse in Norristown, Pennsylvania.

The next days and weeks were a jumble for me. My brother Slug came back from Baltimore to pick up what he could of the cleaning and tailoring business; he also did other odd jobs wherever he could find them just to make ends meet. I remember sitting outside the courthouse the day Dad was sentenced—he got six months, I believe—afraid to go in, afraid to hear what the judge was going to say, afraid to see the look on my father's face if the news was bad.

Someone had to come out and tell me; I think it was Slug. For the first time in a very long time, I cried. I knew we'd survive somehow, but now I felt completely alone. By this time Dolores had moved and Joe had joined the Air Force.

I only went to see my father at the jail in Norristown once, not long after he began serving his sentence. It broke my heart to see him in his gray prison uniform.

I couldn't find anything to say at first because I felt this dam about to burst inside me; I thought the first words out of my mouth would start a crying jag that would go on and on. I didn't want to do that in front of him. Things were bad enough.

"I'm fine," he said. "Don't you worry about me. How're you and Slug doing?"

I told him we'd kept some of the customers and that on weekends I was getting enough cleaning in the shop, making enough deliveries, to get by.

"Slug pretty much handles the business during the day and after school when I'm at practice," I said. "We're all right."

The conversation drifted for a while, then just ended. I'm glad I've forgotten most of that day.

And that was what my senior year in high school was like. I was the star athlete at Cheltenham, I was the most famous kid in the area, I had football and baseball recruiters practically camped out on the doorstep at 149 Greenwood, and now I didn't have a mom *or* a dad. I'd hear the cheers in the gym and on the field, and then at night, when I wasn't running with George Beck and my buddies, I came home to that deadly quiet house. It was like I was leading two lives. Slug was always off working someplace. I'd get up early in the morning, do some pressing in the shop, go to school, then go to practice or a game. Then I'd come home, with dread almost, to the quiet. Slug kept the house immaculate, and he tried to eat with me as often as he could, but there was so much time alone. I withdrew into myself even more. I threw myself into sports with even more vengeance.

What should have been such a wonderful, exhilarating time for me—last year in high school, last stretch of road before the adventure of college—became an alone time, a sad time, a private time filled with a gnawing hurt that would not go away. My coaches, particularly football coach John Kracsun, became surrogate fathers. But it wasn't the same thing as having my dad around. I felt like I went through that last year of high school with an arm cut off.

Dad was still away the day I got my Cheltenham diploma at graduation. Slug couldn't be there either; as usual, he was off working. Just me.

My father was still away the day I left for Arizona State.

By then, I was just glad to get away from Wyncote, even though I'd never been west of Chester, Pennsylvania, and Arizona seemed like it was on the other side of the world. I wasn't mad. I wasn't bitter anymore. I was just leaving *nothing* behind. Frank Kush, the football coach at ASU (and an old friend of John Kracsun), had given me a scholarship and told me I'd be able to play baseball too if I kept a 2.5 average. He told me I'd get tuition, room and board, and fifteen dollars a week in meal money. A friend of mine from the area, Gene Foster (he'd later play for the Chargers), was going to be a senior at ASU the next year.

I said, fine. I just wanted to get out of Wyncote. My father wasn't home. I couldn't pick up my own girlfriend for a date. I was damn, *damn* tired of cleaning and pressing and driving that old truck that I'd loved so much at one time.

Leaving nothing, I felt.

I had two suitcases and one gym bag. My sister Dolores took me to Sears Roebuck and bought me three pairs of pants, three pairs of socks, three shirts, three pairs of undershorts, three t-shirts and two pairs of shoes—one pair of Cordovan smooth-toed dress shoes and one pair of Weejun loafers. I had one gray sharkskin suit and one pea-green sportcoat. I also had one black tie. I had fifty dollars in my pocket. Thirty-five of that was for gas.

One August day in 1964, I just got into Gene Foster's '56 Pontiac, and we started off on a drive across the country to Tempe, Arizona. I didn't look back for a long, long time.

2
BULL IN THE RING

The biggest human being I'd ever seen was walking toward me in Sahuaro Hall, the athlete's dorm at Arizona State.

Actually, the whole dorm seemed to be moving with him. There was a wall on his right in the hallway. A wall on his left. In the middle was this giant, about 6'1" and at least 275 pounds. He had short hair and he wasn't smiling. I wasn't long out of Gene Foster's Pontiac. I'd just dropped my things off in my room, and here's what R. Jackson, college freshman, was thinking on his first day at school:

Whoever this is, I want him to be my first friend in the whole state of Arizona.

I walked up to him—walking *around* him was out of the question—and put out my hand. Mr. Congeniality, Wyncote, Pa.

"Hi, my name's Reggie Jackson."

He looked at me, shook my hand, and gave out this low rumble, which worked its way into a couple of sentences.

"I'm Curly Culp. I'm from Yuma."

I smiled at him. Friendly smile. First-day-of-school smile, you know what I mean?

"Oh, Curly, huh? What's your real name?"

"My fucking name is Curly," he said.

I said, "Okay, you betcha, whatever you say. *Real* nice to meet you. Yes *sir!* Real nice. You play football, right?"

"Right."

"Fantastic. Great. Yeah, football. Me too."

Curly Culp did in fact play football at ASU, offense and defense. From there he went to the Kansas City Chiefs, got even bigger, and eventually helped the Chiefs win a Super Bowl. The moment I met him that day, I knew that Arizona State was a whole new world and I was just one small part of it.

I was certainly one hell of a lot smaller than Curly Culp.

It happens this way with all stud high school athletes. You come from an out-of-the-way place like Wyncote, and in high school you were the biggest, toughest, fastest kid on the block. The girls like you, the cheerleaders cheer you, the recruiters recruit you, the coaches give you special favors. All the while, you are believing this one big thing: Hoo-boy, I am *special.* You can't imagine things ever being different.

Then you show up at college, at a place like ASU that has turned out so many great athletes in so many different sports, from a Culp to other NFL players like Gene Foster and Ron Pritchard and John Pitts; from baseball players like Rick Monday and Sal Bando and Gary Gentry to younger stars like Bob Horner and Floyd Bannister. The list is endless. You find out that *every*body is big. Everybody is strong. Everybody is fast. Everybody is what you were at Cheltenham High School.

Jock shock.

For me, it was Curly shock.

We did become friends, by the way. Curly always looked out for me, which I thought was extremely lucky for me. When I was a running back freshman year, and we'd get down close to the end zone, Curly would just walk into the huddle and say to the quarterback, "Give the ball to Reggie." We only had four plays, anyway.

Then he'd look at me and say, "Follow me."

I'd get the ball and I'd follow him. Scored a lot of touchdowns freshman year. Just basically held onto Curly Culp's shirttails.

One more Curly story.

It was in summer camp before my sophomore year. Curly and I had moved up to the varsity and our coach, Frank Kush, used to have this drill called Bull in the Ring. The temperature was over 100 degrees—it was *always* over 100 degrees in Arizona—and Kush would put the whole team in this big circle. We all had our white practice pants on. Shoulder pads. Gold "Sun Devil" helmets. Either a green skivvy shirt or a red skivvy shirt.

Kush would put one player in the middle of the circle. Then he'd blow his whistle. *Tweet!* And call out someone's name. The player in the middle didn't know where the other guy was coming from. Just somewhere out of the big circle. Sometimes he'd get hit from behind. But from the moment Kush blew the whistle until he blew it again, the two guys would just go after each other as hard as they could, just try to beat the living shit out of each other. Like in one of those Budweiser Light commercials.

When it was over, the player in the middle would *stay* in the middle, and Kush would send someone else in after him. It seemed like I was always in the middle.

Being the bull was a real bad job.

So one day I was the bull; Kush blew his whistle, and I heard him yell out Curly's name. And I just thought: Well, I am going to die. That was it. I could see the stories back in Wyncote: Reggie Jackson, Martinez's kid, star of Cheltenham, was killed yesterday in some place called Payson, Arizona, 'cause he was the bull in the ring.

Except that Curly took it easy on me. He was my buddy, and Kush knew it, and he got all over Curly in front of the whole team: "So you want to take care of your pussy buddy, is that right, Culp? You don't think he can take it, right, Culp? Well, fine! Let's get him out of there and put *you* in the middle, Culp! Let's find out what kind of pussy you are!"

As you may have guessed, Curly did not have the sweetest disposition in the world to begin with. To call him a pussy in front of the team did not improve that disposition one iota.

Curly got pissed.

Kush blew the whistle. Called out a name. The guy went for Curly.

Curly busted his helmet. Just split it up the front.

Guy left. Whistle. Another name.

Curly broke the guy's shoulder pads in half. Left side stayed on. Right side went flying toward Phoenix.

Whistle. Another name. Kid was wearing one of those cage-type face masks.

Curly broke the face mask.

Kush blew the whistle. "I think we'll go on to something else now," he said. It was only summer camp. Kush was about to lose his entire football team to Curly.

Curly Culp was the second toughest person I've ever met in my life.

The toughest was Frank Kush.

Looking back at that first year at Arizona State, what I mostly remember is practicing and studying. I'd go to class. Lift weights after class as part of the football training program. Go to practice. Go to eat. Go back to Sahuaro and study. Get up the next morning and do the same things. It wasn't a bad way to go through school. I didn't necessarily enjoy the regimentation but, looking back, I feel it was good for me.

As a recruiter, Frank Kush had convinced me that playing for him was the best ticket to playing pro football. I'd believed him, and John Kracsun had sung his praises. I could play baseball if I kept a B average, but my mind set was still on football as a freshman. *I was a football player.* And if you were a football player, there was only one way to do things.

The Kush Way.

Frank Kush was from coal-mining stock in western Pennsylvania, and he was always telling us that he had nothing, came up from nothing, but had fought his way up from being nothing because he was tougher than everybody else. We'd all just nod vigorously and say, "Yes sir." He was tough as they come, tough as a bull, though he isn't as big as you might think from his reputation. He has these strong, bowed, hairy legs—he was always wearing shorts and a warmup jacket—and rough, jagged-looking teeth, which you only saw when he had his face in your face and he was yelling at you because the man never smiled that I can remember. He's got a gruff voice and the arms of a longshoreman, and he was all football. I always assumed he ate fingers for breakfast. When you got hit hard in practice, he laughed. When you did well, there was no praise because that's what you were supposed to do.

When he walked by you, you flinched, just waiting for him to say something bad to you, to call you a pussy or a mama's boy. Something. He never abused me physically, never punched me or anything like that (he had to leave ASU in 1979 after allegedly slapping one of his punters; he's coaching the Colts now and doing a hell of a job). He just let the rest of the team beat the shit out of me, which got his message through to me just fine.

I wish I could have played three varsity years of football under him. Because at that time he understood me better than I understood myself. Because Kush knew I wasn't as tough as I thought I was or needed to be.

God, I can remember the whole litany even now. I can hear that gruff Kush voice yelling at me through my helmet.

"You can't take it, can you, Jackson?"

"You're not tough enough, Jackson."

(Never Reggie, incidentally.)

"When are you going to quit pussyfooting around, Jackson?"

"I thought you wanted to be a football player, Jackson. Maybe you should go out for girls' field hockey."

"You're a mama's boy at heart, aren't you, Jackson?"

"Well, Jackson, I guess I'm gonna have to teach you a lesson if you want to be a football player at Arizona State. You guys on the offensive line go over and have a drink of water. Just the center and the quarterback stay here. Jackson, you line up at fullback. Let me have the whole defensive line up on the other side of the line. And let me tell the defense something: You let up on Jackson, and I'm going to work out some drills for you. Now. We are going to run some plays for Mr. Jackson into the line."

And that was what we would do in the heat, always in the heat. Hut, hut. I'd get the ball. No blocking. No faking by me. No juking. Just run into the heart of the defensive line and the linebacker and . . .

Boom!

Fucking hammer every time.

Get up and do it again. I used to have snot running down my nose, tears coming out of my eyes, spit all over my chinstrap, ringing in my ears. Hell, I knew every strap inside my helmet, every piece of padding, because I saw all of it in front of my eyes so often —my helmet was turned around most of the time.

And if I didn't gain at least five yards, Kush would make me do it again. He'd even call out the plays for the defense, as if they needed that. Now how in the hell was I going to gain five yards?

"We're going to run a 161 Trap now, boys."

"We're going to run a Slant Off-tackle, boys."

Hut, hut.

Gimme the ball.

Splat!

One day in spring practice my freshman year, I'd run about ten of those plays in a row, just got creamed ten times in a row. After the last one, I took the football, flipped it to Kush, and said, "I quit. You want me to say I give? Okay, I *give*. I don't have to take this shit. I just became a full-time baseball player."

We were in Sun Devils Stadium, and there were a lot of ex-ASU players like Gene Foster and Charley Taylor watching spring practice, which they'd do if they were in town, but I didn't care about any of that. I just ran. Straight down the field. I was going to run right out of the stadium, through the first available exit I could find. I knew Dad wanted his kid to get a college education, but I was *sure* this wasn't quite what he had in mind.

I didn't know Taylor, who was such a brilliant runner and receiver with the Washington Redskins, was running after me.

He caught up with me about the time I crossed the goal line. And put a bear hug on me.

"You don't want to do this," Charley said.

I said, "The hell I don't. I'm out of here."

Taylor had a pretty good hug on me. He wasn't any bigger than I was, but I had just gotten beat up ten plays in a row. He all but carried me back to the team.

"You are not going anywhere," Charley Taylor said. "You are not quitting because you are not a quitter."

Back to the drill.

Kush: "Heh, heh. I see the mama's boy is back. Everybody back in position. Quarterback and center with Mr. Jackson. I think we'll try the 161 Slant again."

Hut, hut.

Ball.

Hammered again.

I barely picked myself up. But I did pick myself up and started to go back to my position, so I could let the building fall on me again. Taylor was right: I wasn't going to let the sonofabitch beat me.

Kush just wanted to see me get up one more time.

"Okay, get him out of there. We'll give him a little rest before he gets back in there."

Lordy, that man was tough.

At summer camp there was a famous place called Kush's Mountain. A run up Kush's Mountain was another one of his favorite drills. It's hard to explain the mountain to someone who's always lived in a city or who's never been in the West, but it was the damnedest thing you ever saw. It was much, much worse than running up and down the stadium steps, which was another tasty little item Kush had if he was mad at you. Running up his mountain would be the equivalent of running up the steps of the Empire State Building in full uniform with guards—also in full uniform—stationed every few floors to try and knock you on your ass.

It was steep. It was hot. There were rocks and trees and cactus and scorpions and snakes and raccoons and whatever else might happen to scare the living daylights out of you. Every day, Kush would pick out two or three guys to run up that mountain.

You know yours truly was a daily participant.

It was like I had to attend special services at Kush's church every . . . single . . . day.

It would have been cheaper for me to buy a two-week toll coupon.

I survived it all. I played safety for Kush my sophomore year, and I was captain of the defense, which was quite an honor for a sophomore. Kush himself never explained to me why he put me through what he put me through. But my defensive coach, Don Baker, told me afterward that Kush had decided that I was going to carry the ball for him when I was a junior, and he just had to find out if I could take it.

He found out.

I found out.

Despite it all, I was glad to have played for him. I think of all the crucial parental influences in my life. My father instilled in me a relentless desire to succeed and a will to win, and so did Bobby Winkles, my baseball coach at ASU. But Frank Kush made me tough. It sounds simple, but it was so important to me, even if I didn't grasp all of it those days in the stadium when I felt so humiliated and so beaten up, all those times trying to make it up Kush's Mountain. I thought I had grown up tough in Wyncote, but he made me tougher. In high school, I had let some things slide, I had become passive about some of my values. Kush drilled those values back into me, helped me find some steel and will in me that must have been there all along, even if it had gotten lost when my dad went away. I'll always remember Frank Kush for that. I respect him for what he did for me.

I left school after my sophomore year to sign a bonus contract with the Kansas City A's, and by the time I actually went off to do it, it was no big secret around ASU. Reggie's going to sign? It was like saying that Halley's comet appears every so often.

Before I signed, I made it a point to go over to Kush's office and say goodbye.

I told him that I was going, that I couldn't pass up the money or the opportunity, and he told me that he understood completely. Then he nearly bowled me over, as though he were running one last 161 Trap.

"I'm going to miss you," the tough guy said. "You were going to be a hell of a football player for me. Good luck." We shook hands. That was that.

Whenever I'm in Baltimore, if I've got the time, I go over to the Colts training facility and say hello.

Frank Kush.

I'll never forget him.

Can you become more of a man and still not grow up?

I think that's what happened to me at ASU. There is no question in my mind that Frank Kush and Bobby Winkles helped make a man out of me. Kush made me tough and Winkles taught me discipline. They built that foundation in me, would not let me give in. I'm sure that the day Charley Taylor brought me back, Kush was the least surprised person on the field. I'm sure he thought that if Taylor hadn't brought me back, I would have come back on my own.

At least I like to think so.

But I was only being *jock* tough, being jock smart, and I'm not sure that I was becoming people smart. As much as you might hear that sports is a microcosm of society, it really isn't. For all the hurt of sports, for all the drama of sports, for all the triumph and disaster of sports, you are still operating in a very controlled environment, working with people who are different from you and yet not so different. Your greatest bond, of course, is that you have a stake in how well you do. I'd find out more about that in Oakland, more still in New York. No matter how many petty hostilities there are in the clubhouse, no matter how serious the confrontations, the athlete in everyone makes you *get* with the program on the field. At least that's what happens on the good teams, on the teams I've been on. If you can put all the bullshit aside and win, then *everyone* looks better. It's people who like each other, people who don't like each other, people with families, single people—it's professionals realizing that *E pluribus unum* is beneficial.

Arizona State was my first experience living with, being around, a lot of other blacks. Most of the blacks were athletes, but even if we all had shared *black* experiences growing up, the *real* shared experience was about being a black *athlete* growing up. So it wasn't as though I had this fantastic awareness brought out in college about being black. That is simply an ongoing thing, something that happens every day of your life once you get out in the real world. There weren't any startling revelations in the locker room. There rarely are. At least in college.

ASU was sports. Football first. Then football and baseball. Then just baseball. I worked hard in my classes—I changed to a biology major after starting as a physical education major. I had it in the back of my brain that I might want to become a doctor some day.

I went to class and I played sports. I dated one girl my freshman year, one girl my sophomore year. That was Jennie Campos, the girl I'd eventually marry my rookie year with the A's. But what I really was was an athlete, through and through. I wore my cut-offs and football t-shirts to classes, not because I was so proud of being an athlete, I was just being practical. I had to save my nice clothes in case I had a date.

I didn't want to stay out too late on a date, because I might be too tired for class the next day.

And if I skipped a class the next day, then it might get me in trouble with one of my coaches.

And if I skipped too many classes, then my grade average might fall, and then I wouldn't be able to play baseball.

It all came back to sports. I pursued my education because I knew I could fall back on it, but I had by this time become aware that I could make a living in sports. I wasn't going to have to go back to the tailor shop. I wouldn't have to be poor anymore. Sports was going to be my way out.

Arizona was nice. I still enjoy going back to Tempe, and I still have business in the area. The school was nice. My girlfriend was nice. I enjoyed the life of being a good athlete at a major sports school. However, I realize that I may have missed a lot, as I suspect most star athletes do in college. To reach the level of college star, the kind of level reached by a Herschel Walker, a Kareem Abdul Jabbar, you *have* to be extraordinarily focused, driven, almost fanatically one-dimensional. I will always wonder if there's any other way to achieve that kind of success. A lot of good does come out of that obsessive drive—the harnessing of your ability as well as the potential financial rewards—but sociologically you sacrifice quite a bit. The lucky ones can compensate later, when they're more mature, more aware. I can say for certain that I had grown by the time I left ASU. But in most ways, I was still a hick from Wyncote. And believe me, it showed.

My freshman year at school, the big man on campus was Rick Monday, the star of the baseball team, who'd eventually be a team-mate of mine with the A's before he was traded for Ken Holtzman. He was 6'3" and 190 pounds; he could run the 100 in about 9.7; he had an arm like a cannon; he could hit the ball a cold country mile; he was blond with a deep voice. He was a big league ballplayer when he was nineteen years old, and he knew it. I knew it. The school knew it. Every scout in the country knew it. The next year he'd sign a bonus contract with the A's for $100,000.

One . . . hundred . . . thousand . . . American . . . dollars.

As far as I was concerned, Rick Monday had it all.

Even before he signed the big contract. In my mind, he was just everything. I watched the way he moved, the way he talked to people, the way he handled himself. He was only a year ahead of me, and he wasn't aloof exactly, but in the hierarchy of athletes, you just didn't go up to Monday and start talking. I met him a couple of times but that was it. Just met him a couple of times. See, he was *there* already. I wasn't. It was as simple as that.

God, I remember going to the baseball games that spring and thinking Monday was absolutely awesome. In the big leagues, he never became what he was at ASU. But he was something to see. To this day, he remains the best athlete I've ever seen in college sports. I'm talking O. J. Simpson. I'm talking Herschel Walker. I'm talking everybody. Unbelievable is the only way to describe him. In college, to my mind, he was the perfect picture of the sporting hero.

It's even a great name, isn't it?

My baseball career in college really started on a bet.

I had it in my mind, of course, that I'd play baseball there. But in the spring of my freshman year, I began to think about baseball as being a release from Kush and the grueling rigors of football. Spring football practice and the baseball season went on at the same time, and since my grades were good enough, I got permission from the coaches to work out with the football team on Monday, Wednesday, and Friday, then do some work with the baseball team on Tuesday and Thursday.

If that was all right with Coach Bobby Winkles, that is.

What actually got me over to Sun Devil Field was a bet with two baseball buddies, Joe Paulsen and Jeff Pentland. They used to kid me all the time about wanting to be a baseball player. When they weren't kidding me about *wanting* to be a player, they joked about Coach Winkles even giving me a second look. ASU was even more of a baseball factory than it was a football factory, turning out these amazing teams every year under Winkles, and Winkles was every bit as much a legend at school as Kush was.

I kept telling Paulsen and Pentland, "He'll want me, you just wait and see."

They'd laugh and say, "No way."

Finally one day we made a bet. I wanted to take my girl and some of my buddies to a drive-in movie, and you could get in for five dollars a carload, so that was the bet.

One day after football practice, I went over to Sun Devil Field to watch the baseball team. I still had all my football gear on, except my helmet. When practice was over, I introduced myself to Coach

Winkles and asked if I could maybe come over and hit some the next day.

He looked at me sort of funny—I did look a little out of place —but said that would be fine.

I wasn't sure if he knew anything at all about what a good player I'd been in high school, but I told him I thought I could help him the next year and that I'd like to try out.

"I think I can play, sir," I said. Winkles insisted you call him sir.

Winkles said he'd see me the next day.

He did. Paulsen and Pentland were there. I had my football spikes on, my football pants. I took off my helmet and my shoulder pads. Paulsen and Pentland stood by the batting cage, smirking. The baseball team stood off to the side and did the same thing. One of the varsity pitchers—I don't remember his name—went out to the mound.

I swung and missed the first pitch. Then it became like something in the movies.

The guy pitched. I hit one over the palm trees behind the right-field fence.

Another pitch. Another rocket to right.

I missed a couple more.

He threw me another pitch and I hit one over the center-field fence, which was 430 feet away.

Took a couple of pitches.

Then another one to dead center. I got cocky then. For the very first time in my life—I'd never done anything like it in a high school baseball game—I dropped my bat, casual-like, and watched the flight of the ball.

"Okay," I said to Winkles, "do I make the team?"

Winkles said, "I'd like to see a little more of you in practice. But I think we could find a place for you on the freshman team."

I hadn't really thought about that. I was really thinking about the next year. At that precise moment, I was mainly thinking about collecting my money from Paulsen and Pentland.

I told Winkles I would check with the coaches and let him know.

It was a grandstand play, but that was how my baseball career at ASU started. There was the bet. And there was the chance to skip a couple of days of football practice every week, which meant a

couple of days of not getting killed. Surviving. Any time there was
a freshman baseball game, I could miss a football workout. Every
Tuesday and Thursday I could practice with the baseball team,
skipping Kush's tortures and punishments. If there was a conflict
between football and baseball any other time, football won out.

Such was my career really born.

After my freshman year, Bobby Winkles told me to go home and
play summer baseball to improve my skills. I told him I was spending my vacation in Baltimore visiting my mother. Winkles told me
to call up the Baltimore Orioles, say I was with ASU, and to tell
them I wanted to play baseball with an amateur team. I did that;
I talked to a few scouts over the telephone. Being from Pennsylvania, having gone to college, I spoke like I speak. In other words,
no one that I talked to realized that I was black. They sent me to
a team called Leone's (now it's called Johnny's)—one of the most
famous amateur ball teams in the country.

I did as I was told and went to the appropriate ball field. I
mean, there wasn't a black in sight. Everyone kind of stared at me,
but I didn't know what was going on. All I knew was that I was
wearing a pair of football shoes because I didn't own a pair of
regular baseball spikes.

I was told to ask for Walter Youse, an Oriole scout who ran
this amateur team. I went over to a heavy-set guy and asked for
Youse. The person I asked happened to *be* Walter Youse. I said,
"Are you the Baltimore scout?" He said that he was and then I told
him who I was. He looked at me. "You're Reggie Jackson?" I
nodded. *"You're* Reggie Jackson?" I nodded again. I didn't really
realize how shocked he was, though he told me later. But there were
no blacks on this team.

To try out, I had to run a 60-yard dash, throw in the outfield,
hit, and bunt and run to first base for time.

They had me run the dash against the fastest guy on the team.
A white guy, obviously. His name was Skip. I outran him a couple
of times, each time by three or four yards. They had me race him
a few *more* times. I just kept beating him. I ran a 6.3 sixty then.
World class was 6.1!

Then I had to throw to home plate from the outfield and they
matched me up with a kid who had a great arm. But I was young

and I always had a great arm and I could throw bullets for a *month* then. So I outthrew him.

Then they had me hit. They had a guy named Dan Kearns who would have been a big league player as a hitter except he had four or five knee operations. He hit in front of me and he hit *shots.* Then I hit. And I hit shots, too—only mine were about fifty feet further than his.

After that, I had to drag bunt and run to first base. They timed me in 3.4. Mantle had run a 3.3 about ten years before and that was still considered a big deal. The coach thought his stopwatch was broken. They made me run this about eight times—till my tongue was hanging out.

After all this went down, Youse told me to come back the next day, that they might be able to find a spot for me. I did come back and I made the team. Hit over .300 and set all sorts of team records. Eventually, years later, I got to be good friends with Walter Youse. He told me that they'd never had any blacks on the team and they hadn't known what the hell to do with me when I showed up to try out. "But," he said, "the more I saw you that day, the whiter you got."

One other interesting thing happened that summer. Frank Cashen was running the Orioles, along with Lou Gorman. I told Youse that I needed money, $50,000 for my family. At that time, you could not sign a pro contract in one sport and still be eligible to play another college sport until after your second year. Cashen and Gorman were too honest to do any shady deals and they didn't want me to drop out of school. Otherwise I would have started my career as an Oriole.

The world of baseball truly opened up to me in my sophomore year at ASU. Because baseball was fun. In high school, sports had been the release. With Kush, football had been work and survival. Compared to all that, baseball was a *lark.* We went 41–11 in my only varsity season. I hit fifteen home runs in those fifty-two games, a record that stood until Bob Horner broke it about ten years later. I led the team in runs, total bases, stolen bases, hits, RBI. Just about everything. In one of our big games against Arizona, I became the second college player to hit a ball completely out of Phoenix Municipal Stadium. There was a sellout crowd that night, like 8,500 people, and I got this tremendous ovation, the biggest in my life. It was great. Football is much more of a team sport, at least in terms of fan appreciation. But on a baseball field, a lot is individual. You hit a home run, the people in the stands let you know they appreciate it. You make a great catch, they're very happy to let you know how much they adore you. The interaction between fan and player is much more personal.

It was all just fun. No naked 161 Traps against the defense. No dashes up Kush's Mountain. Just the first big batch of dingers in my life, big league scouts around all the time, and my first real sense that I had found my place.

Plus, I was playing for Bobby Winkles.

He was an Army-type guy, Bobby Winkles, a tough little Southerner from Arkansas with a crewcut who'd spit tobacco on your shoe if you didn't watch yourself. He was very regimented. He was the boss, and he let you know that from the git-go. There was no swearing when Winkles was around. You didn't give him any lip. Ever. And he worked us. When you played for Bobby Winkles, you had to run everywhere, run like an animal. Before we ever took the bats and balls out at practice, we'd run for forty-five minutes every day. His favorite was something called the Floor Drill. Run. Stop. Put your arms straight up over your head and jump straight into the air. Sprint now. Stop. Jump. It always seemed to go on and on.

Try it sometime. Especially the jumping part.

If you were the fastest guy on the team—and I was—you had to lead all the running drills, every day. If somebody lagged behind or didn't try, he'd make us do it all over again. He'd say, "Okay, we're going to run it again for Reggie." We'd all groan and run it again. To this day, I always run on and off the field, and that's all Winkles.

I think Winkles took to me because I was a worker. He knew I'd come from a tough background, that I didn't have very much, and he knew I'd had a tough time just getting from day to day in football. And he looked out for me. I wasn't a smart-ass with him. I respected him. He sensed that, and he became a friend.

I'd never played the outfield before, having pitched and played first in high school, but Winkles put me out in center to replace Monday. Before the season started, Winkles pulled me aside and said, "I don't care if you catch a cold, I don't care if you drop balls,

I don't care if you strike out every day. You're going to be out there." Replacing Monday at ASU was like replacing the sun and the moon, but I felt like things would be fine as long as Winkles was on my side.

The first game we played that year I messed up a ball in the outfield, and there was some bickering and some comments after the game from some of the older players. Winkles heard about it and called a team meeting on the spot.

"I'm going to tell you all this one time and one time only," he snapped in his drill instructor manner. "Reggie Jackson is on this team now, he's gonna stay on this team, and he's gonna play center field every day. So get used to it."

For the first time in my life, I felt like a baseball player, and that was because of Winkles's belief in me. He'd coach and manage in the major leagues later on, never with the success he had at ASU. But he was something, and I'll always think of him as my friend. When he got fired from managing the Angels in the '70s, the team was playing in Oakland. I remember going out to the airport and talking with him about it. He was down. It was a switch.

Good, decent man, Winkles, through and through. In my sports experience, he was the closest thing to my dad. I remember my first game in the minor leagues, in Lewiston, Idaho. I struck out, and I ran from home plate back to the dugout. All my teammates laughed.

Someone said, "Hey, Jackson, what the hell do you think you're doing?"

I said, "That's the way Bobby Winkles said you do it, and that's the way I'm gonna do it."

End of conversation.

June 1966. The end of my sophomore year at ASU. A few days before the major league draft. Winkles called the dorm and said he wanted to see me in his office.

I ran.

When I got there, he was sitting behind his desk, looking as tough and proper and Army as always. He said, "Maybe you're aware of this, and maybe you're not, but you're certain to be drafted high in the first round."

I knew many scouts had been coming around. Danny Murtaugh from the Pirates. Tom Greenwade, the man from the Yankees whose claim to fame was signing Mickey Mantle. Dave Garcia from the Giants, who told me I'd be able to play with Willie Mays, my hero. Paul Richards from the Orioles. But I still hadn't really thought about leaving ASU. I figured that the draft was nice, but I'd be back the next year, carrying the ball for Kush, and hitting dingers for Winkles.

I mentioned all this to Winkles.

He said, "You're going to get offered a lot of money. That's what I heard anyway."

A lot of money. I had ten dollars in my pocket. *That* was a lot of money to me. I just nodded.

Then Winkles said, "The Mets have the first pick, and there's no question in my mind that you should be the first pick. But I don't think they're going to take you."

"Why not?"

Winkles: "They're concerned that you have a white girlfriend."

I didn't have an answer for that one, except to sit there in Winkles's office and feel hurt. Jennie? White? In my mind, Jennie was Mexican, and even in a setting like Arizona, she got a hard time sometimes because of that. She got comments because of that, and comments because she was dating me.

But I still couldn't understand why that could be any sort of problem for a *major league* baseball team. It was my first real inkling that if you weren't a WASP in this country, you just weren't white.

Winkles went on. "Anyway, the word I get is that the Mets are going to draft this kid named Steve Chilcott, and it might cost you some money."

Still stunned, I muttered something clever like, "Fine, whatever."

Winkles then told me, "I know you're going home in a couple of days, and I just want you to know whatever you decide, I'm sure it will be best for you, and I'll support you. But before you sign a contract, I want you to call me because there's some things I'll be able to help you with."

I told him I would do that.

I walked out of his office, thinking about the Mets and Jennie and some guy named Steve Chilcott. I had broken every record in sight. The scouts had been fawning all over me for months. If Winkles said I should be the first pick, then I knew damn well that I should be the first pick. Now it wasn't going to happen because I had a white girlfriend? She wasn't white anyway.

Bull. Shit.

I was finding out at a young age that The Man—The (white) Man—had all sorts of ways to hold you down.

I went over to Jennie's dorm room and told her what had happened. Up until that point, it hadn't been very important that I'd been going out with a Mexican-American. I was a star in a very insulated environment—no one was going to give either one of us a very hard time on campus or in the surrounding area.

Jenny cried when I told her the story and said, "Why would something like this happen?" I hugged her and told her I didn't know. What I knew was that there had to be a whole other set of rules about men and women out there beyond Arizona State that I didn't know anything about.

A couple of days later, the Mets took Steve Chilcott first. I'm told he was a catcher. I have no idea what happened to him. What I do know is that things would have been a lot different for the New York Mets if they'd taken R. Jackson. Who knows? Maybe I would have played my whole career there. Maybe all my New York heroics would have been in Queens instead of the Bronx. And if they'd taken me, I suspect the Mets wouldn't have had all those last place finishes.

I'm glad they did.

White girlfriend?

Served the bastards right.

3

BIRMINGHAM: JUST THE KIND OF NIGGER BOY THEY NEEDED

It all happened extremely fast after I left Bobby Winkles's office. I was in Baltimore visiting my mother when it was announced that the Kansas City A's had taken me second, after Steve Chilcott. A scout from the A's named Bob Zuk called and told me Mr. Charles O. Finley wanted to fly me to a meeting in his Chicago office. I told Zuk that I wanted my father to go along, too. Zuk said that was fine.

I called Dad in Wyncote, told him he'd be hearing from the A's and to meet me in Chicago the next day. My dad was back in the cleaning business, scuffling to make ends meet just like always. He was still the one person I knew I could turn to—*had* to turn to—for support.

I also called Bobby Winkles in Arizona. He said that no matter what, I should make sure that the A's took care of the rest of my college education in the contract, that it was spelled out, that I would get at least $2,000 a semester no matter how long it took me to finish.

I flew to Chicago, met my dad at the airport, and we checked

into the Pick Congress Hotel on Michigan Avenue. I dropped the
bags off in the room and took a taxi down to Finley's insurance
offices at 310 South Michigan. Went up to his private office in a
special elevator. Got whisked right in. Twenty years old. Out of
breath. Scared. Doing everything but holding my father's hand.
Sophomore in college meeting the owner of a big . . . league . . .
baseball team.

Meeting this bald, barrel-chested man with a booming voice
and a powerful handshake, not knowing at the time that we would
be beginning a crazy love-hate baseball romance that would be such
a big part of the next ten years of my life.

Mr. Charles O. Finley. Insurance tycoon. Baseball owner. He
put his feet up on his desk, showing off a big hole in the sole of one
of his shoes, and offered me a $50,000 bonus if I signed with the
A's.

I said, "No thank you, Mr. Finley."

Just like that. Didn't even look at my dad.

Martinez didn't miss a beat.

He said, "We want one hundred thousand dollars."

It just came out that way. My dad and I had talked somewhat
about the fact that Rick Monday had gotten $100,000 the year
before, but we didn't really have a plan. We were coming from
nowhere, remember. We had nothing, maybe $100 between us. We
were just feeling our way. All we knew was that I was one hell of
a baseball player, I was the second pick in the United States of
America, and that I had options. Hell, I still had a football scholarship at ASU. I still had Winkles.

Finley said, "I can't pay you that kind of money."

I said, "My. Finley, I don't want to sign for fifty thousand. I'll
just go back to Arizona and keep doing what I've been doing."

Finley looked at us. Still had his feet up. Still had the hole
showing. We looked at him.

"Seventy-five thousand," Finley said finally. "You go back to
the hotel and think about it, and we'll all get together at my house
for breakfast tomorrow."

My father and I talked all night. The money was an unbelievable sum, after all the scraping he'd done, after all the scraping I'd
done in his wake. But I was happy at Arizona State. I had the
scholarship. I thought that obligated me. Everything was so foreign
all of a sudden, happening so fast. The adventure was too big. I felt

that if I finished out my career at ASU playing both football and baseball, I might have even more options when I graduated. Besides, I was in a comfort zone.

Round and round we went.

I called Bobby Winkles and told him that Finley was offering $75,000.

Winkles said, "Take it. Make sure they put college in there like I said, but take the money."

Just like that.

"I don't want to leave," I said to Winkles over the phone.

"Take the money, Reggie," he repeated. "Because it's a lot. And because this is your time. You're ready for pro baseball, and you never know what might happen if you stay."

The next morning we flew in a private plane to Finley's home in Laporte, Indiana, for breakfast. It was a farm, really. Land as far as you could see in any direction. I felt like I was in Oz. There were kids all over the place, cats, dogs, horses. An indoor basketball court. This huge, rolling lawn in back. Finley put on an apron and cooked breakfast for us all on the back patio. Eggs and fresh cantaloupe a la mode. It was the first time in my life I had cantaloupe a la mode. I liked it.

Over breakfast, I said, "Mr. Finley, if you give me the money you offered yesterday, plus two thousand dollars a semester for my college tuition *and* a new Pontiac, I'll sign."

My dad said, "If he gets that, we'll have a deal." Pause, pause, pause. We both were scared as hell.

Finley, in the big voice, said, "Well, there isn't anything more to talk about. We do have a deal. Reggie, you're going to win me a World Series some day."

Two weeks later, I was in the Lewis and Clark Hotel in Lewiston, Idaho. In my mind, I was merely the wealthiest cat in the world. Had a deal that was worth $85,000 in all. Had me a paid-up college education.

Had me a brand new maroon Pontiac.

And I was a *pro*-fessional baseball player. I mean, *wow!*

Lewiston, Idaho . . .

It was like being in Nowhere, USA, but it wasn't very different from Wyncote, really. Small and quiet. Comfortable. A farming town with whites and Indians. The only other black in the town besides me was this wonderful old character we called Chicken Willie. Willie drove the bus, took care of the equipment, served as trainer and traveling secretary. And took care of me.

I was in Lewiston, Idaho, for two weeks. I got to the plate about fifty times, was hitting around .300, and had a couple of dingers. Both of them sailed out of the little ballpark we played in and broke windows in a house across the street. There's no telling how many I would have hit in Lewiston if I'd stayed.

I was having fun. The new adventure and all that. I was also getting acclimated to the idea of being a ballplayer—a real, live, money-earning ballplayer—riding the buses around the Northwest, going back to my one room at the Lewis and Clark when we were at home, looking around, a little bit tentative, a little bit afraid, trying to get a new fix on what it all meant, on how much I was allowed to dream. Making $500 a month and thinking that was a fortune, it coming on top of the bonus.

The last game I played there, I got hit in the head. I don't remember the pitcher's name or the team. Just some big country fastball pitcher who plunked me. I'd been hit in the head before, but never like this. (You never get used to it, incidentally. You get back up and you try to block out the fear and you go on. But there is always that moment when the ball is up in your eyes and you're thinking, "Okay, is this lights out time?") I went down. I wasn't unconscious, but they rushed me to the hospital just to be on the safe side.

I remember waking up in this tiny hospital they had, a little disoriented, with a headache like I used to get after a Kush practice, wondering what I was doing in this room with so many people and what had happened to put me there. I remember being tired. Bill Posedel, a roving minor league pitching instructor with the A's, was standing next to my bed. I didn't know it at the time, but Finley made sure at least one scout watched every game I played.

Posedel was on the phone, and I listened to him in a drowsy, sleepy way.

He was saying, "No, they won't give Reggie a private room."

Pause.

"I'm just telling you what they said, Charlie."

Charlie. As in Finley. As in the big fella.

"They won't give him a private room because he's colored."

Quote, unquote.

Posedel got off the phone. I went back to sleep after he told me I was going to be fine. When I woke up, they took some X-rays and the X-rays were negative. I was released.

And the very next day I was on my way to Modesto, in the California League. It was the next step up in the A's minor league system. The next day. Finley didn't waste any time after Posedel's phone call. No private room for Charlie's bonus baby? His *colored* bonus baby? Well, okay. Fine. Then he is out of Lewiston, like now. I'll always remember Posedel for that.

It was probably for the best. I would have played all kinds of hell with that house across the street from the ballpark if I'd stayed.

But I'll tell you. I did learn one thing in Lewiston, Idaho. I'd hit the first two pro dingers of my life, and I *liked* the feel.

It was in Modesto that I got my first inkling of the dynasty that was a-buildin' in Finley's organization.

A tall, skinny right-handed pitcher from Cucamonga, California, named Rollie Fingers was there; of course he would be the magnificent reliever on our glory teams in Oakland before moving on to more relieving after free agency. Dave Duncan, a cocky, fun-loving guy who would be one of the catchers in the Oakland glory years, was there, and so was my man Joe Rudi. Rudi would be the unsung hero of the three Oakland championships and would turn out to be one of my best friends in baseball, a trusted ally. Rudi, then and now, is a big, sweet, quiet man who is just *there* for you, on the field and off.

We were the Modesto Reds, and we could *play.* Not long after I joined the team we went into Bakersfield to play, and the little paper in Bakersfield had this headline: "CALL OUT THE NATIONAL GUARD! THE MODESTO REDS ARE IN TOWN!" In the California League, they had a first-half champion and a second-half champion. Before I got there, the Reds had won the first half by a couple of games.

The Reds won the second half—we're only talking like fifty-six games here—by *sixteen* games. Duncan hit forty-six homers for the whole year, and Rudi had a bunch. I had twenty-one in the fifty-six games I was there, and knocked in sixty. We just hit the shit out of the ball. We scared some of those kid pitchers to death.

One day we were losing 11–0, and we all just sort of grinned in the dugout and said, "Let's get 'em." We got 'em. Rudi hit three home runs over the rest of the game. I hit two. Duncan hit two. We ended up winning 15–13. It was like that in Modesto. A party every game. A bunch of us lived in this place called the Carvel Hotel for six dollars a day. We traveled around California in buses and laughed a lot. Modesto was my first experience in northern California, an area that I would come to love so much later in my professional life. I would wake up every morning and think, "This *ain't* a bad way to make a living, now is it, Reggie?"

I had money in my pocket. I was surrounded by the best players I had ever seen. I was knocking in a run a day and hitting a dinger about every other. Modesto was the first place I bought myself nice clothes. I can remember buying three alpaca sweaters. Oh, yeah. *Alpacas.* One was mustard-colored, one was gray, another was green.

Remember Banlon shirts? I bought myself a bunch of those. I thought I was the slickest dresser in the minor leagues.

It wasn't like Fingers, Duncan, Rudi and I sat around and talked about this A's adventure that was beginning; we had no way of knowing this was the start of the army for us, the start of something that would be so big in the early '70s. We were still just dreaming about the big leagues. We'd sit around at breakfast in the morning, talk about the big stars, and joke that someday other kids in Modesto would be seeing what Rudi did last night or Duncan or Jackson, in the majors.

One day we drove to San Francisco and I got to see Willie Mays play in person for the first time.

Willie Mays. In the flesh.

I was rooming with a pitcher named Stan Jones, who was a little older than the rest of us. Jones borrowed a car somehow. Another pitcher named Rich Johnson was with us. We drove to San Francisco, about 100 miles, and bought reserved seats for three bucks. And there was Mays.

I don't remember who the Giants played that day. I do remember seeing McCovey, Marichal, Lanier and Perry. But most of all I remember sitting in that drafty park of Candlestick and watching every move Mays made. Making the basket catches. Taking the big swings. Jogging casually off the field. My hero. Mays. The biggest star I could imagine. It wasn't like I sat there and thought about being another Mays. I was only twenty years old, but I knew even then that there was only going to be one. I just wanted to see him with my own eyes. He got a base hit that day, just one, and I was like a little kid.

Saw Willie Mays. Saw him get a hit. Yeah.

Got into the car when it was over, we drove the 100 miles back, and I was happy. I'd seen what I wanted to see.

I have nice memories of Modesto. Because Modesto was my first *taste*. But if you ask me for one vivid memory of that summer, it was that day at Candlestick Park.

My first experience with the South of the 1960s came the next year.

North Carolina first. Camp Campbell, for reserves (I had been in ROTC at Arizona State).

Georgia next. Waycross, Georgia. Minor league spring training with the A's.

Finally Birmingham, Alabama, and the Southern League.

North Carolina and Georgia and Alabama, for a black kid from Pennsylvania who didn't know anything about anything that had to deal with everyday, serious, terrifying racism.

I wasn't in boot camp at Camp Campbell for very long because it was discovered while I was there that I had an arthritic spine from the time I'd broken my neck playing high school football. It was my junior year. I tackled a kid head on, and I broke my neck. Missed the last four games with five fractured cervical vertebrae, spent six weeks in traction, then four more with my neck in a partial cast. To this day, if you watch me closely on the field, you'll see me twitching my neck around, rotating my head and shoulders, trying to get my neck loose. It goes back to that injury. Happened against one of our big rivals, Marple-Newtown.

All I will tell you about my experience, brief as it was, in the reserves—it lasted about four weeks—is that it gave me a pretty fair indication that the military life was not for me. I was cold all the time, I was hungry all the time, it always seemed to be dark outside, and I got yelled at all the time.

Hell, I'd already played football for Frank Kush. If Kush didn't build men, it just wasn't going to happen for old Jack.

When I got out of the Medical Discharge Barracks finally, I got into my Pontiac and drove to Waycross, about ten days late for the start of spring training. Just outside Waycross, I had to stop for gas. It was about ten o'clock at night. I was standing next to my new maroon car, pumping some gas into it, when some rednecks in a pickup truck pulled up on the street in front of the gas station and stopped.

"Heyyyy, nigger."

One voice. Loud. The rest of the guys in the truck were laughing.

I looked around. I was the only one there. I figured I was the nigger in question. I didn't say a word.

"Heyyyy, nigger. You get off our streets and you stay off our streets."

I was by myself in the middle of the Georgia woods at night. I just stood stock-still with the gas pump in my hands and wondered how fast I could get into the Pontiac and get myself out of there.

Then the truck pulled off.

Welcome to the South, kid.

I had had my racial experiences. Couldn't pick up my girlfriend, Sandy, myself in high school. I had a problem finding a roommate when we were on the road at ASU, until a country boy named Glenn Smith from Kansas volunteered to be my roommate. Had been told by Bobby Winkles that the Mets didn't draft me number one because I was a black dating a "white" girl. Couldn't even get a private hospital room for one lousy night in Lewiston, Idaho, because I was "colored."

But basically I had lived a sheltered life. I had been protected by locations like Arizona and Pennsylvania and Modesto. I had been protected for the most part by being part of the athletic community.

I just wasn't ready for *this*. For the deep South. For being called a nigger on a lonely road late at night.

John McNamara—my manager now with the Angels—was the Birmingham manager that year, and that first week at Waycross I politely asked him if he could get my ass out of the South somehow.

"There's other places I can go," I said. "Send me to Vancouver. Send me anyplace. But if Birmingham is going to be anything like here, don't send me to Birmingham."

"Can't do that, Reggie," he said in his quiet way. McNamara

was a good man then and he is a good man now, another of the
decent managers I've been lucky enough to have (they've far out-
numbered the bad ones). "Charlie wants to load up Birmingham
with all his young stars."

Finley was from Birmingham originally and wanted his baseball team to put on a show in his hometown. So that was that. I
managed to get into a couple of intrasquad games, then it was off
to Birmingham. McNamara. Rudi. Fingers. Duncan. A hard-
throwing lefty named Gil Blanco.

And Martinez's son, who was scared to death.

It was a time in the South, 1967, when blacks and whites were
grappling, perhaps more seriously and more dangerously than ever
before, with integration. All the rules were changing. There had
been the freedom marches, the sit-ins. A lot of blood had already
been spilled and a lot of bad blood was building. Martin Luther
King and all the wonderful things he stood for loomed over the Old
South, threatening traditions and emotions. It was a strange combination of hope and change: The South was turning away from the
blatant racism of the past toward an angry, simmering racism that
lingered below the surface, threatening to explode at any moment.
A year later it did explode, of course, when Martin Luther King
was tragically assassinated.

That explosion hadn't come yet, when I arrived in Birmingham. But I felt the uncomfortableness, the awkwardness, the fear.

I was in the heart of Dixie.

Rudi, Fingers and Duncan were all living in the same apartment complex by the time I got to Birmingham, and the first week
or two I slept on a couch in Rudi's place. I figured I'd get myself
settled, get acclimated, then go about the business of looking for an
apartment of my own.

Wrong.

Joe and I were sitting around his place one night, and he said,
"Dave and Rollie and I are thinking about moving."

I didn't know what he was talking about. Hell, we'd all just
gotten there, and while the accommodations weren't exactly the
Ritz, they were clean and nice and convenient.

"Why would you guys want to move?" I asked innocently.

After beating around the bush, Joe said, "Because they've threatened to throw me out if you continue to stay with me."

The light bulb went on. I thought of the rednecks in the pickup truck in Waycross. Apparently it wasn't enough to get the niggers off the street. They wanted them out of the house, too.

"They can't do that," I said to Rudi.

"Well, they can, Reggie. But I told them that if you go, then we all go."

We were all twenty and twenty-one years old in a strange world that none of us, white or black, really knew anything about. Joe was from California. Rollie was from California by way of Ohio. I was the Wyncote Kid. We didn't know anything about being ethical or philosophical in matters like these. We were kids. We were ballplayers. We were teammates. We figured we were just passing through Birmingham on our way to the majors.

We couldn't live together?

What was that?

What kind of place was this?

I finally said, "I'm not gonna let you guys do that. Four people shouldn't have to move because of one. Just tell the landlord to give me a few days, then I'll be out of here."

I moved to an apartment hotel called the Bankhead that did rent to "coloreds." One room, neat. Bed. Table. Chair. Small black-and-white television set. A small stereo I'd picked up. Telephone. That was my world, that and the maroon Pontiac. I'd drive to the ballpark, I'd hit line drives, I'd run like a deer, I'd drive back to the Bankhead. If the speed limit was twenty-five, I drove twenty. If it was fifty, I drove forty-five. If it was seventy, I drove sixty-five. I didn't want trouble in any way, shape or form.

As I tend to do, I kept all this inside. No one really knew what I was going through. No one knew that I was doing something I'd never done before (or have done since)—I was *living timid.*

When I got home at night I wrote letters to my family; I called Jennie in Arizona every other night. The phone was my best buddy. I watched television, I listened to some music, I went to bed. I'd get up the next day and drive to Rickwood Field, where we played our home games.

When we were in Birmingham, I ate just about every meal in my room or in the Bankhead coffee shop. I wanted to hang out with my buddies, but I didn't want to make things hard on them, so I stayed to myself. I remember one of the first nights I was at the Bankhead, I went out to dinner alone, a place called the Red Lion Inn, I think. All I wanted to do was have a steak.

Not many of the tables in the place were occupied, but the headwaiter took a long time to seat me, and as I walked through the room, I could feel every eye in the place on me. I didn't look left or right, just sat down, ordered the steak right away, and asked for a soft drink or something and some french fries.

The waiter came back with the steak quickly. Too quickly. As he held it in front of my face, I could see that it had barely been cooked.

Then the waiter just dropped the plate on the table, from a height of about three feet. Just dropped it. The steak flopped onto the tablecloth. The silverware went flying, water glass tipped over. Big racket. Loud fuckin' racket.

"Nigger," the waiter said, "don't you *ever* come back here."

I said, "Yes sir," hot-footed it out of the Red Lion Inn, *ran* the five or six blocks back to the Bankhead, and ordered room service.

It was fear, pure and simple. I wasn't going to force any social change—that never even *occurred* to me—I was just going to survive, keep my nose clean and survive. When you'd been raised the way I'd been, all you needed or wanted were the essentials to survive. Food. Clothing. Shelter. There was food downstairs at the Bankhead if I needed it. The sheets were clean. I had all those hours at the ballpark every day when I could feel at ease with my buddies. I could call Jennie at night—my phone bill every month was at least sixty dollars—and watch television and write letters. There was money in my pocket and there was my car—even then I took inordinate pleasure in working on my car. So I made a very conscious decision to lay low, take myself out of the line of fire of the racism as much as possible. And survive.

Thank God Martin Luther King didn't feel that way. But I sure did.

The guy who owned the Bankhead was white, of course. Everyone in Birmingham in 1967 seemed to be white. The owner's daughter was a cute girl named Sally, about my age, and she took to me. I think she saw how lonely I was, knew I was having a hard time; I also think she was more than a little attracted to me. The first couple of months she used to call and ask me if I wanted to eat with her.

I don't know how many excuses I fabricated in that time. Twenty. Thirty. Maybe a hundred. I appreciated the offers, but I had become perfectly aware that dining out in public with a white girl in Birmingham was a suitable excuse for getting beat up, or lynched.

Sally never gave up. But I never gave in.

John McNamara tried to help out as much as he could, and so did my teammates, but what could they do really? Change the color of my skin? I knew they cared, however, which helped. When we'd be on a road trip and we'd stop at some diner for hamburgers or something to eat, McNamara wouldn't compromise. It was simple for him: If they wouldn't serve me, they weren't going to serve anyone. He'd just take the whole team out of the restaurant, we'd get into the bus and we'd keep driving until we found a place that would serve us all. To my mind, McNamara was a giant that season. There'd be times during his managerial career in the majors —Oakland, San Diego, Cincinnati, now California—when it would be said that John McNamara was too nice, as though that were some sort of fatal and crippling disease. I just wish the people who said that could have seen how strong he was for me in 1967.

At the end of that season, some of the local influential people wanted to throw a big party for us at one of the local country clubs, and they let McNamara know that it would be a lot easier on everyone if I just, well, disappeared the night of the party.

McNamara: "You know, that is an excellent idea. Really excellent. But you ought to know that if Reggie isn't there, it's going to be awfully lonely for you people throwing the party, because I'm not going to be there either, and neither is one member of this baseball team."

I got invited.

That's what John McNamara was about. He was and still is like blood to me. It goes way beyond a player-manager relationship. It all goes back to '67.

So I rode the buses all during the summer and thought about getting home in one piece at the end of the season. All-night bus rides and three dollars a day in meal money. Charlotte and Knoxville. Montgomery and Macon. Evansville, Indiana. Greasy hamburgers, cold coffee, warm soft drinks, sleeping sitting up with the window open, ninety-nine degrees and ninety-nine percent humidity. If you left a sandwich on the bus when you went to play a game, you'd come back to find the roaches had eaten it. Nameless little towns that you knew you'd never see again hurtling past you in the night. Rolling with the punches all along the way.

The racism was always there, but you almost got used to it after a while, because you knew you weren't going to beat it. Not in the South. Not then. And it was so crude and blatant and pitiful that there were times when it actually did make me laugh.

One night in Knoxville, Gil Blanco, who was Mexican, convinced me to go to this out-of-the-way nightclub he knew about. I couldn't see how Knoxville was going to be much better than Birmingham when it came to race relations, but Blanco kept bugging me and bugging me so I finally went with him.

We got to the nightclub. They had one of those little peepholes in the door, like in the old gangster movies. The peephole opened.

Blanco: "Uh, can we come in?"

The hole opened a little wider so the eye could see who was with Blanco.

The hole closed. From behind the door, we heard this disembodied voice say, "Ah cain't be lettin' no nigras in heah."

I just started to laugh. There was no escaping it. It was everywhere.

I said to Blanco, "Gil, man, you go ahead and go in if you want to. I'm just gonna pick myself up some fried chicken and go back to the hotel." Which is what I did. I ate a lot of fried chicken —just to feel comfortable in the South.

Even in the rattiest little nightclub dive in the rattiest part of Knoxville, Tennessee, it was always there.

Ah cain't be lettin' no nigras in heah.

Do me a favor and please pay attention to this next story.

I met Bear Bryant that year. His son, Paul Jr., was the general manager of the Birmingham team; he used to come to the games sometimes. He came into the clubhouse after I'd had a pretty good day. I'd hit a dinger and a triple as I recall (I led the league in triples with seventeen that year; I could really run then).

Paul Jr. took me over to his father and introduced me as a former football player from ASU, just to give us a common bond.

The Bear was exactly the way you always saw him on television. Tall, physically overpowering, a deep voice. Deep-set eyes. Craggy face. Porkpie hat. He was the most famous man in Alabama then, just as he was the day he died.

I shook his hand and said, "Nice to meet you, Mr. Bryant. I've heard a lot about you." I said it very softly, very respectfully. I didn't raise my voice much that year in Birmingham.

Bryant smiled, looked away from me over to his son, and said very matter-of-factly, "Now this is the kind of nigger boy I need to start my football program." (He was still a few years away from integrating the Alabama team with black players.)

I'll never forget that moment in the clubhouse at Rickwood Field. I was the kind of "nigger boy" he needed to start his football program. The funny thing is, I knew he didn't mean any harm with those words. Later on in my life, people would call me "boy" in unguarded moments and I'd feel like punching them. But I sensed that this was different. This was the best he could do, his way of paying me a compliment. He was drawing on his own experience, his own life, and trying to be nice.

"Yessir," Bear Bryant said, "if I could just have one like you, I could get it done real easy at school."

I was growing up. And I mean *fast.* Most of my energy was poured into baseball and survival, but I was beginning to learn about people. The word "nigger" coming from Bryant that day was just different from a voice behind a door in Knoxville or at the Red Lion or from some crazies in a pickup. It just was. Bear Bryant was a Reggie fan for some reason that day and for the rest of his life. When I was living in New York and he was passing through, he'd always find a way of saying hello to me.

I liked the Bear. I really did. I wish I could have known him better.

You've heard about players being up in the majors for a cup of coffee?

In June of '67, I got called up to the Kansas City A's for a cup of coffee, but I didn't even have time for cream or sugar.

It was just a way of moving from one kind of scared to another.

I was scared in Birmingham because I was twenty-one and black.
I was scared for my three weeks in Kansas City because I was
twenty-one and *in Kansas City.*

I was three years out of Cheltenham High School. I barely had
one year of minor league ball under my belt. But I had gotten off
to a good start in Birmingham with the bat—I'd only end up with
seventeen dingers that year, but when I hit them, they stayed hit;
there were some railroad tracks behind the rickety old fences at
rickety old Rickwood, and I hit some Ruthian shots on those
tracks. One day John McNamara took me aside and told me to get
the first flight to Kansas City. The team wasn't doing well, Finley
was getting a lot of heat because he was moving the team to Oakland, and he wanted to draw some attention away from himself.

Slugging Reggie Jackson, just twenty-one, was the attention.

I stayed up three weeks and was barely noticed. Those three
weeks were pretty much a blur of excitement and jitters and where-
the-hell-am-I and what-am-I-doing-wherever-I-am?

The A's were playing the Indians. I was in left field. I'd prayed
for a righty, but the righty was Steve Hargan, one of the best
pitchers in the American League then. I was oh-for-four.

The next day I got Sudden Sam McDowell, the hardest throwing lefty in the game and a guy who didn't have much control. I
was thrilled to get a grounder to short off him. Later that game I
got my first big league hit, a triple to right-center field off Orlando
Pena.

For the rest of my cup-of-coffee tour, I struck out just about
every third time.

I would love to say that all my childhood dreams had come
true by being in the majors. I would love to say that I was like a
kid in a candy store. But it was like I was there and I wasn't there,
like I was standing off to the side watching this overmatched hick,
age twenty-one, try to act like a major leaguer.

A blur. And before I knew it, I had been beamed back, like
a character in an old "Star Trek," to Evansville, where the Birmingham team was. I was relieved and crushed at the same time. I felt
like a fool and a failure. It was the first time in my life—*ever*—that
I had failed as a jock.

When I got to the clubhouse, McNamara took me into his
office since he could see the mortification just dripping off me.

He told me, "You didn't let anyone down, and I don't want

you to worry about anything. If this is the toughest thing that ever happens to you in your life, then you're going to have a pretty nice life. You know and I know that you're going to be back with the A's sometime soon, and when you are, you'll never play in the minor leagues again. So just go into the clubhouse, face your teammates and be a man, and we'll all get on with the rest of the season."

That's what I did. Evansville pitched a lefthander named Jerry Nyman that night, and I ended up tripling off him in the seventh to knock in the winning run in a 2–1 game. We went on to win the pennant, and the Dixie Series against the Dodgers AA team in Albuquerque, and after the season I got called up in September for one more cup of coffee with the A's.

And on September 15 at Anaheim Stadium against a pitcher for the Angels named Jim Weaver, I hit my first major league home run. It went about 400 feet to right.

It felt real good. Who am I kidding? It felt *great*.

I finished out the season with the big club, ending up with a measly .178 average for thirty-five games. But I'd had my taste, and I'd had my first dinger, and John McNamara was right. I never saw another day in the minor leagues.

I never had to go back to Birmingham. I have spent a lot of my time in the South since then, with the Yankees having spring training in Fort Lauderdale, and my work with ABC for the "Superstars" television series in Florida. But I've never gone there on my own. I've never felt comfortable there. Because of the summer of '67 in Birmingham, I will probably feel like an alien in the South until the day I die.

4

MR. CHARLES O. FINLEY

I played eight years in Oakland for an owner named Charlie Finley. If they ever have a Tough SOB Wing in the Hall of Fame, he will be the very first person in it. However, I have to say I kinda liked Charlie Finley. We fought all the time, like a contentious father and a headstrong son. The only simple contract negotiation we had was the first one, at his office in Chicago and then at his home in Laporte. After that we did a lot of tricky negotiating in person, and we did a whole lot of yelling in the newspapers. But we also laughed a hell of a lot. He'd take his best shot, I'd take my best shot, then we'd shake hands until the next bout.

What did Ali and Frazier have? Three fights? Charlie O. and I could have three in a day: breakfast, lunch and dinner. And they were all beauties.

He could be vindictive and he could be impossible, but I always thought Charlie was honorable at the core, a businessman who was mostly interested in the bottom line. Looking back, just about every one of our fights was about money. If Charlie could pinch a nickel on you, he would. Once he got away with pinching the nickel, he'd shoot for a dime. Then a quarter. In that sense, you had to battle him every step of the way. But it was his nature. He was a country boy from Birmingham who built an insurance empire from scratch and just felt he had to scuffle every day of his life, even after he'd built the best baseball team in the world in the early '70s.

His habits were the habits of a hungry man, and he could never break them, but I could relate to him and the habits. Charlie always had his shirtsleeves rolled up. And I must admit, he did have a creative baseball mind.

Night All-Star games? Charlie's idea. Night World Series games? Charlie's idea. Colored uniforms? Charlie. Players with mustaches and beards? Charlie was the first to say it was just fine. He was the first man to groom minor league pitching prospects as relievers; he did that with Rollie Fingers. He was the first man to see speed as a consistent force in the arsenal of a major league team. Charlie even wanted to use colored baseballs—I've still got a box of orange balls at my home in Oakland—and I think he's right about that, too. They'd be a lot easier to pick up, just like colored tennis balls are. He was always a step or two ahead of everybody else.

He was tough, and there was no bullshit to him. No bullshit whatsoever. But believe me, every day was an adventure. If you didn't learn about hardball business working for him, you just weren't paying attention.

People are always asking me to compare Finley and Steinbrenner. I gave you a little of Finley's background. Well, George was different. He came from a different arena—he inherited his wealth. He is a cuff links guy, not a rolled-up-sleeves guy. The analogy I've always used is one about gunfighters. Charlie was the fastest gun there ever was. He knew it. You knew it. When he called you out, he meant it. He'd show you his gun, and if he told you to meet him at dawn at the OK Corral, he wasn't bluffing. When you got to the OK Corral, you'd better be ready and you'd better be quick. Or Charlie would plug you right between the eyes. He didn't have to tell you he was tough; it was just there, all over him. And even when you beat him, even when you'd end up with that extra $10,000 in a contract squabble, he'd grin and say, "I'll get you next time." He meant it, too.

George wanted to intimidate you because he didn't really want to fight. He didn't want to look you in the eye and fire. He'd just sort of pull back his vest and *show* you his pearl-handled revolvers and try to scare you off, because he didn't want to draw. There were very few face-to-face confrontations with Steinbrenner; he'd always use intermediaries whenever he could, or leak a story to the press. Charlie only leaked when he went to the men's room.

Charlie would come looking for you. Or pick up the telephone and say, "Okay, what is this shit you're trying to pull?"

You could be sitting in Charlie's office, having another huge argument about money, and all of a sudden he'd say, "Time for lunch." He'd push all the papers on his desk aside, walk over to the refrigerator, and fix up this wonderful impromptu meal. Raw clams and oysters (he loved that stuff). His special dip: horseradish, mayonnaise, vinegar, Tabasco sauce and ketchup. Fix it all right there on the desk.

I'd say, "Uh, Charlie, you're trying to cut my pay here, and I'm not too crazy about you doing that. Don't we have a little more to talk about?"

Finley would look at me like I was crazy and say in that gruff, booming voice, "Jeezus, Reggie. It's two o'clock in the afternoon. Man's gotta eat. Now do you want some of this or not?" He'd grin. We'd eat. He'd clear the plates away and put all the fixings back in the refrigerator, then we'd go back to trying to knock each other's block off.

He was always like that, even after he traded me to Baltimore at the start of the 1976 season and nearly broke my heart. I was going to be a free agent at the end of that season, and he knew I was finally going to hold him up for the big money. He knew I'd test the waters in the draft. But I hadn't made up my mind about leaving and when he traded me, it was like losing my family, the way I'd lost my family back in Wyncote when I was six. I was deeply hurt.

And yet he was still honorable. When I'd signed my original bonus contract with the A's, he had worked out some investments I'd all but forgotten about. The first time I came through Chicago that 1976 season with the Orioles, Charlie got word to me that he wanted to see me.

We met in a little park across the street from his office at 310 South Michigan. It was lunchtime on a beautiful afternoon and the two of us sat on a park bench and talked.

"I still owe you $45,000 on your original contract," he said, "and I want you to know that I haven't forgotten it. I've talked to your people, and some of the papers have gotten lost, but I'll make good on the money, because I owe it to you."

I really had forgotten about the money. I remembered that we'd had a long talk about the market when I signed, and that he'd told me there were ways to move the money around. But that had been ten years before.

Ten years but he hadn't changed much. He crossed his legs, and I noticed there was still a hole in his shoe. His shirtsleeves were rolled up and his tie was undone. Charlie O. being Charlie O. Kelly-green sports jacket in his lap.

We sat in the park and watched the pretty women walk up and down Michigan Avenue.

"You doing all right in Baltimore?" he asked finally. A dad asking his kid how first semester away at college was going. "You comfortable?"

I said, "I am. I miss the guys and all, but it's a pip playing for Earl Weaver, and everybody on the team has gone out of their way to make me feel at home. I'm not sure if I'll stay after this season, but it's a real nice place to play."

We talked a little bit about the A's. Charlie said that most of the big guns on the team were in the last years of their contracts, and there was no way he could keep them. Charlie knew that free agency was going to be the end of it for him. After all the years of paying the short money to get by, the Fingers and the Bandos and the Rudis, guys like that, were going to head off to *greener* pastures. He'd lost Catfish to the Yankees after the 1974 season because of a contract foul-up that made Cat a free agent; that was the beginning of the end. Now I was gone, along with Ken Holtzman. It was coming apart on the old gunfighter, and he knew it on that bittersweet afternoon in a Chicago park.

"Cat doing all right with the Yankees?" he asked.

"Cat will *always* do all right, as long as he keeps throwing those darts," I told him.

Long pause.

"We had some time, didn't we, Reggie?" he said.

I said, "We had all of that."

"You're all going to do all right," he said, not in the gruff voice now but quietly, more vulnerable than I'd ever seen him. "And every time you hit another home run, or Sal, or Joe, or Cat wins another game, it's going to be a feather in my cap."

I didn't say anything. A couple of months before, after he'd traded me, I'd been more furious with him than ever before. I'd been angry and felt betrayed. Now I understood, as I'd probably always understood on some gut level, that it had been more than just business for Charlie O. But free agency was nipping at his heels like some sort of mad dog, and he was scuffling, just like always.

"You should be proud of yourself, Reggie," he said. "You're going to make a lot of money, and you can bet that you haven't played in your last Series."

"It's all going to work out for everybody," I said.

Charlie grinned his grin.

"And don't forget about our deal."

"Which one was that?"

Charlie O. said, "You always promised me that you'd loan me a quarter of a million if I needed it."

"Promise still goes."

We shook hands. He went back across the street to 310 South Michigan and I walked back to my hotel. We'd come a long way since our first meeting at 310 back in 1966, flying by the seat of our pants the whole time.

I have no doubt that if I called Charles O. Finley tomorrow and told him I needed $10,000 in a hurry, he'd send it by Federal Express.

Lord, the man was cheap, though.

In all the years I was with the A's, he always had this skeletal administrative staff of eight or nine people working in Oakland. They were the detail people who just kept things going while Charlie handled personnel from his Chicago office. He was the chairman, the president, the GM, the scout and the ticket manager. Not a nickel was spent that he didn't know about. He knew about the phone bill in the trainer's room. He knew how many sanitaries we used. It was wild. Charlie used to have this fourteen-year-old kid named Hammer sit in the owner's box at the Oakland Coliseum and call him during home games to tell him what was going on.

There was no one to sell season tickets; Charlie didn't want to spend the money to hire someone to handle that. He figured if we won, we'd draw. Wrong.

There were a couple of seasons we started without a radio or television contract.

Carpet on the floor in the clubhouse? What was that? I never saw carpeting on the floor of the home clubhouse until I got to New York.

You couldn't get autographed baseballs from Charlie to give away or take home with you. You had to steal them.

You got two caps to wear all season long. Two dozen bats to use the whole season. Even when we were winning championships in Oakland, guys got crazy when they'd break a bat, hit one off the fists on a cold night. Because if you had twenty-four bats going in to the game, you had twenty-three left after it, and it might only be April.

When I got to the Orioles in '76, I was just amazed when I'd see guys use half a roll of tape and then throw the rest away. Throw away *half* a roll? Charlie'd have you shot for that in Oakland if he found out about it. You'd go into the trainer's room and you'd get your ankles taped, and then the trainer would very carefully put the rest of the roll of tape on a shelf, like it was gold.

There were no new uniforms from one season to the next. I remember starting 1975 with 1972 pants. And a jersey from 1974.

That was the season after we'd won our third World Series in a row.

Charlie O.

The first game of the '73 Series against the Mets, we found out that the complimentary seats for wives and family were in the upper deck. Closest place to heaven in New York or northern California. Charlie didn't change that little plan until Sal and I and a few of the other guys raised holy hell after the game. I remember finding out during that Series that the Mets had chartered two planes: one for the team, one for friends and family. That sounded like the height of luxury to me. We had one plane. A 727 with ninety-eight seats, which barely accommodated the people we had on board. When we flew to New York, I was in one of the stewardesses' seats for takeoffs and landings. We never made a nonstop flight in our collective lives—we were always stopping somewhere to refuel.

And all the while, we were just a bunch of raggedy-ass ball-

players who kept kicking butts and taking names. Charlie O. made
us tough. We were like a pick-up team from the baseball ghetto, and
nobody wanted to come into our neighborhood and play. We were
always mad at Charlie because we were the best baseball team in
the world and we knew he was paying us slave wages. But we had
a way of turning that mad on the rest of baseball. Teams just hated
to play us, especially in Oakland. It was cold, and the ballpark was
always empty. It always seemed to be forty degrees in Oakland. But
we were playing hardball. Catfish and Vida Blue were throwing
bee-bees, and Bando and Jackson and Rudi were sitting there in the
middle of the lineup with one of their twenty-four bats, and Bert
Campaneris and Billy North were scurrying around the bases, and
Rollie was waiting out there in the bullpen, twirling the big mustache.

Oh, yeah. The insurance man from Chicago definitely made us
tough.

I guess that was the plan all along.

Did I mention that the man was cheap?

Did I mention that he would squeeze a nickel out of you?

My rookie year with the A's was 1968. I hit twenty-nine home
runs—there were some incredible shots in there—and I began to
pick up the reputation as one of the best young sluggers in the game.
It was an exciting time. Bando was there, and Rudi and Fingers and
Cat. Monday was playing in center. Dick Green was at second,
Campy was at short, and we were all having fun because you could
see that the makings of something great were there, even if the
money was short. I'd gotten married to Jennie during the All-Star
break. I was twenty-two years old. I felt that the twenty-nine dingers were only the beginning. I sensed that a whole new life was
starting.

After the season, Charlie offered me a contract for $16,000.
Sixteen thousand dollars.

I know, I know. It was fifteen years ago. There was no such
thing as free agency. I had only one year of big league ball under
my belt. I knew that Charlie wasn't going to give me the moon.

But I still kind of thought that twenty-nine dingers translated
into more than $16,000. Gary Walker was my agent and my busi-
ness partner by then, a man who was and is one of the closest friends

of my adult life. I'd met him when I was at Arizona State. He is decent and fair and honorable, but he is also tough, and so I sent him in there against Charlie.

Our basic position was this: Stick the sixteen grand.

We must have scared the hell out of Charlie. He went all the way up to $18,000.

"I just can't go any higher," Charlie told Gary. "That's my final offer."

The two of them haggled all through the winter and into spring training. I held out for the first two weeks of spring training, and Gary finally got me $20,000 for the 1969 season.

We went from there.

In 1969, Reggie Jackson went from being a fledgling Oakland celebrity on a coming ballclub to a national celebrity. That was the year I took a run at a mythical lady I called "Ruth Maris." I hit forty-seven home runs in 1969, and I hit forty-five of them before the first of September, before the pressure of the fans and the media and the whole damn country caught up with me. I started fast and never let up until I just burned out at the end. I was twenty-three years old, and all of a sudden that burning spotlight was on me. I was trying to be a good husband and not doing such a spectacular job of it as my world changed so drastically. I was trying to feel my way with this extraordinary burst of celebrity. I held everything in until September—I am good at holding things in, up to a point—when the bubble burst.

My teammates banded around me. I tried to deal with the crush of interview requests in every city as best I could. Microphones were shoved in my face for the first time, hands reached across coffee-shop tables trying to get my attention, fans grabbed and screeched for autographs. People called me in the middle of the night, actually came to my room. It got to the point where I had to register at hotels under an assumed name. I began to crave peace and quiet away from the ball park. Meanwhile Charlie was calling me all the time, being supportive, acting as cheerleader.

"Just keep trying to fight your way through this storm of attention, Reggie," he'd say. "Keep the windshield wipers on and keep driving."

I just wasn't ready. I would be ready for the pressure and the glare and the heat in all the seasons that would come—for the rest of my life, really—but I just wasn't ready for it in the summer of

1969. I was four years away from Arizona State, from the time when I was a football player first and a baseball player second. I was still a kid in a grown-up's clothes in so many ways.

So I just died in September. Didn't even win the home-run title. Harmon Killebrew ended up with 49 and Frank Howard ended up with 48. I finished third. I also had 118 RBI, I scored 123 runs to lead the league, I hit .275 and even stole thirteen bases. But I was a wreck by the time the season was over, tired and beat-up. I knew I could have done more if I'd been stronger and more mature, even with all the fireworks going on around me, but I was still proud of the numbers I'd put in the books. And I was still only twenty-three.

Charlie offered me $35,000 for the 1970 season.

I wanted $60,000, and Gary thought I should ask for $75,000. They went at each other the same way they'd gone after each other the year before. I went to stay with Gary at his home in Tempe and tried to stay out of it as best I could. If Charlie could be all business, so could I. By February, as everyone was getting ready to go to spring training, Charlie had moved up to $40,000, but he wasn't budging from there. The game would eventually change on old Charlie, and he'd reluctantly change with it as the salaries began to rise and the team became more successful, but in good times and bad he always had a firm salary structure in his head and moving him away from it was like trying to stop the USS *Arizona* by throwing spitballs at it.

The *Arizona* didn't stop in February. Didn't stop in March. Spring training was going on without me, and I was worried about that and more than a little scared, because I knew forty-seven home runs was going to be a tough act to follow.

Charlie's position was constant: "Catfish and Reggie are my two most important guys. I've got to keep them at the same level. And Catfish is making $40,000."

I finally signed for $45,000 plus $400 a month for an apartment on the second of April and proceeded to play the season like a man who hadn't had any spring training. That year I had only twenty-three home runs and hit .237.

Charlie cut me back to $40,000 for 1971.

And the game was on.

In 1971, I hit thirty-two home runs. Held out the next spring and finally signed for $55,000. Same as Catfish.

The salary structure was still holding.

In '72, I hit twenty-five home runs, but we made the playoffs and beat the Reds in the World Series. In a burst of generosity, Charlie moved me up to $75,000—same as Catfish.

It just kept getting better. In 1973, I hit thirty-two home runs, knocked in 117, and hit .293. We won the World Series again, this time over the Mets. I was MVP in the American League. I was MVP in the Series. I was on top of the world. Charlie offered me $100,000 and never budged. Guess why? 'Cause that's what Catfish made. But I won $135,000 in salary arbitration.

1974: I hit .289. Had twenty-nine dingers and ninety-three RBI. We won our third world championship in a row, taking four out of five from the Dodgers. I was the leading vote-getter for the All-Star team that year.

Charlie offered me the same $135,000 I'd gotten the year before.

Charlie: "You went down, down, down, Reggie. In good conscience, I can't give you a raise for the kind of numbers you put up this year."

This was on the telephone one day during the winter. I didn't have an answer for that one.

Gary was always a lot better than I was when it came to debates about finance.

Charlie: "I probably should cut you for the year you had, but I'm a generous man at heart, despite what you think. So what the hell. I'm going to keep you at 135 grand because hundred-thousand-dollar ballplayers are supposed to hit thirty homers and drive in a hundred runs."

He always said he was paying me in '74 for what I did in '73 and that he was paying me in '75 for what I did in '74.

We took him to arbitration. I asked for $160,000. He stayed at $135,000.

He won. But generosity overwhelmed him and he gave me a $2,500 raise.

In 1975, I hit thirty-six dingers. I knocked in 104. I hit .253. Catfish had gone to the Yankees by then, and something big had gone from our team, but we still managed to make the playoffs before being swept by the Red Sox. I still believe we would have won the fourth World Series if we'd had Cat, but we didn't, so the streak ended at three. I hit .417 in those playoffs.

Charlie: "I'd like to offer you a raise, Reggie. But I can't. Your batting average is embarrassing. You still strike out too much. I know you drove in 104 runs, but I don't feel they were *important* runs. Maybe if we'd made the World Series, I could give you a raise. But we didn't. So I can't. I'm sorry. I feel bad about this. But I just can't." He never mentioned that my thirty-six homers had led the league. (I hit two the last day of the season to tie George Scott.)

I went to spring training in 1976 without a contract, and Gary and Charlie kept dickering. He wanted me to sign before the start of the regular season. I wouldn't sign, not after the year I had, not for the money he was offering. Plus, for the first time, I had an option.

Free agency had come to baseball the previous winter. An independent arbitrator named Peter Seitz had thrown out baseball's traditional reserve clause in cases involving Dave McNally and Andy Messersmith. Up until then, once you signed a contract with a team, you were bound to that team forever. Seitz, in the McNally and Messersmith cases, basically said, No way on forever. Suddenly if, after your contract was done, you didn't up and sign another one, then you were free after the one option year. It was, of course, the most historic ruling in the history of the game, and it has made a lot of us rich. Thanks to Curt Flood, Andy Messersmith and Dave McNally.

I didn't know in the spring of '76 *precisely* how that was going to affect me after the '76 season—the Players Association and the owners would do a lot of serious fighting before the details of the first free agent draft were worked out—but free agency was definitely in the wind.

For the first time, I sensed that Charlie O. didn't have Reggie M. by the balls anymore.

The thing is, though, I didn't want to leave. Oakland was home. I loved northern California. The A's were family. We hadn't won the World Series the year before, but the nucleus was still there, and I figured we'd start another streak in 1976.

Charlie still wouldn't move off a salary of $140,000 (he had finally offered another $2,500 raise).

Gary and I came back with a counterproposal: a three-year contract starting with the '76 season. A total of $525,000, with $150,000 for the first year, $175,000 the second year, $200,000 the third. I just wanted $50,000 a year in actual salary, with the rest of it being deferred.

Before the start of the season, Finley traded me to Baltimore.

Charlie was bottom line right until the end.

There was no question that Charlie wanted to be the star in Oakland, even after he'd put together this magnificent baseball machine piece by piece. He didn't care whether the team got promoted; he was popping off and promoting himself. Television contracts? Radio contracts? They were afterthoughts with him. He always wanted it to be Charles O. Finley and his Oakland A's. Like it was an orchestra and he was the leader. Like it was Les Brown and His Band of Renown. Charlie always wanted to be right there in the forefront, saying this and that, wearing his Kelly-green coat, waving his baton.

But he knew his baseball. Oh, yes, he did. No matter what the contract problems were, he was always figuring out ways to make us better. He had this innate sense about people and chemistry and the kind of nucleus he needed to have a winner. He did a lot of things, Charlie did, but he never messed with the nucleus.

He had Jackson and Bando and Rudi. He had Gene Tenace and Dave Duncan, then Ray Fosse, as his catchers. He had Campaneris and Dick Green in the middle, and then when Green retired he went out and got Phil Garner. There was Rick Monday in center; then Charlie saw the need for another left-hander so he traded Monday for Kenny Holtzman and Bill North. Holtzman gave the starting pitching depth and balance, and North took over in center. Then Angel Mangual played center. He'd go out and get a Mike Epstein or a Don Mincher to play first. Balance, Charlie always understood balance. However, his first slip-up caused his eventual downfall.

Later Steinbrenner would make moves just to make moves, to keep himself in the news; he was always doing things for effect because he was in New York City, and he had this idea that you had to do things for effect.

Charlie was always tinkering to make us a little better. Help the nucleus. Keep the balance just right. He was always poking around the waiver wire in all his years in Oakland, looking for that

one extra pinchhitter who might make a difference. A Rico Carty.
A Felipe Alou. A Matty Alou. A Manny Sanguillen. A Billy Williams. I used to joke in Oakland that if you stuck around the A's
long enough, you'd pretty much get the chance to play with anybody you ever heard of. Players on the way down or on the way
out would get one last stop at drafty old Oakland Coliseum. Charlie
did it with pitchers, too. A Mudcat Grant one season. A Sonny
Siebert the next. A Jim Perry. Guys who might be good for one win,
or two, or three.

If Charlie could get them for bargain basement prices, he
would. I'm sure when he saw a name on the waiver wire he thought
he could use, his eyes lit up like a kid on Christmas morning. He
said he used to read that waiver list like it was his income tax return.

The managers would change—Hank Bauer, McNamara, Dick
Williams, Alvin Dark—but Charlie kept the whole thing going,
until free agency mugged him and he couldn't compete anymore,
at least not the way he had. We had the hitting in the middle. We
had speed up top in Campy and North. There was always enough
catching and plenty of defense. The starting rotation was a dream.
The right-handers were Cat and Blue Moon Odom; the lefties were
Holtzman and Vida Blue. Paul Lindblad was our left-handed reliever, then Charlie added Darold Knowles. Rollie was the stud.

Yeah, we were Charlie Finley's Oakland A's. Gold socks and
high stirrups and white pants. Gold shirts sometimes, green shirts
sometimes, white shirts on Sunday. Kicked ass and took names.

He loved it all. We fought him. We fought each other. But
somehow we managed to laugh a lot also. Remember that old line
the Packers used to have about Vince Lombardi? "He treated us all
the same—like dogs"? That was the way we were with Charlie.

And not one of us would have missed a minute of it. We were
the meanest junkyard dogs who ever played the game of baseball.

It never changed between us in the eight years I played for him in
the big leagues, through all the dingers and battles and championships. Contract time was a constant. His best lick followed by your
best lick. Wipe the blood off your lip and go play the season.

After I finally settled on the deal in 1972, after I finally bled
$55,000 out of him for a thirty-two-dinger year in '71, Charlie

called me up on the telephone to congratulate me on this fabulous
new contract. I assume *he* assumed I was doing cartwheels.

"There's just one little thing I'd like to ask you, Reggie," he
said.

I felt like saying, "Whatever it is, it's going to cost you five
grand, Charlie."

I actually said, "What is it?"

"I'd prefer if you didn't mention to anybody exactly how much
I'm paying you," he said.

"Charlie, you've got no problem there," I told him. "I'm as
embarrassed about this contract as you are."

We both laughed then, Charles O. Finley the hardest.

5

BUT HOW WE PLAYED THE GAME...

I f there had never been free agency, if Peter Seitz hadn't made his ruling for McNally and Messersmith, if Charlie hadn't lost Cat because of a contract technicality, if Jackson had played his whole career in Oakland, and Bando and Rudi and Campaneris and Fingers, too, there is no doubt in my mind that the Oakland A's would have won eight or nine World Series in the 1970s, maybe even into the '80s. We were that good. When we left, most of us were still in our prime. We were talented and mean and hungry, and we might just have turned out to be the greatest team of all time.

As it was, when you talk about the great teams, we certainly have to be among them.

We played as well as we had to because we always had October in the backs of our minds. There were years when we could have won our division by ten games, or fifteen or twenty; I believe that. But there was this sense in all of us that when we had a three-game lead, it was all right, it was fine, because we knew it was over. We'd wander from a one-game lead to a six-game lead, never worrying, never fussing. We knew we would do it when we had to. We had

Charlie's nucleus. We were all business. We did it right off his blueprint.

North: Switchhitter. Good lead-off man. Steal fifty bases for you a year.

Campy: Good with the bat in the second spot. Move North around. Get on himself. Steal fifty bases himself.

Bando: Captain. Leader. Manager on the field. Clutch man. Hit twenty-five homers. Knock in 100 or close to it.

Reggie: Clean-up man. Made you pitch to Bando in front of him and Rudi behind him. Get his thirty dingers. Get his 100 ribbies.

Rudi: Unsung man at bat and in the field. Hit .290 falling out of bed. Get his twenty homers. Make every play a man could possibly make in the outfield. Get eighty to ninety RBI.

Gene Tenace: Catch some. Play first some. Knock in eighty runs. Get 100 walks. Hit as many clutch homers as anyone on the team.

Dick Green: Glue of the infield at second. Good bunter at the bottom of the order.

Five straight Western Division titles. Three straight World Series in the middle. Doing it the same all the time.

North would get a walk. He'd steal second. Campy would bunt him over. Sal would hit a sacrifice fly. All of a sudden, we wouldn't have a base hit, but we would have a run. And know what? Catfish was pitching. And Fingers was just sitting and waiting in the bullpen. Before a team would get up to bat, we'd have them on the ropes. They knew it. We knew it. It's just the way things were. When Cat was pitching, we knew we were going to be in the game, every time. It's a wonderful way to start the day. He would give up one run maybe, two at the outside. All we had to do was get him a lead by the seventh.

Because then Rollie was going to stroll in from the outfield with the chain in his hand to bolt the door.

Taking care of business.

We'd save all our emotion for contract fights with Charlie or fights with each other. On the field, we were not emotional. Just went about our jobs and got it all done. There were no pep talks, no rah-rah stuff, no pounding guys on the back. Oh, every once in a while Sal would get up in the clubhouse and straighten some things out. I remember a time in 1974—Alvin Dark was the man-

ager by then—and there had been some bickering from some of the
guys about not being used often enough, or correctly. Sal called a
very, very brief team meeting.

"Hey, look, I'm sick and tired of hearing guys bitch about
not getting into games at the right time, not being used right,"
Sal said.

When Sal talked, people listened. He was dark and menacing
when he wanted to be. He was also built like a tree stump.

"That's not the way we do things around here," he said. "Let
me just spell it out for some of you. If you're a left-handed relief
pitcher and you come in to face a right-handed hitter, get him out.
If you're a left-handed pinchhitter and you come up to face a lefty,
get a hit. Just do it. And shut the fuck up about it. Okay. Do we
understand each other?"

That was about it.

We didn't want to hear a lot of dialogue about guys screwing
up. If the game was 3–3 in the eighth and North or Campaneris had
to steal a base, then they were supposed to steal the damn base.
Make it. Do not get caught. Don't come back to the dugout and
tell us that the pitcher had a great move or the catcher made a great
throw. If North or Campaneris stole the base and got to second,
then the next guy got him to third. Throw a little flare to right.
Don't worry about getting jammed or breaking your bat. Get the
guy over to third. You hear? Just do it.

And shut up about it. Just like Sal said.

We fought all the time. I've always said the same thing: When a
fight would break out in the A's clubhouse, no one would even look
up from their card games. You'd just be sort of bemused.

Who is it today?

Anybody know why it started?

Whose turn is it to break it up?

Oh, shit, I gotta do it. Okay, I fold for this hand, but I'll be
back for the next one. Somebody come and help me.

We were all young. We were all cocky as hell because we could
beat anyone. We were always mad at Charlie. Couldn't beat up
Charlie. Had to beat up each other.

Billy North and I got into it one day in 1974. North was a

feisty little guy with a hair-trigger temper, and one of the reasons why he was such a winner on the field was because he had a lot of piss and vinegar in him. I had introduced him to a girl; then one night at a bar when he wasn't around, the girl started coming on to me. I sort of brushed her off, but when the story got back to North, it was Reggie who had come on to the girl and not vice versa.

Whoops.

North let it simmer for a few weeks, then confronted me one day in the clubhouse and accused me of trying to "steal his woman." I told him it wasn't true. He wanted to fight, I could see that. I didn't want to fight. One of the reasons was I was standing there in my birthday suit with nothing on but shower thongs.

It wasn't exactly my fighting outfit.

North called me a "faggot," which was sort of ironic since at that particular moment he was accusing me of trying to snake his girl.

I didn't much like being called a faggot anyway, so we went at it. Typical clubhouse fight. Wrassling and jostling. Roll around on the floor. Grunt a lot.

Then somebody got up from a card game and broke it up.

It was always something. Rollie and Blue Moon got into a fight during the '74 World Series. I can't even remember what it was about. Joking led to instigation which led to cursing which led to, well, wrassling and jostling. I got into a fight with Mike Epstein in '73 over ticket allotments for players. Another time Blue Moon went after a reserve outfielder named Tommy Reynolds with a Coke bottle. Another time it was Campy and Vida.

When the fighting was done, we'd just go out and win again. Later on, when I was with the Yankees, Goose Gossage and Cliff Johnson would get in a bathroom brawl. That was in 1979. Gossage hurt his hand and missed half the season. In New York, it was as if the Japanese had invaded Coney Island. You guessed it: Cliff got traded.

Around the A's, it would just have been part of the daily routine: Batting Practice, Brawling, Infield, Game. And another victory.

•   •   •

Gene Tenace was one of the rocks on the team—a smart, solid, down-to-earth guy from Ohio; family man; never a troublemaker; good sense of humor. We used to joke that he was Sal Bando's shadow. Didn't matter where you were. If you saw Sal, you saw Geno.

Tenace (he liked to call himself Tenachi) was hard-nosed, and would play hurt, and he loved to come up in the clutch. The first year we won the World Series, over the Reds in seven games in 1972 —that was the one I spent on crutches, having torn up my hamstring scoring the tying run in the fifth playoff game against the Tigers—Gene was MVP.

The next year, in the World Series against the Mets, Gene gave me the closest thing to a pep rally I ever had in Oakland. It was before the sixth game. We were down three games to two, and Tom Seaver was pitching for the Mets. I'd been having a good Series— I'd end up being MVP for that one—and I guess Gene just sensed that it was time to shine.

We were standing at my locker in the clubhouse, getting ready for the pre-game introductions. Gene walked over to me and put his hand on my shoulder. My teammates called me "Buck" then. The big guy. To this day, the old A's call me Buck.

"Buck," Tenace said, "I sure would like to play tomorrow."

And walked away. That was the entire speech. Buck, do something today. Get us to the seventh game and then we'll take our chances.

I went three-for-four that day with two doubles and a single. We beat Seaver. It was over then. We had Cat going, and I've already told you what we felt like when we had Cat going. In the seventh, I had a big dinger off Jon Matlack.

We won our second Series in a row.

I'll never forget that moment with Tenace before the sixth game.

Buck, I sure would like to play tomorrow.

Sal Bando was the Godfather. *Capo di capo.* Boss of all bosses on the Oakland A's. We all had our roles, we all contributed, but Sal was the leader and everyone knew it. He didn't make a big deal out of it, but when something needed to be said, he said it. He is a hell of a man, Italian through and through. When we used to go into

Cleveland his whole family would be there, and it would be kisses all around. Salvatore Bando. His wife's name is Sandra Fortunato. His son's name is Santino Leonardo Bando.

Sal Bando was and is my friend. He was ahead of me at Arizona State, and we always had that in common, having played for Bobby Winkles, having all Winkles's baseball values drummed into us. He always understood me, Sal did, and I always thought we complemented each other extremely well as teammates. He hit third. I hit fourth. It is not such a bad deal in a man's career to hit behind Sal Bando, then Thurman Munson. They were the two best number-three hitters I ever played with. Pitchers couldn't pitch around them, and they always seemed to be on base, so I always got good pitches as a result.

In the early years in Oakland, Sal and I spent a lot of time together socially. He and his wife, Jennie and I. We lived in the same neighborhood in Hayward, California. We drove to the ballpark in his Buick. He was stable, he was bright, he had a ton of character. And there was nothing flaky about him.

Except his temper.

Hoo-boy, did Sal used to get pissed off. In that sense, he was Jekyll and Hyde. He wouldn't show you a lot of it when he was actually on the field, but in the dugout after a strike out, he was the ultimate, maximum, all-out red ass. He'd go through a half-dozen batting helmets a season, at least. It used to make Charlie crazy, because as I've already mentioned, Charlie was cheap with equipment. A half-dozen batting helmets. Two, three dozen bats. He would just destroy things. When he'd come back to the dugout after striking out or popping up or not getting a runner across, everyone would just scatter. Like toward San Francisco.

Rollie used to rib him about it all the time. Everything was fair game for ribbing with the A's, even where Sal was concerned. Even with the captain. The Rollie and Sal Show was a regular part of every bus ride.

"Hey, fat boy," Rollie would call out. "Oh, fat boy. How much private property did you destroy today? Oh, fat boy, you've got to learn to control that Italian temper of yours."

Sal's comebacks were always the same.

"Fingers," he'd say, "I would respond to your silly insults, but I'm not sure you would understand what I was talking about."

Sal used to come out of the pitching meetings shaking his head about things Rollie had said. We went into Baltimore one year, and it was when Frank and Brooks Robinson were tearing up the American League. Sal asked Rollie how he intended to pitch to them. Infielders want to know what pitches a guy is going to throw to a certain hitter in a specific situation so they can position themselves properly.

Sal wanted to know if the count was such-and-such, was Rollie going to throw a fastball in or a slider out, that sort of thing.

Rollie said, "I'm going to pitch those suckers the best way I know how."

Sal: "But how are you going to pitch Frank and how are you going to pitch Brooks?"

Rollie: "Tell me again. Which one is which?"

Sal leaned forward, not sure whether Rollie was kidding or not.

But that was it.

The thing was, Rollie's best was usually good enough, no matter what he threw. Or which one was which.

In so many ways, the Oakland experience was the college experience I'd never had. We had all come from different parts of the country with different sets of experiences to go on this fantastic voyage together. I was from Wyncote. Catfish Hunter was North Carolina through and through. Blue Moon Odom was from Macon, Georgia; he'd had a lifetime of experiences like the ones I had in just that one summer in Birmingham. Rudi and Rollie were from California and Gene and Sal were from Ohio and Dick Green was from North Dakota and Vida was from Louisiana. We gave different things to each other, made the personalities and experiences mesh, learned from each other, won together. We all grew up together.

The eight years in Oakland were the best baseball years of my life, despite the difficulties with Charlie, despite the fights, despite the fact that I was learning to cope with celebrity the same as everyone else. It was like we were safe in Oakland. It wasn't New York. It wasn't Los Angeles. The spotlight wasn't the same until we got to the World Series, and then we handled it because we were just so . . . damn . . . good.

Our experience was the one we shared, day in, day out, going from place to place and beating people, joking about our brawling image, doing more brawling, flying commercial when richer teams were chartering, busing from New York to Baltimore when we knew most teams flew, bitching about our salary problems together, calling each other "Fat Boy" and "Buck," never realizing that on such a fundamental level this was the fun part, that we'd all go on to make more money in other cities, and we'd win independently of each other as we had when we were together. But it wasn't going to be the same. The rest of our careers was the real world. An experience everyone hopes for—thank goodness I had the opportunity.

Occasionally, the growing up parts would take place away from the Oakland experience. Such was the case after the 1970 season when I was lucky enough to play winter ball for Frank Robinson in Puerto Rico.

That season, 1970, had been a terrible time for me. I had had the contract fight with Charlie all winter and spring, not signing until April. I had dropped from forty-seven homers to twenty-three. My batting average had been .237. I had separated from Jennie, and I was doubting myself. The forty-seven-dinger year had been a party, at least until September. I had *arrived.* From April through August, I had the country talking about Ruth and Maris. I was twenty-three years old and the world seemed to be my oyster.

Then . . . *crash!*

Reality set in. Charlie suggested winter ball, and I agreed. I wanted to see if I could get my swing back in Puerto Rico. And I wanted to play for Frank Robinson. It seemed a good time to get away from Oakland, where everything had temporarily become depressing.

Even at the best of times in college, there is a rotten semester.

Frank Robinson had always been a hero of mine. Not like Mays had been, but close. He was tough. He hung over the plate fearlessly. They knocked him down, and he got back up, sneered at them, and hit home runs. He was a winner, in Cincinnati and Baltimore. He'd won the Triple Crown and been MVP. He was going to the Hall of Fame and everybody knew it. He was in his heyday when I came up to the big leagues, and I respected the hell out of him. He had *done* what I was *trying* to do.

The name of our team that winter was the Santurce Cangrejeros team. We were known as the "Crabbers." The owner was a man named Hiram Cuevas, and I remember he looked a lot like my dad, which was sort of a cross between Adam Clayton Powell and Cab Calloway. Nice man. Easy smile. Glad to have me there.

Robinson knew what kind of year I'd had. Hell, everybody did. He could see that I was wearing my doubts and insecurities like an old suit. The first couple of days in San Juan I stayed at the Hotel San Juan, then Frank had me move into his apartment. He was all business about the rent, same way he was all business and professional about everything else.

"I'm the manager," he said. "I make more money down here than you do. I'll take the big bedroom, you take the small bedroom. I'll pay seventy percent of the rent, you pay thirty percent."

I listened and nodded. When Frank talked in that high-pitched voice of his, you listened and nodded a lot.

I only played three months for him and lived with him for two, but I learned a lot in that period about being a pro in good times and bad, about being a leader, about leading by example. Frank had no time for pouters. He'd never been a pouter himself. He had no time for whiners. That word wasn't even in his vocabulary. He was a mature man, and he wanted to show that to me so I could become more mature myself.

When I'd get into a slump, he'd pull me aside and say, "Just keep doing the best you can."

I'd put my head down and mumble something about doing lousy.

"You're having a slump," he'd snap right back. "Everybody has slumps. Keep your damn head up. If you're going to be a leader in this game, you've got to lead all the time. If you want to talk after every at-bat, we'll talk after every damn at-bat."

And that is what we did. Every time I started to get down on myself with the Santurce Cangrejeros, Frank Robinson would be all over me.

"If you're going to lead, lead all the time."

Same refrain.

"Don't lead for twenty-nine days, then throw your helmet and hang your head and pout on the thirtieth. Be a man. Be a pro."

I left the Santurce team a better professional, a better man, than when I'd come. Frank Robinson came into my life at a perfect time for me, and I'll always have a special feeling for him for the way he took me under his wing. I've tried to do it for others in the years since. I watched out for a guy named Champ Summers when he came up to the A's. In New York, I moved a rookie named Dennis Wirth right into my apartment when he was feeling his way.

It all goes back to Frank.

In the '71 season I had thirty-two dingers and never looked back.

Fifth game of the American League Championship Series. Second inning. Tiger Stadium, Detroit.

It was the day the Oakland A's won their first pennant. It was the day I ran myself out of the chance to play in my first World Series.

I walked and stole second. Sal flied out to right, and I took third. Mike Epstein got hit by a pitch. First and third. One out.

Gene Tenace struck out.

Two outs.

Dick Williams, always a ballsy manager and always one tough SOB, put on the sign for the double steal. Epstein was going to take off for second. I was supposed to watch Bill Freehan, the Tiger catcher. If he threw the ball down to second, I was supposed to take off as soon as the ball went past Mickey Lolich, the Tiger pitcher. If Freehan bluffed the throw, I was supposed to be close enough to third so I could get back safely. It was a play we executed beautifully all the time. Now we had to do it in an all-the-marbles game for the pennant.

Freehan gunned it down to second, and I was running.

It was a cold October day at Tiger Stadium, and about halfway home, I felt a muscle pull in the back of my leg.

Hamstring. Shit.

I kept going. It was still early in the game, but we were down a run. We needed the run. Hell, we were the A's. If you tried to steal the base, you were supposed to steal the damn base. I kept running, and about twenty feet from Freehan and the plate, I could feel my leg pull up, and the hamstring just tear completely.

How do you know you've torn it?

You just *know.*

Freehan was blocking the plate, and I half-slid, half-jumped into him, screaming as I went, because I knew I'd hurt the leg, hurt it seriously. There was a hell of a collision between Freehan and me.

Safe. 1–1.

I just lay there on the ground, my leg knotted up underneath me like a pretzel. The team gathered around me, and finally they took me off the field on a stretcher. I was crying with the pain.

I watched the rest of the game, which we ended up winning 2–1, on a television set in the clubhouse. I was propped up in the trainer's room when the champagne celebration began. Somebody had already found me some crutches. Dave Duncan came into the trainer's room carrying a bottle of champagne in his hand, and when he saw the crutches, he started to cry.

He wasn't playing much at the time. Tenace was the first-string catcher now, and Duncan knew he wasn't going to get much of a chance to play in the Series against the Cincinnati Reds. Dave and I had come the whole way together, from Modesto to Birmingham to Oakland, now to the Series, and as we hugged each other and sipped champagne in the visitors' clubhouse at Tiger Stadium, we just wondered how things could go wrong. This should have been our greatest day, and now the World Series was going to go on without us.

There is always that cruel athletic mix of triumph and tragedy lurking at the edges of every game you play. Just look at the loser of a contest as soon as it's over.

"You've got to play in the World Series, Reggie," Duncan said. "You gotta do it for me, for both of us."

I said, "I don't see how I can, Dave. The leg is a mess, I just know it."

After a while I got up on the crutches and hobbled over to the Tiger clubhouse and congratulated Billy Martin on the way his team had played against us. It had been a terrific series from the start, and I just wanted him to know I respected the job he'd done with an older Tiger team.

Martin shook my hand, thanked me for coming by, and told me he was sorry about my leg.

It was a nice moment.

(Later on, when Billy and I were acting like Egypt and Israel in the Yankee clubhouse, I would wish Billy remembered the moment a little better. But it never came up.)

We flew to Cincinnati that night and I went straight to the hospital; the doctor told me that I'd not only ripped the hamstring but a lot of the muscles around it, and that he was going to put the leg in a cast. That made it official. I was going to be a spectator at my first World Series. Shit. Shit. Shit.

The night before, Rudi and Duncan and I—the Modesto Three, the Birmingham Three—had gone around to a lot of the guys' rooms just to talk about the fifth game against the Tigers, just to let everyone know that we were all together and we were going to win that deciding game. And now we weren't together at all, except in spirit.

If someone had told me that night in the hospital in Cincinnati that I'd be known as Mr. October someday, that I would set all sorts of World Series records and have the greatest night the Series had ever seen, I wouldn't have known whether to laugh or cry. I was hurt and miserable, and I felt cheated.

Both teams had workouts the next afternoon at Riverfront Stadium, and Johnny Bench came over to me and told me how bad he felt that I wasn't going to be playing. I told him I appreciated that.

"If we're going to win this thing," Bench said, "we want to beat you guys at your best. And you guys won't be at your best with you on the sidelines."

I said, "Look out for yourself, anyway," and Bench laughed.

Then he said, "What are you doing tonight?"

Me: "I thought I'd sit in my room and watch television and be depressed."

Bench: "Well, that won't do. This is my town. You're going to have dinner with me."

The night before the 1972 World Series, Johnny Bench took me out to dinner. It was a gesture on his part that I can't ever forget as long as I live. From that moment on, I thought of Johnny Bench as a Hall of Fame human being, in addition to being one of the most magnificent catching machines in the history of baseball.

That is Memory No. 1 from the 1972 World Series.

Memory No. 2 is standing off to the side after we won the seventh game. Guys were spraying champagne. Guys were laughing and crying and hugging and cursing and dancing, and I just could not get into it. I hadn't made any contribution whatsoever. I hadn't been to the plate, I hadn't even swung and missed. Nothing. It was one of the most painful, ambivalent moments of my life.

I felt a little like I did walking home that day in Wyncote after the Dixie Series, telling myself every step of the way that I'd be a major leaguer someday.

In Cincinnati that day, I made a silent vow to myself that the next time the Oakland A's were in a World Series—I wasn't sure it would be the next season, but I had a strong feeling—I was going to be *right there.*

I was.

I hit .310 against the Mets in '73. Got nine hits. Went three-for-four in that sixth game and had the dinger off Matlack in the seventh.

Walked away with the MVP award.

I said that we all laughed a lot in Oakland. Vida Blue laughed as much as any of us.

He had come up at the end of the 1970 season; then in '71 he took the American League by storm, winning twenty-four games as well as the MVP award and the Cy Young. He'd have his own contract problems with Charlie later on, and Charlie would burn a lot of the fun-loving kid out of him, but Vida always had one of the sweetest dispositions you ever saw. And Lord, could he throw a baseball. He would just stand out there and throw fastballs and grin at you and dare you to hit them. Everybody liked Vida. He was a dugout instigator like the rest of us, but always in an innocent way. He had this smile I was sure you could see all the way back in Mansfield, Louisiana, his hometown.

That was why I was so shocked and saddened later on in his life when he was involved with cocaine. I felt he had betrayed his talent, betrayed himself. But when I heard, I understood so much better why things had seemed so strange between us in the years when he was pitching for the Kansas City Royals, after coming over from the Giants.

I always wanted to say, "Hey, man. It's me, Buck. What's bothering you? You can tell me. We were *together,* man. Tell me."

I never asked. He never said anything in our brief encounters.

Then I found out about his drug problem, and it was like putting two and two together. I understood. Completely. But too late. I wondered what in the world had happened to that sweet ol' guy from Mansfield.

I have rarely taken a drug in my life. I can't say that I've been perfect. I will drink my beers and have a glass of wine now and then. But the whole thought of it is sickening to me. Everything I have in life stems from the fact that the Lord gave me this skillful body. I have to think He gave it to me for a purpose. I'll never abuse this body with drugs. Never will. My eyes, my strength, my coordination—those are my instruments, the tools of my trade. I will not disease them with drugs. And I can't have respect or sympathy for anyone who does. You do drugs, you get arrested, you do time? Fine, I say. You deserve everything you get. Not because you're supposed to be setting any kind of example for the world, but because you have violated yourself, your body, your God-given talent. When He gives you the ability to run fast or hit a ball or jump over all the other players on a basketball court, then He enters into a contract with you in spirit. You do not break that contract. If you do, don't come crying to anyone.

I am usually a little cynical about baseball players—all athletes really—who have these well-publicized victories over booze and drugs. It has almost become a fashionable hobby, and half the time I don't really believe a guy is cured at all. It seems like every other day someone is driving past one of the drug or alcohol rehabilitation clinics, stopping for lunch, calling a press conference afterward, announcing he's cured of liquor or cocaine, and driving on. And everyone cheers. Rehab chic.

This is too important a problem in our society for me to ignore. It has to be addressed. It is just so damn stupid to do drugs. It goes all the way back to the admonitions you always heard in childhood: Don't touch the stove, it's hot. Watch that hot water, son, it'll burn your fingers off. Don't smoke cigarettes, they're bad for you, they'll stunt your growth. When I was growing up, no one had to tell you *not* to do drugs because drugs didn't exist. At least not twenty-five years ago in Wyncote, Pa., they didn't. But drugs would have been part of that long lists of do's and don'ts we all grew up with.

And the rules, at least to me, always seem to apply double or triple if you are an athlete. If you're an athlete, you're supposed to get your rest. Don't stay up late, man. We got a game tomorrow.

There used to be this saying we always heard from the coaches in the minors: You're going to run into wine, you're going to run into women, you're going to be around smoking. You can get away with one. Two will shorten your career. All three will end it. So be careful what you do when the game is over.

If you reach for the sixth beer in a six-pack, if someone offers you cocaine and you take it, you know you're treading on thin ice. You should see the red light go on. You should know you're heading into the danger zone.

You should stop.

I see it happening to athletes more and more, and it just sickens me. They look around and say: I'm the one who can handle drinking to excess if that's what I want to do; I can handle the dope. They are such fools. They deserve what they get, and they get what they deserve.

Dick Green was our Bucky Dent. With the Yankees, Bucky played shortstop, and I used to say he was outstanding at doing a necessary job. He made all the plays. He got his bunts down. He chipped in big hits when he got the chance. Greenie was the same way.

As I remember it, it seems he was always hitting .220 and always fielding close to 1.000 at second base. He turned singles up the middle into outs. If there was a runner on first, he turned a single up the middle into a double play. He was the baseball workman. His uniform was always baggy and sloppy; it always looked like it was a couple of sizes too big and hadn't been washed since Truman was president. Even his shoes looked too big.

But he never made an error that counted that I can remember. He was as much a leader as anyone else on the team. Then when the season was over, he went back to his family, his moving and storage business.

Between April and October, though, he was a rock at second base and a sneaky contributor at the bottom of the order.

A real Oakland A, Greenie. Miss him.

We were controversial because we were good. And at the time that we were punching out all of baseball, we were different. We had those funny-colored uniforms. We had that crazy owner, that Finley guy. We wore long hair and mustaches and beards. We fought with one another.

But we would have been just another goofy sporting oddity if we couldn't back it up on the field.

The funny thing was, we didn't think of ourselves as being controversial or different. We just thought of ourselves as being the A's. It wasn't until we'd get out on the road, go to Chicago, go to New York, that we'd get a sense from the media that we were the hottest show around. As we kept winning World Series, we understood that fame was enveloping us, we understood that fans around the league found us exciting and intriguing, but we'd look at each other and say, "What's the big deal? What's changed so much?" Charlie was still bleeding us at contract time. Blue Moon was always mixing it up with someone in the clubhouse. Rollie was still calling Sal "Fat Boy." Kenny Holtzman was still talking about money all the time. Greenie's uniform still didn't fit.

Maybe it was because we were in Oakland. Maybe it really was like being in another world. In 1974, in the same month, I was on the cover of both *Time* and *Sports Illustrated.* I was still only twenty-eight years old, and I was pulling off a double play very few athletes have pulled off before or since. And don't get me wrong: It was a very pleasant ego massage.

But it didn't change my life a whole hell of a lot.

Time called me the leader of "The Wild Bunch." That was a nickname we'd picked up because of a popular movie of the same name. That was nice. Except that when I was in the clubhouse, I was still "Buck," and everybody gave me a ribbing about being called the leader because we all knew that Sal was the leader.

So I just kept hitting home runs, and Campy kept scurrying around the bases, and Sal and Joe and Gene kept knocking in their runs, and in October of 1974 we won another World Series. Like it was a rule.

The thing about making history is you rarely figure that out until someone tells you. We were all too busy having the time of our lives to know that we were accomplishing things individually and as a team that would be remembered as long as people played Mr. Doubleday's game.

.   .   .

There was always something inevitable about the A's, from the time
we came together and saw day in and day out what we could all
do on a ballfield. There was always the sense that Sal was in charge,
but Dick Williams, who came along in 1971 and managed us to the
first two world championships in '72 and '73, was the right drill
sergeant for us at the right time. He might have made us jell a little
sooner than we would have without him. We respected his reputation because he'd managed the Red Sox to their "Impossible
Dream" in 1967. And the man was a *tough* son of a gun. Dick
Williams was never interested in winning any popularity awards
with anyone, as far as I could see. Williams was macho before the
word began to take on a life of its own; he had a gravelly voice that
sounded like he'd been gargling with razor blades most of his adult
life, and he never—ever—worried about hurting any feelings with
his cocky band of young warriors.

He was the master of the game of fundamentals, and he was
as big a reason as any why fundamentals became our badge of
armor. Hit the cutoff man. Get the bunts down. Make every relay
perfect. Do not—*do not*—screw up a relay. And do not miss a sign.

Vida used to sit in the dugout when he wasn't starting and
watch everything Williams did, try to hear every negative comment
he made about anyone. If Williams would throw down his cap or
throw down his cigarette and call someone a horse's ass, Vida
would walk down to the water fountain where Williams sat with
his coaches and say, "I'm gonna tell Greenie what y'all said about
him. I'm gonna tell him as soon as he gets off the field."

Smiling that big Vida smile so they just couldn't get mad.

But he'd tell. Sometimes Williams would do the bad-mouthing. Sometimes it was a coach of his named Irv Noren. It was just
a part of the program.

One day I kicked a ball around in the outfield and wasn't too
happy about it, and when I got back to the dugout, Vida was
waiting for me, smiling.

"Buck," he said, "Buck, get over here right now 'cause they
got it on you."

That was the expression for the bad-mouthing: "They got it on
you."

Noren had made a comment about my fielding.

I let it slide.

A couple of innings later, Greenie was up and, for one of the few times in his career, didn't get a bunt down properly. Noren made another comment, this one about Green not being a good enough hitter to mess up bunts.

I said loudly, "Who the fuck does he think he is?" Meaning Noren.

It just rubbed me the wrong way on this day, and I let it fester. When the press came by my locker after the game, I made a statement, in full earshot of everyone, that went something like this: "I am sick and tired of some fucking no-account coaches on this team who bad-mouth players and are a pain in the ass and aren't much good for this team."

Something diplomatic like that.

We were flying to Baltimore that day. We'd lost the game 3–1, and I'd been hitless. When I got on the plane, Williams was sitting in the front of the plane reading a newspaper, his reading glasses down at the end of his nose like they always were.

As I passed his seat, he just said, "Superstar, my ass." He'd heard about my remark.

I didn't take *his* remark the way, oh, Norman Vincent Peale might have.

I stopped right there. "Hey, man, who the fuck are you to be talking to me like that?"

Williams put the paper down and just stared at me, blood nearly coming out of his eyeballs.

"I've followed the damn game my whole life, and I remember when you played, and you didn't do *shit*. So don't lay any of your sarcastic superstar shit on me. You just leave me alone from now on. You write my name down on the lineup card and leave my ass alone."

Williams never said a word. In my Baltimore hotel room that night, Finley called me.

He said, "Hey, Reggie, we're trying to win here, so I'd appreciate it if you wouldn't insult the manager in front of the team if that's all right with you."

I was still steaming and didn't say a word.

Finley: "If you weren't so instrumental to this team winning, I'd fine you and suspend you for what you did today. But I'm not going to do either. But what I am going to do tomorrow is extend

Dick Williams's contract, so you better get used to playing for him and keeping your mouth shut."

The next day he extended Williams's contract, I went off on a hot streak at the plate, and Williams and I never had a problem.

I just figured as far as the A's went, it was a mild incident. Hell, we didn't even get into a fistfight.

Fingers was the team wit. Later on in New York, I'd come across Graig Nettles, who, although he seemed to mix his humor with bitterness, was one of the quickest men with a one-liner or a comeback I'd ever heard. But he wasn't any funnier than Rollie. When I think back on all the bus rides we took in my Oakland years, the thing I remember most is sitting in the back and laughing at something Rollie Fingers said.

One night we landed in Kansas City. The airport in Kansas City is about forty-five minutes out of town, it was three o'clock in the morning, and we were all bone tired and just wanted to get to sleep. Except for Rollie. Rollie just carried on this nonstop conversation with the bus driver all the way into town.

"Hey, bussie, could we drop the governor off now so you could drive this thing a little faster?"

"Hey, bussie, I don't want to say we're going slow here, but the moths are hitting the *back* window."

Finally he concluded with what we all later agreed was the most descriptive bus driver line of his career, which was saying something for Rollie.

"Uh, bussie, are you aware that not only is there a three-legged dog keeping up with us—but that he's also screwing the exhaust pipe?"

Catfish was the country boy. James Augustus Hunter from North Carolina. He was Dodge pickup and family and taking the dogs out in the fields. But there was a quiet intensity about him, and he was a winner. And he had guts.

He had much better stuff as a pitcher than he got credit for. He was supposed to have just an average fastball, but that was bull; I found out in '75 when I had to face him for the first time. He had a terrific fastball, a mean slider and fabulous control. Ron Guidry would remind me a lot of Cat when I got to the Yankees. But no one was Cat. To my mind, he was the premier pitcher of our generation when he was in his prime. I faced Tom Seaver. I faced Jim Palmer. If I had to pick one man to win one game, it would be Catfish Hunter. I mean it.

We were friends. Catfish kept to himself; it was his nature. And every four or five days, he'd go out and beat somebody 2–1. It was just understood that he would do his job and get us between twenty and twenty-five wins a year. Cat didn't make a big production out of that because he didn't make a big production out of anything.

We'd end up winning three world championships together in Oakland and two more in New York, and if I have any regrets about our relationship, it's just that he wasn't more supportive of me when I had so much trouble in the Yankee clubhouse later on. I thought we had a bond, I thought we were old Army buddies, I thought he could have done something to take care of me. Never did.

Maybe I expected too much.

The closest thing to trouble Catfish Hunter ever caused was on a flight to Milwaukee early in '71, right after Williams had taken over as manager. He was sitting with Paul Lindblad in the back of the plane, and they noticed this megaphone back there. Catfish just took the megaphone and hid it under his seat. Cat raised dogs back home in North Carolina. Figured he'd take the megaphone home and use it to call his dogs.

As we were getting off the plane, one of the stewardesses told Williams that the megaphone was missing. Now Williams was new to us, and we'd heard he'd had problems in Boston with Carl Yastrzemski, the Red Sox's biggest star, so I guess he wanted to establish right away that he was going to be tough with us, no matter how many stars we had.

He threw a big-time tantrum when we were all on the bus.

"Okay, you fuckers," he screamed. "You want to play games with me? Fine. I can play games, too. Now someone stole a lousy megaphone, but we don't steal things around here, so we're going to give it back. *Now.* I don't have any time for smart asses around here. I've tried to be nice all spring, but I'm going to tell you something you were going to find out anyway: It is very, very easy for me to be a prick. I am going to go back to my seat in the front of the bus now, and we are all going to sit right here until the megaphone magically appears."

We all knew it was Cat, but nobody was going to, uh, rat on the Cat. There was this long silence. Then suddenly the megaphone began to make its way up the aisle. Rudi handed it to me, and I handed it to Sal and Sal handed it to Rollie. Until it got to Williams.

That was Catfish Hunter's major indiscretion for a career. Blue Moon seemed like he was always in a fight with someone. North and I fought *au naturel.* There were about a thousand other fights.

Cat tried to sneak a megaphone off an airplane in Milwaukee one time.

That was his entire life of crime.

By 1974, we were in our heyday, smack in the middle of it, a truly *great* professional baseball team. We could do no wrong. We played the game and won at will. In the fourth game of the playoffs that year, we got one hit and beat the Orioles anyway. I doubled off the left-center-field wall in the eighth that day to knock in Bando, and we won 1–0. That was the only hit we got, but we got thirteen walks that day, and we won.

There was no big celebration afterward. We had a couple of bottles of champagne, read the scouting reports on the Dodgers on the flight west, just started getting ourselves in the right frame of mind to beat the Dodgers and win our third in a row.

When we got to Los Angeles, we read in the newspaper how the Dodgers were going to take us apart.

What?

There were a lot of comments from the Dodger players. Catfish wasn't that good. We were overrated. Reggie and Campaneris were the only two A's who could start for the Dodgers.

Huh?

Didn't they know who we *were?*

Before the first game, I sidled up to Sal at the batting cage and said, "Did you read that stuff in the papers?"

Sal said, "Uh-huh."

Me: "I say we should dispose of these people quickly."

Sal: "Buck, that sounds like an excellent idea."

We beat the Dodgers in five games that year, and in the fifth and final game there was one play that I thought epitomized exactly what we were about. If I had to go back over the years and select one vignette that just eloquently described the greatness of the Oakland A's of the early '70s, it would be this one.

Bill Buckner hit a rocket to right-center field, between Billy North and me. North was scooting over to his left, and I could see he was going to get to the ball first so I angled in behind him to back him up. And he did get to the ball first, but it skidded off the outfield grass, which was slick that night.

The ball hit him up on the left arm.

Buckner was heading for second by then, and from the way he was running, I knew he was going to try for third.

The ball bounced away from North, but I was there, backing him up the way you were supposed to back guys up on the A's.

I fielded it with my bare hand.

I was throwing the ball toward the infield before I even looked. Because I knew Green would have come out to take the relay. And I knew where he would be.

He was there. The throw came to him chest-high. Perfect. Greenie took it, wheeled, and threw a perfect strike to Sal at third. Bingo! Buckner was out. Our lead was safe. We were going to win another World Series.

Catfish would leave that winter. I'd stay one more year and then Charlie would trade me to Baltimore. Holtzman got traded along with me. The rest of the heroes became free agents after '76. We'd lose in the American League playoffs to the Red Sox the next year, mainly because we didn't have Cat to be the stopper.

That night against the Dodgers was our last great night as an Army, even if we didn't know it at the time. So we punctuated our glory years with this perfect defensive play, this Oakland-type play that we had been making for years.

Be there for each other.

Do the job.

Don't make mistakes.

No excuses.

Jackson backed up North. Jackson threw to Green. Green threw to Bando.

Oh, yes. How we played the game. . . .

6

JENNIE CAMPOS ...
JACKSON

I have always wanted consistency in my life.

This sounds so odd because of the career I've had as a baseball player.

It has not been serene. It has not been normal by anyone's definition of the word. It seems that my career has been played out to a disco beat. But it was not always what I wanted or the way I would have wanted it to be.

What I have wanted is consistency, ever since the day back in Wyncote when my Mom and Dad split. I have wanted to be liked. I have wanted to be loved. I've wanted to be in a family-type atmosphere. In so many ways, that's why the Oakland years were such warm, happy ones for me, despite the rocky weather and the turbulence and the seat-belt sign being lit the whole time. For the first time in my life, I had that family atmosphere. That clubhouse was my home. We fought, but we fought the way brothers would, and when the fight was over, it was over. I was safe there. I was becoming a success in baseball and a success in the business world. I came to own a car dealership in Oakland, which seemed to put

the Good Housekeeping Seal of Approval on my lifelong passion
for cars. (The count is around sixty now. I've actually had to buy
a few warehouses in California to store them.) During the New
York years, the real estate business in Arizona with friend Gary
Walker began to grow by leaps and bounds. My life was always
changing, but I had that safe base: the A's clubhouse. I had my
family.

I had a nice home in Oakland and some nice friends—Ev,
Gary, Steven. I was happy.

I have always strived for consistency. I haven't always had it,
but it was in my nature to want it. Steven Kay, an Oakland lawyer,
has been my lawyer for ten years. I've been associated with Gary
Walker since Arizona State in 1966. Matt Merola has been my
agent since 1969. An Oakland man named Everett Moss has been
my best and most trusted friend for fifteen years; he now works with
me in Oakland and wherever I travel. I'm with the Angels now, and
I hope to be with the Angels for the rest of my life. I value their
loyalty to me, and I want them to value my loyalty. When I finish
playing, I want to take off my uniform, put on a suit, and go to work
for Gene Autry in the front office. I hope I can have some type of
ownership position by then.

I tell all this as an introduction to telling about my attempt at
being a husband. I wanted consistency there, too. I wanted a wife
and family.

I failed. I wasn't a very good husband. A lasting relationship
with a woman was out of the realm of my experience because of the
way I grew up. I guess I was also devoting too much energy to
becoming a good baseball player.

I feel there is a misconception about me where women are concerned. I think it's caused by the lifestyle I lead, the image I have
and the one that's been created by the media: a Fifth Avenue
apartment in New York, Rolls-Royces and Mercedes and fine cars
all around, huge celebrity, personal wealth. All the trappings, all
the things that fit the image. And I'm a hell of a flirt. But during
the baseball season, if it's 1:30 in the morning, I'm going home, and
99 percent of the time I'm going home alone. I don't like to bring
strangers home with me. Not because I'm above it all, but because
I'm afraid of letting something infringe, encroach, on my job. I need

my rest, and I don't want a strange person sleeping with me. It would just beat me down. When I am dating someone, I am usually dating *her*. I love being with a good woman, talking to her, learning about her. But if I had led the kind of dating life most people think I've led, I would be about 5'2" now, weigh 120 pounds, walk with a cane, and be just about ready to give you my Mr. October death rattle.

I don't whore around.

I don't see the sun come up in somebody else's apartment. I see the sun come up when I'm going out to work on a car.

In the last few years of my life—*just* in the last few years—I've learned a lot from the women with whom I've spent time. I've learned for the first time to put my problems aside and deal with their problems. I used to think in all the familiar clichés, think of women as the weaker sex, as very dependent. Now I've changed. I'm not saying that this is some sort of landmark achievement for the feminist movement. I'm just saying I've learned. I am human, with weaknesses and failings and insecurities. Women are human, with their own weaknesses and failings and insecurities. It doesn't matter if they don't like sports. I used to think that if one person in a relationship was a visible achiever, then the relationship was too one-sided to sustain itself on any kind of lasting basis. I know now that just isn't so, not with work, patience and understanding. Each person has their own contribution to make.

I have learned these things, but I have learned them as I approach the age of forty.

People think I use and abuse women, that I have one in every port, that I fly women all over the place, that they are toys to me, that every woman I go out with has to be blond. And that is just not true. Maybe there is a part of me that is more attracted to a white woman than a black woman, but I don't believe that; besides, who cares anyway, and those that do don't matter anyway. Maybe, as I said earlier, that is a psychological heritage, a legacy, that goes back to a fundamental mistrust of women that began when my parents split, a mistrust I have spent a lifetime trying to overcome. But I have not gone through life parading beautiful blondes in front of the world just so I could show them off as exhibits, objects. Toys. Not my style.

It just hasn't happened that way. I haven't always been the

most enlightened of modern men, and there is a part of me that is still scared to death at the prospect of committing myself fully to a woman. But I have worked at it. I have tried to make myself more aware. When I got to college, I knew nothing at all about women. Just didn't know. I was a virgin when I got to Arizona State. I was a virgin the night I got married to Jennie Campos.

We dated my sophomore year at ASU. We dated throughout my first two years in the minors. We slept together, but we never made love. I assumed that wasn't to be done. She would come visit me when I was playing for Birmingham, and I'm sure my friends thought we were sleeping together. But that's all we were doing. Sleeping together. I am not trying to pass myself off as a paragon of virtuousness or clean living or the Christian ethic. I just thought, with my limited experience, that that is the way you did things in this world. In that sense, I was a product of the '50s. Different world then.

I got married in 1968 because I thought that's the way you were supposed to do it. I was a rookie with the A's. Sal Bando was married. Joe Rudi was married. Dave Duncan was married. Gary Walker was married. I had been going steady with Jennie since my sophomore year. I was earning a nice living. I missed her when I was away. She was a pretty, dark-haired woman with a fabulous smile; she loved me, she was nice, she had a bright and cheery disposition, she was down-to-earth, she was sincere, she was supportive. She was clearly willing to put our relationship first.

If I had been keeping score, I wouldn't have been able to find any minuses about it.

My friends all thought it would be a good idea if I got married. It just seemed right.

So I got married. July 8, 1968. The All-Star break.

It didn't matter to me that I still didn't know anything about women. Understand them? I could barely talk to them. I could barely talk to myself. In so many ways, I was still the withdrawn kid from Wyncote, keeping it all in. I thought there were experiences that Jennie and I had shared. She'd had difficulties in her life because she was Mexican-American. It wasn't being black, but as I've said, if you're not a WASP in this country, you're not completely white. And she had grown up without a parent; her father had died when she was young. There should have been that emotional base for us. But there wasn't.

I could not give. I could not share. The sharing and giving I was accustomed to in my life were in male-oriented, jock-oriented situations. I had no frame of reference where women were concerned. There was no dominant female influence in my life because my mother wasn't at home with me. By the time I got married—because it was the All-Star break we had no honeymoon, I just went right back to the team; I guess that's revealing in itself—I had established contact with my mother again, but I was just not given to reaching out to a woman.

In the back of my mind, I was still struggling with the fact that I was raised by a man.

In the back of my mind, I was also still scuffling to make enough money. I was so geared to playing baseball and making money that my relationship with Jennie just got lost. And I really can't fault her. We were married for three and a half years, together only for one and a half really, and during that time she did her very best to make things work.

But *I* couldn't make it work. It wasn't philandering that did it; I didn't have another woman until the third year of our marriage, by which time we were separated. I was simply ill-equipped to deal with a marriage on a day-to-day basis. When I started hitting all those home runs in 1969 and the pressure began to drown me, I wasn't able to share the pressure with her and find a safe haven when I got home. We lived in the same area of Hayward as the Bandos and the Rudis. All of us would get together, and I would watch the other couples, then watch Jennie and think that we should be the way they were, but know that we were not. There was a level of communication between the other husbands and wives that I knew we didn't have.

Jennie did not nag. There were no big fights, just silences.

Jennie: "Is something the matter?"

Me: "No."

Jennie: "Is there something you'd like to talk about?"

Me: "I'm fine, really."

Jennie: "I want to help."

Me: "I know. Good night."

I didn't know how to tell her that I loved her. I didn't know how to give her that one night of the week when the two of us could be alone. I didn't know how to help with the dishes or tell her what it was like to be interviewed all the time and analyzed all the time. I had all these stupid misconceptions about marriage, '50s misconceptions. She did the chores. I went to the ballpark and made my living. I came home. We ate. We went to bed. In that sense, I was a feminist's horror.

Perhaps the biggest misconception of all was that a man couldn't show weakness, that he had to be big and strong and tough all the time, even in private moments with his wife. It was the only way I knew. Had to be tough.

Father was incarcerated when you were a kid? Be strong, be *hard.* Keep the business going. Keep the grades up. Be a star athlete. Don't let up.

Frank Kush says you're not tough enough to play football for him? Show him. Take the dirt out of your mouth and stop crying and run up his damn mountain again.

People calling you nigger all the time in Birmingham? Hold it in, keep your mouth shut, play your way through it.

Be a good enough player that you didn't have to take any shit. Make enough money so that The Man couldn't mess with you. *Ever.* And ever!

I brought all of that baggage into my marriage. I had thought that if you had the pretty girl as your girlfriend, and she loved you, and you thought you loved her, then it would all come together as soon as you started playing house.

It just doesn't happen that way. You work to make yourself a great baseball player. You work to make yourself a success in the business world. And you work to make a successful marriage. It isn't enough just to be the breadwinner and for your wife to be a caring and supportive helpmate. You have to *talk:* husband to wife, man to woman. Human being to human being. You have to let the guard down.

I had never let my guard down, not totally. I have a hard time doing that to this day. I am not the only kid in the history of the planet who came from a broken home, but I am still a kid who came from a broken home, and that experience has reached out and tapped me on the shoulder again and again throughout my adult life.

Reggie Jackson, married in July of 1968.

Divorced in February of 1972.

Jennie Campos Jackson deserved better from me, a lot better.

There have been a few very nice women with whom I have shared my life since Jennie. But not *all* my life. It comes from not being able to completely trust. I'm now better than I was at trusting, better at letting the defenses down, but no one is calling me Mr. October when it comes to the business of living with a woman. Maybe some day. I'm looking forward to that day.

In 1977, a very nice woman named Dayna came from California to live with me in New York. I had been divorced for several years, and I was willing to take another crack at the whole business.

Of course, 1977 was the first Yankee season, a season I will tell about, a season during which I thought I was having a walking-around nervous breakdown. The members of the Yankee team didn't want me around, and I felt I had made a terrible mistake coming to New York. I was fouled up with the team, the media, the city, Billy Martin, trying to justify in my own mind the contract George Steinbrenner had given me. I was used to the clubhouse being home in Oakland, and now I didn't have that. Baseball became my only release.

I made the same mistakes with Dayna I had made with Jennie.

I was miserable. And I'm sure that made her miserable. In August she finally left and went back to California. I wanted to go with her, just split, leave the Yankees, leave baseball, just go and hide. But I didn't. *Get the job done*—that was the credo again. Do it alone, but get the job done. The survival instinct in me has always been the strongest instinct of all.

It bothered me a lot when she left, *but I did survive.* And that was the reason I ended up hitting three home runs in the last game of the World Series.

The day Dayna left, she took my hand and said, "I can't take it anymore, Reggie. I can't watch what the city and the Yankees and this life is doing to you. I have to get out of here. I'd like to stay and help, but you don't want that for me or you."

There was a lot I wanted to say to her, a lot I wanted to explain. A lot that was inside me. But I was not very good at talking to her. I was not great at talking to members of the opposite sex.

I was never able to tell Jennie that I loved her in a way that sounded sincere. Couldn't. Wouldn't. Didn't.

I am at a point in my life now where I am thinking again about marriage and about starting a family, about settling down once and for all. My friends tell me to wait until I have finished playing baseball. People like Everett Moss, who has been like a brother to me in Oakland, tell me that as long as I'm wedded to the game, to being Reggie Jackson, there can never be enough of me to go into a marriage.

Everett says that when I put down the bat and glove for good, then I will be ready, and I'll make it work this time.

I think he's partly right. But I know I can make it now if I want to.

I'm thirty-eight and I realize the day will come when I will not have the security of being embraced by the game of baseball. And I look forward to going to a *real* home for the first time.

7

PROCEED DIRECTLY TO THE EARL OF BALTIMORE. PASS GO. COLLECT $200,000.

C harlie Finley had become a desperate businessman by the spring of 1976. He knew that all his years of colorful parsimony were coming to an end, because free agency had arrived. He knew that if he didn't pay us now, then we might just start leaving Oakland like someone had set off an air-raid siren.

Jackson would be a free agent at the end of the '76 season. Ken Holtzman would be a free agent. Bando would be a free agent. Fingers would be a free agent. So would Rudi, Tenace, and Campy.

All of them had extremely long memories.

We didn't know it for sure at the time, but old Willie Nelson should have been standing on a chair singing about turning out the lights.

'Cause the party was over.

My contract fight with Charlie that spring was more acrimonious than usual. We went back and forth on the $140,000 that he had offered, and finally he automatically renewed my contract with a 20 percent pay cut, down to $112,000, which he was entitled to do by the terms of the contract and baseball law.

I'd hit thirty-six home runs in 1975, remember. I'd knocked in 104. Not only was he refusing to give me a real raise, *now* he was cutting me, as a show of spite. You can do that in a man's option year. Hardball all the way.

Still, I was having a good spring; at one point I hit four dingers in a row. We had a new manager, Chuck Tanner (Charlie'd gotten rid of Alvin Dark because we didn't make it to the World Series); Tanner had such a positive sunny attitude about life you couldn't help but like him. I was used to fighting with   Gary Walker was used to fighting with Charlie, who'd rejected our offer for the three-year contract with most of the money deferred. But I figured something would get worked out.

I'd helped win the man five divisional championships, three pennants, and the two World Series I'd played in. I had been one hell of a return on his original $85,000 investment. I'd been MVP for the American League, MVP of a World Series; I'd made the cover of *Time,* made the cover of *Sports Illustrated.* I'd made money for Charlie. He'd made money for me, if indirectly. In my mind, we were a team, a bickering team but a team.

I'd hit 254 dingers for the man in eight seasons.

I couldn't believe he would not keep me if he had the chance to keep me.

Wrong.

Charlie was going to play his hand all the way.

Gary Walker called me up on the telephone on April 2, 1976. I was in my home in Tempe, Arizona.

Gary said, "I hope you're sitting down."

"Why?"

"Because Charlie just traded you and Holtzman to Baltimore for Don Baylor and Mike Torrez."

Gary must have thought the line had gone dead.

I sat there on my bed looking at the receiver as if it had just turned into something unrecognizable.

Traded? Me? Away from the Oakland A's?

Say *what?*

Bad connection. Had to be.

I said, "Say that again."

Gary: "It's true, Reggie. He's traded you."

I pondered that for another fat moment and said, "I ain't going."

"What?" That was the best Gary could come up with.

"You tell Charlie and you tell Baltimore and you tell anybody else who cares to listen that I am about to go on vacation."

I sat there by myself for a long time. Emotions? Stunned was having a fight with angry. It was so clear what Charlie was doing. He was making examples out of Holtzman and me. The deck had gone cold on Charlie, and he was playing it the only way he knew how. Hard line.

He was basically saying this: You want to hold free agency over my head to get more money, to get a long-term contract? Fine. Go do it. But here's what I'm going to do, gang. I'm going to uproot you before you can uproot yourselves. I'm going to take you away from your families, I'm going to take you away from your buddies, I'm going to boot your asses out of Oakland. Oh, by the way. Thanks for the memories.

He was sending me away from the only real home I'd ever known, the Oakland Damn A's. I'd grown up a lot in my years working for Charlie. I'd learned a lot about life, about business, and about myself. I had learned to deal with celebrity. I had been married and divorced. I'd been given the chance to give my father and my family some real money for the first time in their lives.

But I did not want to leave Oakland.

Did. Not.

Gary called back.

"You cooled down any?" he said.

"A little."

"What will it take to get you to go to Baltimore?"

"Two hundred thousand dollars. If I'm going to get jerked around, then they're going to have to damn well pay me to get jerked around. I think we can win a pennant in Baltimore, but it's going to cost them."

Gary said, "I'll see what I can do. But I think you should lay low for a while. This is no time for you to be making any big decisions. You really should get away."

I got away. I stayed around Tempe for a couple of days, saying goodbye to the guys. It was an emotional time. It really was saying farewell to family when I had to look at Bando, Rudi, and Fingers, shake their hands, *know* that it was over. The ride on the merry-go-round was finished. We'd grabbed the brass ring in a way few teams ever had. We had taken the Oakland A's, made them famous, and moved them uptown.

When I said goodbye to Sal, he said, "Give 'em hell in Baltimore, Buck."

Get away. That's all I wanted to do.

I spent a couple of days in Oakland, then flew to Hawaii and checked into the Hawaiian Hilton Village. I figured I could find a degree of privacy there that I couldn't find on the mainland. They also knew who I was at the Hawaiian Village, they knew about Reggie and the A's and the fact that we'd been world champs a lot. They knew that my holdout was big news every day in the sports section. But they pretty much let me keep to myself.

I just walked on the beach, eating meals in my room, running some, just trying to work through the bitterness and the hurt.

Damn you, Charlie, I kept thinking. You hard-ass sonofabitch, you didn't have the decency to pick up the phone and call me.

Damn you.

After a while I got tired of being in Hawaii, flew back to Arizona, and holed up at Gary's house in Tempe. The press couldn't find me there, and Gary screened all my calls while he kept negotiating with the Orioles. I wanted to play, but I knew I was in no shape emotionally to play.

And there were a lot of calls from people who very much wanted me to play.

Bob Zuk, the guy who'd originally signed me to an A's contract, called.

Brooks Robinson and Jim Palmer of the Orioles called and told me how much they were looking forward to playing with me, how much the team needed me.

Bowie Kuhn, the commissioner of baseball, called to say that the game needed me.

American League president Lee MacPhail called and said the same thing.

Hank Peters, the Orioles' general manager, called either Gary or me every day.

Earl Weaver, the Orioles' manager, called and told me to get my ass to Baltimore, because he had this huge vacancy in the cleanup slot that I could fill.

Jerry Hoffberger, the Orioles' owner (he'd later sell the team to Edward Bennett Williams), called.

We just kept haggling about the contract. The Orioles knew I was going to be a free agent, but they had given up two frontline ballplayers for me in Baylor and Torrez, and they wanted more than a one-year return. Gary and I kept telling them that they could either have me for one year at $200,000 or five years at around $250,000 per.

Back and forth.

But I wasn't budging. I was giving them a take-it-or-leave-it offer. All the years of working for Charlie Finley had taught me a rock-hard stance. I was giving the Orioles a taste of *his* medicine. I had been taken away from my home, I had been taken away from the West, I had been taken away from my team and my friends. I hadn't even gotten a phone call from Finley. I couldn't make him pay, but *someone* was going to have to pay.

The Orioles were going to.

Finally Hank Peters flew to Arizona for his final sales pitch. Gary doesn't fly, so the meeting had to be in Arizona. We met for dinner at the Tempe Racquet and Swim Club.

Peters is a quiet, pleasant man who looks a lot like a college professor in his horn-rimmed glasses. He is also one of the two or three most brilliant baseball minds around. He worked for Finley in the '60s, running the farm operation. Now he was running the Orioles. That meant he had a big part in two of the more successful baseball operations of this generation.

We sat there at a table in the Tempe Racquet and Swim Club and went back and forth a little more.

Hank said, "Reggie, the fans are going to love you in Baltimore. We can win it all with you, but we've got to get you in uniform before the season gets away from us. You're going to like living in Baltimore. I know you've got some family there. [My mother and sisters Dolores, Tina and Beverly lived there.] The team can't wait for you to get there, because they know you're the one who will get us over the hump."

I said, "I understand all that, Hank. But I'm not moving on the money."

"It's a lot of money," he said.

"I know that. Gary knows that. But I'd like to have some security. I want to be in just one place. I want to hang my hat with the Orioles for the rest of my career. Or I'm just going to sit here in Arizona and see what happens. I'm not mad. I'm not upset. That's just the way it is!"

I went over to the bar for a beer, and Gary and Hank worked out the terms. I was to get $190,000 for the first year in Baltimore. There would be an unsigned contract for the second year worth roughly the same money. I had until the end of the '76 season to make up my mind about that. If I wanted to test free agency, I could just leave it unsigned and go someplace else.

I never did re-up for the second year.

Which meant that I had only one season playing for Mr. Weaver, the Earl of Baltimore.

I showed up in Baltimore for a press conference on May 2, and I showed up thinking of myself as an interim Baltimore Oriole, even if I did have that contract for 1977 in Gary's safe back in Tempe. That didn't mean I wasn't going to play hard. I had tremendous respect for the Oriole organization; everyone in baseball did. It was stable, it was polished, it had Earl Weaver, and the Orioles were at the top or near the top every season.

They played good, sound, fundamental baseball, the way we had in Oakland. I was excited about playing there. But in the back of my mind, I always knew it would only be for one season. I was going to become a free agent. I was going to find myself a windfall. The Oakland experience had burned me, turned me into a full-fledged baseball mercenary for the first time. I felt I had been used by Charlie. Now I was going to use the system myself.

I did not get an apartment. I lived in the Cross Keys Inn, a huge hotel/mall, the entire season. I had become a baseball gypsy.

Somehow, some way, I was going to get mine, get even.

After the press conference I went down to the field and had a long batting practice. Mentally I was finally ready to play, but not physically. I needed swings. In baseball, you do not fall out of bed and start hitting dingers. A baseball swing is a very finely tuned instrument. It is repetition and more repetition, then a little more after that. Even with a free swinger like myself, mechanics are everything.

I hit that day until my hands were bloody and blistered. That meant one more day off. I knew that would be it, because the season was already a month old.

And like Earl said, there was this big hole in the cleanup slot. It had my name on it.

Earl Weaver smokes too much and drinks too much. He has a voice that sounds like broken glass. He is short, feisty, has a ferocious temper, especially with umpires, and doesn't know when to keep his mouth shut. He has never been accused of being a diplomat and has never set out to win any popularity contests with his players.

He is also one of the few baseball geniuses I have ever met. He'll be in the Hall of Fame someday, and I enjoyed just about every day I played for him. In all my years of playing ball, I have had three managers I consider special managers for whom I wanted to give something extra just because I liked them so damn much. John McNamara was one. He was always more than a manager for me, in Birmingham and with the Angels; he was and is like family. Dick Howser was another, because I respected him and he respected me, and he acted as a buffer between George Steinbrenner and me.

Then there was Earl, with whom every day was an adventure, a joy, even if I didn't help him win that pennant in '76. Maybe things would have been different if I had started out the season in Baltimore, instead of waiting until May. Maybe we would have beaten the Yankees.

With all of that, I wouldn't have missed playing for Earl for the world.

That is not to say that we didn't have our little, uh, confrontations at the start. I was still mad at Charlie, see. And Earl was just Earl. So some fireworks occurred.

Some fireworks occurred almost right away, as a matter of fact.

It happened on an airplane.

Things are always happening with me on airplanes.

Earl had a rule about ties and sports jackets on planes. Now I had already looked around and noticed that the Orioles didn't much resemble the A's in terms of length of hair and beards. In fact, there was *no* long hair. There were *no* beards. I didn't know about the tie rule until I boarded a flight to Milwaukee early in the season. I actually thought I looked pretty good that day: crewneck sweater, buttoned-down white shirt, designer jeans, new loafers, black leather jacket serving as a coat. Mr. Slick.

Earl was sitting in the front of the plane, where managers sit. I think they passed that rule right after the Wright Brothers invented the airplane.

He didn't make a big fuss. He just said, "If you don't put on a tie, you can't make the trip, Reggie."

It is all the Big Game. It has always gone on between managers and players, especially managers and *new* players. Earl had wanted me desperately, but he was the boss and he had rules, and he had to show the rest of the team right away that those rules applied to the new kid.

Everything had been fine until then. The players had gone out of their way to welcome me: Brooks Robinson, Bobby Grich, Lee May, Mark Belanger had all pulled me aside to tell me how glad they were I was around. But still I knew everyone was watching me.

And it all seemed so silly. Dress code was a foreign concept with the A's. It was nothing to see Vida, for example, get on a plane wearing blue jeans and a t-shirt. In Oakland, nobody cared what you looked like as long as you got the job done.

So very calmly, I turned and walked off the airplane.

It was a charter. At the gate area, I checked one of those computer schedule boards and there was a commercial flight leaving for Milwaukee about thirty minutes after the Orioles' charter. I was about to buy myself a ticket—it was like $120—when Brooks Robinson came walking off the plane after me with a tie in his hand. He'd borrowed it from the United Airlines rep who flew with the Orioles on their United charters.

Brooks, who is one of the great gentlemen to ever play baseball, said, "Hey, why don't you just put this on and get back on the plane? Everything will be fine, Reggie. It's no big deal. We know you're still feeling your way here, we know you're still upset about being traded. Just be a part of the team. Earl has a certain way of doing things, and we're all pretty much used to them. Come on."

I put the tie around the outside of my sweater, as sort of a mock gesture, and went back on the plane with Brooks. I didn't say anything to Earl. He didn't say anything to me. We flew to Milwaukee. When we got there, we bused to the Pfister Hotel, an elegant old lady of a hotel where most teams stay when they're in Milwaukee.

When I walked into the lobby, Earl was waiting for me. Apparently he'd been composing his State of the Reggie Address since I'd walked off the plane in Baltimore.

This was the Earl you've seen in the highlight films. This was Earl auditioning for a cockfight. He put his hands on his hips and he looked up at me—he's got a lot of Jimmy Cagney in him, Earl does—and he gave it to me in front of the whole team, as well as the rest of the people passing through the lobby of the Pfister Hotel at that particular moment.

"Look," he said in that raspy, cigarette voice. "I want you on my ballclub. I need you to win. It's very important to everybody that you get along with me and I get along with you. And I'm a big booster of yours, Reggie. I really am. But you've got to understand one little thing."

His voice went up a couple of octaves here, and he punctuated every one of his next eight words with a stubby little index finger.

"I . . . can't . . . have . . . you . . . shitting . . . in . . . my . . . face!"

I said to Earl, "If I thought wearing a tie was that important, I'd wear one to hit and I'd wear the sonofabitch out to right field."

His finger jabbed with every word of the next sentence.

"I'm not trying to turn you into a fucking cadet, but . . . do . . . not . . . shit . . . in . . . my . . . face."

I wanted to laugh. He was so damn serious, but his words sounded so damn funny. I didn't laugh, though. Not even a smile. That would have been all wrong. I just said, "I know what you're saying, and I've always respected you when we've been on opposite sides of the field, and if it's that fuckin' important to you, I'll wear a fuckin' tie."

We grinned at each other and shook hands.

Our run-in got a lot of attention in the press.

That night I hit my first home run as an Oriole, a grand-slam, to bring us from behind and get us a 7–6 win. Jerry Augustine was pitching. I just remember Grich walking in front of me to load the bases, then tattooing one to right field. The ball bounced back onto the field, and one of the ball boys gave it to me. I took it back home and gave it to Hank Peters.

Even if it was only going to be for one season, I was an Oriole, and I wanted Hank to know that it was nice to be aboard and that I'd play my ass off for him.

I'd even wear a fuckin' tie.

Incidentally, when we got back home after the road trip and I checked my mail, I'd received over two dozen ties from fans.

On the thirteenth of June that season, my Oakland A's years came to a symbolic end.

If the trade hadn't done it, my Oakland home burning down certainly did.

We were in Arlington to play the Texas Rangers. I was asleep in my hotel room about three in the morning when Everett Moss called. He got right to it. He usually does.

"Got bad news, Jack," he said.

I said, "Well, how bad is it?"

He said, "It's bad. The house caught fire and burned to the ground. Everything's gone."

I took a deep breath, swallowed, and pictured that wonderful two-story place on the hill in Oakland, just across the Bay Bridge, with its sensational view of San Francisco Bay and the city of San Francisco; the way it all looked at twilight, with its spectacular color shows every day that it wasn't raining or foggy; how San Francisco looked like some ominous movie set when it *was* raining and foggy. Snapshots rushed through my head one after another.

Everett was telling me it was all gone.

I finally said, "Everything." It wasn't a question. I just needed to hear it out loud; I needed to say it to believe it.

"Yes. But no one was hurt."

"Did the garage burn?" The garage was separate from the house, and I had a couple of cars in there, a cherished 1940 Chevy and a Porsche.

"The garage didn't burn down," Everett said. "The cars are fine."

"How did it start?"

"Nobody knows, Jack. It just started and took everything with it."

I asked Everett if he thought I should fly back to Oakland. He said there was nothing to fly back for, because it was all gone. The only thing left for me to do was talk to the insurance people.

I was devastated. This house had been filled with memories. I have never been big for trophies and things like that; I've given a lot of them away to my father and other members of my family. But the house was the thing. I loved that house. That was my A's house, paid for with my A's money, filled with emotional bits and pieces of the glory years.

The thing that really stands out in my mind is that I lost my Most Valuable Player trophy—I assumed in the fire. But to top it off, the next winter I got a phone call from someone who said they'd return it if I gave them a reward and a trip to New York. I never did get it back.

I would later build a new house on the same Oakland hill, with the same view of San Francisco, and it is a fine place. But it will never be the same. I remember the night vividly. It was as if the fates were saying, "Okay, kid. Close the chapter on the A's years, as painful as that may be. Let's get on with it."

I called Hank Peters the next morning and told him what had happened. Hank was class as usual.

"Do whatever you have to do," he said in his calm, professorial way. "If you have to go home, fine. If you think you can stay with the team and handle things, then stay with the team. Selfishly, I hope you can stay with the team because the club is doing well, and we need you. But I'll back you up whatever you decide."

I decided there was nothing for me in Oakland. I didn't really want to see the rubble. So I stayed with the team. We played that night. We won and I even hit a home run. We traveled that night to Baltimore and the next morning I got about my business on the phone. I called Gary. I called Matt. I spoke to the insurance people and the builder. My poor girlfriend Dayna had just moved into the house two weeks before with everything she owned, but she was traveling in Europe; I tried to get hold of her to tell her what had happened. I spoke to Everett all day long, every hour or so.

And was late getting to the ballpark.

By about ten minutes.

Earl knew nothing about my house burning down.

He read me the riot act in the clubhouse.

"I thought we'd gotten this all straightened out," he screamed, pacing in front of my locker while I just sat there with my head down. "Goddamn it, you're not bigger than this team, Reggie. I am not going to let you get away with this kind of shit. Who the fuck do you think you are?"

I never said a word. I felt like crying, to tell you the truth. I felt beat up. My house was gone, my girlfriend was in Europe, I was living in a hotel in Baltimore, I had really tried to get with Earl's program, and now he wasn't even giving me the chance to explain. I did not say a word. Usually I had a response of one kind or another, but not on that day. I just got dressed as quickly as I could and went out and took batting practice. I don't know how I did it, but I homered again that night. That was my sixth consecutive home run in six consecutive games, which tied an American League record.

There is a postscript. The next day Earl found out what had happened. He pulled me aside in the clubhouse, and I could tell he felt rotten about what had happened.

"I'm sorry about yesterday," he said. "I just didn't know."

That was that. Earl and I never had a problem from that day on. Hank Peters later told me how sorry Earl was about the incident, and how much he appreciated that I stayed with the ballclub and kept playing, despite what I was going through. Earl, the little man, was big enough to apologize.

The thing that really stayed with me after it was all over was the thought that God may have wanted me to restructure my life. I was so into my house and the things in it and He took everything away from me. He hurt no one, though, and left me with all my physical abilities. I decided He wanted me to reconstruct my life, my entire philosophy of life, and start over.

I liked playing in Baltimore. I liked the polished, professional atmosphere. I liked my teammates. I still missed the guys in Oakland; in a way I'll always miss them because we had been to war together and we'd won. But I was appreciated in Baltimore. Mark Belanger took me under his wing as a friend. I had a damn good year: twenty-seven dingers, .277 average, ninety-one RBI, even twenty-eight stolen bases in just 134 games.

But what I liked the most, what I will remember best, was sitting watching Earl Weaver do his act in the dugout and on the field.

He was just plain wonderful every day.

We were playing in Oakland one night, and Vida was pitching a two-hit shutout. It was about forty degrees, just like it always is in Oakland at night. Vida was throwing his bee-bees, it was the top of the ninth, and we were behind 2–0. Two outs. Belanger, who wasn't a very good hitter—no one was against Vida—was batting second that night, Grich was batting third, and I was cleanup. The count was one ball, no strikes on Belanger. Grich was kneeling, freezing, in the on-deck circle. I was on my way to the bat rack because I was "in the hole." The guy in the hole is the batter after the man on deck. Belanger needed to get on and Grich needed to get on before I got a chance to hit, but I figured I'd get ready anyhow.

Earl was sitting down at his end of the bench, little legs kicking over the side and not reaching the ground, towel wrapped around his neck to keep warm, jacket zipped up all the way, smoking as usual; he smoked a cigarette about every six seconds in the dugout.

As I passed him on the way to the bat rack, he said, "And where the fuck do you think you're going?"

I turned around because I knew something funny was coming. I didn't know what. I just knew it would be funny.

I said, "I'm getting ready to hit."

Earl spit.

"You're not going to hit."

I said something witty like, "Huh?"

And Earl said, "Now, Reggie, you know and I know that there is no way in the fucking world Mr. Mark Belanger is going to get a hit off Mr. Vida Blue tonight. Are you shitting me? Put the bat back. Go inside. Quit freezing. 'Cause he ain't gonna get no hit off Vida."

I just laughed my ass off. That was Earl. He wasn't being nasty. He was just being matter-of-fact, being Earl. It was a long season. You were going to lose some. We were going to lose to Vida on this night, as soon as he struck out Belanger. Earl didn't see any reason for me to go through the rituals of getting ready to hit.

Earl just didn't have any bullshit in him.

Another time we were in Milwaukee. Larry Hisle was the hitter. There were runners on first and third with one out. The run on first was the tying run at the time. I wasn't playing that day because I'd hurt my right hand. Al Bumbry was out in left field, and he caught Hisle's fly ball on the warning track. Now, he has got no chance in the world to get the runner out at home. A moose with a broken leg could have scored on Hisle's fly ball because it was so deep. Bumbry throws toward home anyway. I say *toward* home, because his rainbow of a throw barely made third base on the fly.

Earl went crazy, because the runner on first tagged up and went to second while the rainbow was floating toward third base like the Goodyear Blimp. He didn't care about the runner scoring; that was going to happen anyway. It was the runner getting to second. So he started to run up and down the dugout in front of the bench. He used to do that from time to time, scurry around like some crazed munchkin, but this was a special tantrum. He ended up on the top step of the dugout, the end toward left field, staring at Bumbry. He took off his cap—he was always taking off his cap —and he grabbed a fistful of his gray-white hair. I mean, a whole fistful.

I happened to be sitting close to him. He turned to me and screamed, "Did you see *that?*"

He was on a roll so I just nodded.

"Could you have thrown that man out, Reggie?" He was talking about the runner who scored.

He was still holding on to his hair.

I said, "I don't think I could have thrown the man out, Earl."

Earl (still shouting): "I know that!" He paused for a moment, to catch his breath. "So what the hell is Bumbry *thinking* about, letting a man go to second like that? *Nolan Ryan* on a good day couldn't have thrown that sonofabitch out at the plate."

He jumped off the top dugout step then, grabbed his hair one more time, threw his cap back on, and pranced down to the other end of the dugout, where he sat down with the little legs kicking over the side and pouted.

I just wanted to roll around on the dugout floor and laugh.

When Bumbry came in off the field, Earl went through the same act again. Exact same act. Lord, the man was funny as hell, even when he wasn't trying to be.

Weaver is a great manager. Despite his antics and his temper, he had this knack for making ballplayers think they were better than they actually were. He actually *forced* you to have a good opinion of yourself as a ballplayer. He let you know that he *believed* in you. He made you get more out of yourself.

Despite all that I had accomplished in Oakland, that worked with me. When I got to Baltimore, I knew I was one of the best home-run hitters in the game and had some stats to back that up, but I also felt that I had just been one of a number of good players with the A's, part of that neat ensemble. From the first day, with only those two interruptions for our quarrels, Earl kept telling me that I was going to be another Frank Robinson for him. He made me believe I was the second coming of Robinson, something I could never have dreamt of on my own. That was his pitch to me.

I was going to bat cleanup every day. I was going to carry myself like a team leader (which Frank himself had taught me in Puerto Rico). I was going to knock in the big runs.

Earl: "I'm just going to write your name down fourth every day and not worry about you."

I don't know whether Earl realized that Robinson had always been one of my heroes, but the Robinson pitch was certainly the right one for me.

I just loved playing for him, loved watching the way his mind would race during games, loved listening to him talk about all those index cards he kept with all those statistics and tendencies written on them. He had this knack for taking that information off the index cards and playing certain hitters against certain pitchers and making it all work. I've never been a big fan of the platooning system, and we'd hardly done any platooning at all in Oakland, but Earl made me see for the first time how the lefty-righty percentages could work.

Earl has a romance with the home run while despising the bunt at the same time. Earl has never liked to play for just one run or use the sacrifice bunt to move a runner around because Earl is always playing for the three-run homer. He didn't have me bunt, and he never got too concerned when I was striking out because his philosophy was that I could hit a 425-foot homer against anyone at any time.

My kind of manager. Live by the dinger and die by the dinger.

It was great fun playing for him. I enjoyed every minute of every argument he had with umpires. I loved the back-and-forth between Earl and Jim Palmer, on the mound, in the dugout, in the clubhouse, on the bus. They were the oddest couple imaginable, what with Palmer being tall and good-looking, the picture of the all-American hero, and Earl coming on like an insurance salesman in a polyester suit. They could disagree about everything from pitching to the weather.

A very pleasant year.

But I didn't stay in Baltimore.

Maybe I should have. Looking back, maybe I could have had a successful *and* serene career if I had forgone free agency and stayed with Earl and Hank Peters. Maybe the Orioles would have won the World Series the Yankees did in '77 and '78.

I didn't take the serene route.

I never have.

On the last day of the season, Earl came up to me in the clubhouse, pumped my hand, and said, "Whatever you decide, I'm glad you were on my team this year. And I'd love to have you on my team *next* year."

I told Earl I appreciated that, and I wouldn't have missed playing for him for anything.

I said, "I don't know how all this will turn out, but I owe it to myself to see what's out there."

I saw what was out there.

George M. Steinbrenner.

8
JUST BUSINESS

I t has always meant a lot to me that people have recognized me as a great baseball player. But I have always wanted them to realize that I have also been successful as a businessman in the Real World, that I could compete in the Real World as a businessman. I have always wanted that respect from the time I started to make real money. It has been important to me that people could look at Reggie Jackson and say, "He's made it off the field as well. He has taken advantage of his situation. He's not dumb. He works when he's not playing ball."

And I work. Hard.

I've been generally disappointed with the way athletes have pursued their business careers. I can say this because I am an athlete and I've spent so much time with them. I've become a wealthy man because of baseball and because of business—and because I work all the time. Constantly. I've carried it to extremes. However, I don't think it's necessarily a good thing to be as taken as I am with the hunt for success. I've also been lucky in business because I've been around real good people who have led me in the right direction. I didn't realize how fortunate I was in business until I had the year I had in '83. In '83 I looked the end of my career in the eye. I suddenly knew it was a year, or two years, or six months away. And when you actually have to live it, it's different. Suddenly you're saying, "Damn! What do I have in the bank? What's coming in? What'll I do?" Because it might be over. That's a feeling you can only understand if you experience it. I say this because I hope that some athlete will catch what I'm saying. It's like dying: nobody dies at the right time. Everybody feels, "If I just could've done that one more thing!" Your career is the same way. It doesn't end the way you want it to. It just ends. BAM! It's over. You're never totally prepared. That's why I've never been able to understand guys who hunt or play golf or travel all winter, who think that's all there is. It's not the time. Hell, you'll be out of this game while you're still plenty young enough to do all that.

The first company to hire me as a spokesperson was Puma Shoes in 1973. I also worked with a man named Jim Woolner to create the Puma baseball shoe. It was extremely successful.

When I came to New York, of course, the stakes escalated.

The first company I signed with in New York was Standard Brands for the Reggie Bar. They later merged with Nabisco, for whom I still work. I do public relations mostly. Speak on behalf of the company, sometimes to sales people, usually to outside people at charity dinners or occasions like that.

Nabisco has an impressive stable of athletes: Frank Gifford, Bobby Orr, Rod Laver, Alex Webster, Davey Marr. I have a real loyalty to the company. They've taken good care of me. They also got me when I was pretty rough and crude, not very polished. But they stuck with me through bad times and good, and for this I have to thank Ross Johnson, their chief operating officer.

Panasonic commercials have probably done more for my image than anything else I've done. They're very visible and they've shown my lighter side.

I also have a long-term deal with Pony Shoes. I help design the shoes I endorse. I care about what I wear so I tell them what the need is in a shoe and they listen, then construct it. I completely designed a baseball shoe for Pony that they call The Anaheim model. It's rubber-soled like a turf shoe; the top part is like a

baseball shoe; the raised heel was originally because I have bad
Achilles tendons, but it turns out people like the raised heel. It's
really caught on.

I'd only stay in the business of baseball if I could own part of a team.
I'd like to do that. I'd like to be involved in putting together a team
of ballplayers whose talents and chemistry could mesh to form a
winner. It's easy to see talent—that's why there are so many high-
priced free agents—but it's very hard to recognize chemistry. The
Orioles' front office can read chemistry. Finley knew chemistry. In
football, the Dallas Cowboys have recognized it for a long time. So
have the Celtics in the NBA. Shula in Miami. Al Davis of the
Raiders. The Dodgers organization. The Yankees, for the time I
was there, had chemistry *and* talent.

Chemistry is being able to understand what complements one
thing or another. To build a ballclub, for instance, you need good
right-handed starters and good lefty starters. If you have to choose,
go with a lefty because they're rarer. If you have a lot of good six-
or seven-inning pitchers, you'd better get yourself a real good short-
man. If you have some quiet people who don't like the press, who
can't be volatile take-charge guys, you get some people like Dave
Winfield or Pete Rose. I don't think Mike Schmidt, for instance,
cares too much for publicity. But he was always the biggest star the
Phillies had so he naturally attracted attention. Well, Schmidt had
great years after the Phillies got Rose. I think it's because Rose was
able to take some of the heat off Mike when it came to dealing with
the media. Rose is terrific at that; he thrives on it. Schmidt doesn't
seem to like it. If you've got a lot of high-profile starts, you'll
probably need a low-key manager. Billy Martin was the perfect
manager for the A's, for instance. He got the attention, the heat;
he dictated the flow of the chemistry, and he didn't have any
veteran stars to disrupt that flow. They needed a leader, a father
figure, and he fit the bill perfectly for a while.

Chemistry: understanding what talents can complement other
talents and how personalities can blend to form a cohesive team
unit.

As I said, it's easy to see talent: a guy runs real fast, someone's
got a good swing, a guy's got a ninety-five-mile-per-hour fastball—
a machine'll tell you that. But a guy may have major league talent

and not have major league character. Or mental toughness. That's the tough thing to pick. Will this guy stand up to pressure? Does that guy want to put himself through the tough physical and mental strain it takes to be a winner? Playing baseball is *hard*. It's physically and mentally demanding and it takes a lot of dedication and discipline. Too many young players today forget that. They're twenty-four, twenty-five years old, and they're making $300,000 a year; it's easy to forget that they've got to work hard to keep up the level of excellence that *got* them to that point. You've got to find guys who can handle the roller-coaster ride, the highs and lows. When you put together a team of guys who know how to lose *and* win, who've got the heart *and* talent, that's chemistry. And that's the kind of ballclub I'd like to put together if I ever stayed in the game of baseball as a businessman. You must find players who can accept success and tolerate but never accept *failure*. I call it *coping*.

I believe I have exploited myself, my name and my talents, in a good way, to the benefit of myself, my family, and my future family. In doing this, I feel I have made a contribution as a black man. I don't beat my chest about it. I don't stand up and say, "Hey, I'm black. I made it." It's obvious that I'm black, and I don't have to say it. My father taught me that class isn't supposed to bellow. But it's important to me that I be thought of as a classy businessman—a classy *black* businessman—by professional people, both black and white. I want to be a good man first, but I know I will be perceived as a black man so I want to be a *good* black man. I've always thought: Black babies are born and people see them lying in their cribs in the hospital and the first thing that comes to their mind is "black." Then they check to see if it's a boy or a girl. With white babies, it's just boy or girl. You go from there. You are always going to be different, no matter how much money you have. You always have to work a little harder. Not a complaint, just a fact.

That is why the black, even the successful black, is always worried about The Man. There is always that vague feeling of being threatened even if you achieve financial levels you never dreamt about while you were growing up poor. And all blacks in my time grew up poor. That's why I feel blacks should stick together economically the way Jewish people do, the way Italian people do, the way Mormons do, and others. It's something we should aim toward. What you're looking for is what I've always called "Fuck-you Money." You're never quite sure how much that is, because it has to be enough so you won't ever be squeezed again. This is not a reverse racism of any kind. This is just being practical.

Friends will say to me, "When are you going to have enough? When will you stop?"

And I just say, "I want to have enough to give and enough to keep."

If a friend has a car repossessed and doesn't have enough money to get it back, I want to be able to get the car back. I want to have the ability to pick and choose. I want to live my life on my terms when I'm finished with baseball. I don't want to be exploited the way many athletes have been. As an athlete, particularly a black athlete, it becomes an extra commandment: Watch your pennies and save your dimes. Growing up black, which as I've said means you're probably poor, it makes it easy for me to understand why modern-day athletes will go for the money above anything else. Yes, as my dad said, your education is something they can never take from you. But his dad and his dad's dad and his dad's dad's dad and everybody else I know always said, A bird in the hand is worth two in the bush.

That is why I have always worked so hard to meld my athletic career in the proper way with my business career. Never was that melding more apparent than in 1976 when I became a free agent and signed with the New York Yankees. It was the proper decision, both athletically and financially, at the time. I had been preparing for it for a long time, thanks to D-A-D and to three valued and trusted friends: Gary Walker, Steven Kay, and Matt Merola.

In 1966, while I was still at Arizona State, a fast-talking, good-looking blond guy named Gary Walker tried to sell me some life insurance. I turned him down.

In 1968, we formed a company together that still exists—United Development—and Gary Walker, who is one of the most brilliant and decent men I have ever known, set about the business of making me a wealthy man.

He was persistent from the start. Even after I turned him down on the insurance policy, he kept coming around. He gave up on selling me insurance, but I enjoyed his company and he enjoyed mine. He was older than I was, he was out in the business world, he had a beautiful wife and child—he was different from most of the people I was hanging around with at ASU. He wasn't a jock, is what I'm trying to say. And he was always honest with me.

We were having lunch one day in Tempe after we'd known each other for a few weeks, and Gary said, "Listen, I want to be your friend. I like talking to you, I like being around you. If you decide you want to buy some insurance from me, fine; if you stick to your guns and don't want to buy any, that's fine, too."

I said, "That's a good idea. I hate insurance, but I like you, too."

He was different from anyone I'd ever known. He spoke in sentences and communicated in paragraphs. His brain was always in a sprint; we'd be talking about three or four things at the same time before I realized we'd gotten off the first topic. And I liked the fact that he was an impromptu, extemporaneous type of person. He hated making plans as much as I did. Gary's the type of person who will call up at seven o'clock and ask you to have dinner in fifteen minutes. Then he might not show up, might just change his mind on the way to the restaurant. You had to expect the unexpected with him. We could be going to dinner in two cars, Jennie and I in one, Gary and his wife, Lynn, in the other, and Gary might just decide to go home. He'd call the restaurant and tell you.

Or he'd call me up on the telephone and talk for twenty minutes and then suddenly say, "I'm tired of talking. See you."

Our personalities just sort of meshed. There has always been depth to Gary; he has always seemed comfortable with himself. The relationship between us has been the way friendship is supposed to be: You don't have to watch what you say around Gary, worry about handling him this way or that. You can be yourself completely around him, let your guard down. Up until that point in my life, I'd never had a friend like him.

I gravitated toward him. There was so much I wanted to learn. He has been a salesman all his life (his father had sold insurance for Central Life before him), but he doesn't have the air of a salesman. He is a devout Christian as well, and I have a great deal of respect for that. Gary is the person in my life who has made me more devout as a Christian.

In 1968, right after I got married, we decided to form United Development, and Gary began syndicating real estate out of his second bedroom. He wanted to call it United because he was white and I was black; he wanted to show people that blacks and whites could work together in business and be friends and successful at the same time. Gary's an idealist; he's interested in other people's welfare. He feels very strongly that my success in business—and *our* success as a black-white team—is important as a symbol to show that it *can* be done. We had tough times at first. He had to loan the company money and so did I. At one point, Gary even had to mortgage his house. But he was determined to make it work, as friend and partner.

He has always been as determined when it came to negotiating my baseball contracts, which he started doing before the '69 season. And he has never charged me a cent for that. Not with Finley. Not with the Orioles. Not with Steinbrenner or the Angels. Just would not hear of it. It was something he wanted to do for me, something for which he had a flair.

Gary Walker has made me rich beyond my dreams in Arizona real estate. Syndicating real estate goes something like this: You see a plot of land that you want, say forty acres of it, and the cost is $500,000. You need to put $100,000 of that down. So we would put down $10,000 of our own money, then Gary would go out and get nine other investors to put up $10,000 apiece. We'd be the general partners, they'd be limited partners, and we'd go from there.

Gary saw the development of the Phoenix area coming long before anyone else did, and he has made it pay off. At the present time, we have about 800 investors. We do business with companies like Hughes and Mobil. When we started out, he used to say, "You're not going to touch this until you're retired. This is rainy-day money."

At this point in my life, thanks to Gary, I could probably withstand, oh, about 100 years of financial rainy days.

He has been magnificent as a friend, though he remains as quirky as ever. I remember when I first met him, I just could not believe the car he drove. It was an awful '61 Falcon, and I thought he would have been better off selling it to the school so the student union could use it as a trash can. Ugly-looking white thing. Plus he won't fly. In fact, he hardly ever travels away from the Phoenix area. He is Gary. He likes where he lives, he likes being with his family. He believes in loving his wife and being a good husband to a great woman. His wife, Lynn, is wonderful. In my mind, Gary is a successful man.

And I'm proud that he has a son named Reggie Jackson Eric Walker.

He was with me, via telephone, every day of my traumatic first season in New York when I thought I was on the verge of breaking down so many times. It was Gary who stressed that I should read the Bible. It was Gary who gave me pep talks.

"Don't retort," he'd say. "Don't talk back to Martin because he isn't worthy of that. Just let your talent perform. Let the world see that talent. Behold—"

Constant sermons, constant support. From Arizona, he was the foundation of my spiritual life that year. If I had a bad day at the plate, he told me I would bounce back the next day. Somehow I did. When I would moan that I was having a bad year, he would quote me statistics from other years and tell me I was going to be fine.

I would not be where I am today, in business or in life, without Gary Walker. He will be my friend until the day I die.

Steven Kay, my lawyer friend from Oakland, structures my deals for me. Gary will go in and settle on a dollar figure, then Steven will come in like the cavalry and set up loans, interest rates, payment schedules and deferred money. It is the same with Steven as it is with Gary: He is a friend and we work together. If a man can't be my friend, then I don't want to be in business with him. It's that simple.

Dr. Harold Kay was the team physician when I got to the A's, and one day I mentioned in the clubhouse that I needed some advice from a lawyer about some deal that Gary and I were contemplating. Dr. Kay told me his son was a lawyer. He arranged a meeting, and Steven and I hit it off right away.

He was a little hyper, the way Gary is, but I could see right away that he was a doer. Same as Gary. He can go over six things with you in about two minutes and get them all across to you perfectly. When I signed with the Yankees, the contract was for $2.96 million. Steven looked over the contract and said, "We will want a $250,000 loan right away at six percent interest, we will want the money paid out over fifteen years, we will want $650,000 of the contract paid out up front, including the bonus. The Yankees don't want to give more than $200,000 a year in salary? Fine. Then we'll want $150,000 on the first of January and another $50,000 on the first of June. Any questions?"

He is that kind of guy, slick and polished, a beautiful dresser in his lawyer's three-piece suit. I might add he is also a devil with the ladies.

Steven Kay is Jewish. It's funny when I think back on it, but my father used to talk about me getting a Jewish lawyer when I got older and had a few bucks. There was no meanness or bigotry about it; my father was from Philadelphia, and he used to talk about Philadelphia lawyers, and Philadelphia lawyers to him meant Jewish lawyers. When I was growing up in Wyncote, a lot of my friends were Jewish and their fathers were doctors and lawyers. My dad used to say, "Jewish people know money. They know what's going on with money. When you grow up, get yourself a Jewish lawyer." And that's what I did. That's the way I was brought up. Steven Kay and I would have been friends regardless, of course, but the fact that he's my lawyer has always made Dad very happy.

We joke about my dad's instructions about a Jewish lawyer all the time. It has, in fact, always been a running gag with us. After he structured my Yankee contract for me, I bought him a Mercedes. A 450-SL. He went crazy when he saw it because he'd always wanted one but never thought about buying one for himself. He had only charged me his basic lawyer's fee for working on the contract, and I thought he deserved more so I bought him this car.

He sold it a year later and I got furious with him.

Cars don't mean as much to him as they do to me, and he thought he could put the money to better use. So he sold it. I wouldn't speak to him for a month.

When I finally did start returning his phone calls again, I told him I really shouldn't have been surprised because what he did with the Mercedes expressed a typically Jewish attitude.

Steven laughed and said, "Your father would be very proud if he could hear you talking like that."

Steven just does magic with money—he takes it out of your hand, turns around, makes some phone calls, waits a while, turns back around, and gives you more money. But he tells me all the time that he has to do a good job with my money because he is now known as "Reggie Jackson's lawyer."

"That's why I've got to check and double-check and triple-check everything," he says. "If you go broke, I look bad."

.   .   .

Matt Merola is my New York agent, in charge of selling the Reggie
Jackson name, getting endorsements, getting me on television.
When you see me endorsing Panasonic products, Murjani jeans,
Pony sneakers, Ellesse sporting wear, Pentax cameras, or Remco
toys, that's Matt's department. When you see me working for ABC
Sports on "Superstars" or the World Series, that's Matt. Same with
a guest shot on "Archie Bunker's Place" or "Love Boat." I like to
say that Gary and Steven are in charge of dollars and cents and
Matt's in charge of me.

He is the most un-agentlike person in the world, a good-
looking Italian in his forties with sleepy eyes and the sweetest
disposition you've ever seen. Matt was just as important as Gary
in getting me through the difficult early period with the Yankees,
all but holding my hand half the time. He'd eat breakfast with me
in the morning at a little place on Madison called the Nectar Coffee
Shop, which is right around the corner from my apartment. He'd
wait for me at the Stadium after games, drive me to Jim McMullen's, have dinner with me there, drive me home. He was a saint
the entire time, a friend, a brother, a godfather. To this day, Matt
calls me every morning of my life.

You want to know how un-agentlike Matt is? In the office of
his company, Mattgo, he answers his own phone. And takes care
of a small but lucrative list of clients, which includes me, Tom
Seaver, Cathy Rigby, Nolan Ryan, Bob Griese, Dave Kingman,
and Gale Sayers. Do not be fooled by the easygoing manner, his
manner in general. Matt Merola is sharp as a tack and doesn't miss
a trick.

One day in 1976 when I was with the Orioles, I was sitting
around after a game against the Yankees, bullshitting with some of
the New York writers. Phil Pepe from the *Daily News* was there,
and Steve Jacobson from *Newsday* and Henry Hecht from the *Post.*
I'd had a good day with a dinger and a couple of other hits, and
I was feeling my oats. It was one of those baseball moments when
you're just happy with all of it: the team, the weather, the standings,
yourself, life in general. You feel like a little kid who's fooling
everybody because *they're* paying *you* to play ball for a living, when
you'd be just as happy to have it the other way around. I was as
full of stuffing as a Christmas turkey.

And I said the following thing to these New York guys: "If I
played in New York, they'd name a candy bar after me."

I just said it off the top of my head.

If I played in New York, they'd name a candy bar after me.

Everybody laughed.

Except Matt.

He started shopping for it as soon as the ink was dry on my Yankee contract in November.

The idea was not greeted with overwhelming enthusiasm. He'd call candy company after candy company, and there were no takers. He finally took one last shot in the dark with Standard Brands.

Bingo.

Not long after I signed with the Yankees, Matt and I met with Ron Cappadocia and Peter Rodgers. Ron was in charge of the confectionary division of Standard Brands while Peter, at the time, was in charge of United States consumer products. Ron Cappadocia was exactly what you'd expect from his name: three-piece suit, well groomed, authoritative, very Italian looking. Peter Rodgers looked like a Madison Avenue executive should look. Along with that look, he had an English accent which, to me, made everything he said *sound* brilliant, whether it was or not. We also met with Ross Johnson, then Standard Brands's chief executive officer. Ross is a high-powered businessman, in command of his thoughts, forceful in his presentation, never hard-selling you, a good listener, very attentive, very persuasive, one of those people you could see running everything up to and including a small country. We all went back and forth with Matt talking about the kind of money we were looking for and with Ross, Peter, and Ron listening and saying they thought I was one athlete around worthy of such a deal.

After several months of negotiation, the Reggie Bar was born. I had come a long way from stealing a Clark Bar back in Wyncote.

The Reggie Bar would only last a couple of years, but the deal was a sweet one for us, spread out over ten years and worth almost as much as my Yankee contract. There were problems getting it off the ground, which I'm told is standard operating procedure for any product like it, and it would later die in infancy, in part because of the merger between Standard Brands and Nabisco. Perhaps it didn't get the support it needed. In the end, the Reggie Bar was short-changed, I think.

But it was very tasty, if I do say so myself. Chocolate, caramel and nuts. I remember when I did the first commercial, I had to take bites from more than seventy-five of them. Good thing I liked it.

It did have one great day at Yankee Stadium. Home Opener, 1978. Remember how I hit four home runs on my last four at-bats in the '77 Series? Remember how I hit three in a row on three swings in the sixth game at the Stadium? I guess you do.

I hit another one my first time up in that '78 Stadium opener against the White Sox.

And Standard Brands was ready with its Reggie Bars.

They had passed out 50,000 of them to the fans as they came through the turnstiles. And when I took my position in right field in the top of the second, after the dinger, those Reggie Bars started to rain out of the right-field stands. The people were chanting "REG-gie! REG-gie!" just as they had on that October night six months previously. That I could understand.

The rainstorm of candy that came next, I didn't understand.

It was just a few at first, and when they landed near me, my first reaction—I promise you this—was, "Oh, shit. They don't like them. I hope Standard Brands isn't watching this."

Then they were coming from everywhere, thousands of them, hail wrapped in orange, covering right field. I picked up the first few and tried to stuff them in my pocket, but all of a sudden they were everywhere. The people kept chanting and the candy bars kept coming, and the game was delayed for about fifteen minutes while the ground crew came out and cleaned up. I finally just started laughing like hell.

Matt told me later he just sat and watched from the Standard Brands box like a proud papa, because this was just about the top of the Empire State Building if we're talking about a single act of pure promotion.

I was as happy for him as I was for myself. Like I've said, Matt has always been a saint, especially when I needed him. When we'd have these fiery meetings with Steinbrenner and his people later on, Matt was always sitting right there next to me, acting as referee, trying to calm the situation, being a friend; Matt has always been the soother. We've been together for fifteen years now, and we've never had anything more than a handshake agreement.

There have been times when people have told me that I didn't need Matt anymore, that I'd outgrown him. I always say the same thing in response: "We start together, we end together. You get me, you get Matt." It will be that way forever. He has been terrific. A

fine human being. Prompt. Organized. Efficient. A detail man who
doesn't worry about details being great or small. Jack of all trades,
master of all trades. Matt's as comfortable making a plane reserva-
tion for me as he is making a deal with ABC.

He is another one of those people without whom I never could
have made it in New York.

So that is Team Jackson. Me. Gary. Steven. Matt.

One day in 1976, we decided to take the show to Broadway.
For better or worse, I guess that's where it always belonged.

The whirlwind courtship with George Steinbrenner and the Yankees that began on November 4, 1976, took just three weeks.

It started out with the Yankees and twelve other teams—
Montreal, Los Angeles, Atlanta, San Diego, California, Baltimore,
the New York Mets, San Francisco, Pittsburgh, Oakland, Chicago,
Philadelphia—drafting for the right to negotiate with me.

It ended with George Steinbrenner and Gary Walker and me
making our deal in the Hyatt Hotel in Chicago on the day before
Thanksgiving. The final flourish to the deal was George giving me
$60,000 so I could buy a Rolls-Royce Corniche. Contrary to popu-
lar belief, George didn't offer to buy me the Rolls; it was something
that *I* wanted. It didn't matter to him *how* I spent that sixty grand.

I've got to level: It was a fun three weeks.

I had been romanced before in my life as an athlete, by college
recruiters in general and Frank Kush in particular, by Charlie
Finley, by the Baltimore Orioles. But it had been nothing like this.
There were other fine players in that '76 draft, players like Grich
and Rudi, Don Gullett and Wayne Garland, Don Baylor, Rollie
Fingers, Sal Bando, Bert Campaneris, Gary Matthews. Still, the
most valuable property in the game is the slugger, the guy with the
dingers. And luckily, that was me. I had home runs in my portfolio.
I had the reputation for controversy from the A's. I had three
World Series rings. I was just six months past my thirtieth birthday,
right smack in the middle of my prime.

So all these teams wanted to throw money my way and tell me
how wonderful I was. Call me a crazy old romantic, but it sure
sounded like fun to me.

Gary drove up from Arizona (remember, he doesn't fly) to

handle the nuts and bolts. We had established a figure of $3 million for five years, and we didn't intend to budge much from that. Again, we had learned our lessons well from Charlie Finley. We weren't trying to beat anybody up, we just wanted them to know what the check for dinner was going to be before we sat down. Gary would drive from city to city and I'd fly, and we'd meet with the team and listen to what they had to say. Then Gary would drive to the next city and I'd fly, and we'd go through the whole thing again. There wasn't any urgency to all this, but I had it in my mind to get back to California for Thanksgiving, and I wanted to be working for somebody by then.

We didn't weed teams out; they did that themselves. San Diego offered $3.4 million, but we wanted that $250,000 loan, and they only wanted to give a $100,000 loan. Goodbye, San Diego. Goodbye, Ray Kroc and all your McDonald's hamburgers. I flew up to Montreal to meet Charles Bronfman, who owned the Expos. He impressed me tremendously. And when he took me to his home, I was overwhelmed. I'd never seen a house like that in my life. It seemed like it was 100,000 square feet. There was a big movie room, a great entertainment room, a tremendous sliding roof that opened the house up to the outside. Bronfman was a nice man, and his whole family treated me well. While I was there, I also saw John McHale, who ran the Expos. They made a fabulous offer that worked out to almost $5 million for five years; Steven Kay dropped the phone when he heard about it. I liked McHale and I know I would have enjoyed playing for the Bronfmans. I also thought Montreal was beautiful, but I decided that I wanted to play in the United States, old patriotic me.

On and on it went. The Orioles were slow to make an offer. They'd come in later with an offer almost identical to Steinbrenner's, but by then I fancied the idea of playing for George, taking my run in the Big Apple. I'm still not sure what would have happened if the Orioles had made their offer the day after the draft because 1976 had been such an enjoyable year, and I really did think Hank Peters was a decent, honorable man.

The Dodgers came in late, too. A couple of years later, after the Yankees had beaten them in the '77 and '78 World Series, I had a feeling the Dodgers may have rethought their position.

By the time I had rejected Canada, and the Padres had haggled about the loan, and the Dodgers and Orioles were just a bit too tardy, I had had lunch with George Steinbrenner at "21" in New York.

And I've got to admit, that hot lady called New York and that smoothie Steinbrenner swept me off my feet.

My first impression of George Steinbrenner was class. I had been in Montreal the day before, and I flew into LaGuardia Airport (Gary was on the road). George was there with a limousine. And he was George. Mr. High Roller. Looked you in the eye. Had the uniform on that would become so familiar to me: blue blazer, gray slacks, blue shirt, Yankee tie. Killer-gray hair. Clean shaven.

He put out his hand and said, "Welcome to New York. Let's go have lunch."

We got into the car and went to "21." I'd never been there—never even heard of it, to tell the truth. On the way into town, he told me it was one of the "in" spots for the city's shakers and movers. He said it was good that I had a tie on. I asked why and he said, "You have to wear a tie at '21.' " Right away I knew that the limo was easing me into a brave new world.

I had never worn a tie to lunch in my entire life.

I was amazed when we walked into "21" because it looked like a saloon to me, with its checkered tablecloths, cheap-looking furniture and ordinary wood floor. I thought, Geez, it isn't even carpeted. I decided that had to be what "in" looked like in the big city. We hadn't worried much about "in" or chic in Oakland and Baltimore. To me, when someone said chic, I thought they meant chick, and I looked for the color of her hair.

George was at his best that day. He sold tradition. He sold the pinstripes. He sold himself. He sold the city.

"You can own the town, Reggie," he said. "There will be so many business opportunities for you out there you'll be able to pick and choose like you're at a long buffet table. With your charisma and personal charm, you'll be even bigger than you already are. And we can win with you. We can bring a world championship back to the Yankees, where it belongs. You and I are going to make a great team."

I asked him about the various pressures of living in the city, about the media, and George just laughed.

"The way you can talk, Reggie," he said, "dealing with the media will be like eating ice cream."

George had brought a few of his buddies to lunch that day. Larry and Zack Fischer, who seem to own half the buildings in New York. Tony Rolfe, also in the real estate business, was there, too. And Bill Fugazy, the limousine man. They were dressed the way I'd always imagined New York businessmen would dress—hair neatly trimmed, glasses tucked into inside suit pockets, monogrammed shirts, cuff links. I felt like I'd walked onto the set of the movie *Network*. These guys seemed to represent all the business and radiate all the action of the Big Apple.

Fugazy was there mainly as Steinbrenner's yes guy. Anytime George said something, Fugazy would nod and agree that "Yes, that's the way it is." He also told me that any time I needed a car, I should just call him and he'd supply me with one. I didn't have the heart to tell him that the only time I could see myself riding in my own limo would be on the way to my funeral.

It was something. It truly was.

Talk about bein' out of your fuckin' element.

Of course I was dazzled. Overwhelmed is more like it. But I couldn't wait to get back to California, have a tuna sandwich, some corn chips and a smoothie.

I remember that, as we were leaving, I looked at a pipe in the smoking case by the front door. It was sixty dollars. *Sixty dollars.* For a pipe! Shocked, I kind of stuttered to the cashier, "Uh, well, sorry. Maybe next time." Larry Fischer immediately said, "No, go ahead. Take it. A present."

I mean, everybody was workin' that day.

At the door, George said, "Let's just you and me take a walk."

We did. If you have never lived in New York or visited New York, then it is difficult to explain what walking the city streets is like on a fine Indian-summer November afternoon. New York can just put its arms around you and give you a bear hug on days like that. It's warm. It's smiling. Friendly. You can feel the vitality, the urgency, the romance of the city just pouring up out of the cracks in the sidewalk like steam on a cold day. There's nothing quite like it.

Everywhere we walked that day, up into the Sixties, crossing Fifth Avenue first, then moving to Madison and Park, people were stopping us.

"Hey, George. Hi, Reggie. You gotta play for the Yankees. We need you."

Cab drivers were leaning out of windows, yelling back even as they pulled away.

"Hey, Reggie. Come on, man. This is your kind of town."

A group of kids getting out of school converged on us and asked for autographs.

It was like a two-man St. Patrick's Day Parade, and I loved it.

Every block or so, George would turn to me with this earnest smile that looked like it would last for months and years and say, "This is what it's like. This is the greatest city in the world, isn't it? Can't you feel how much it wants you?"

I have to admit I was doing some smiling myself. Some people would suggest later that George staged all those bursts of affection that came at us that day. I don't think any of it was staged. I think it was just New York. George Steinbrenner was good that day, very good, and I looked at him as though he were the unofficial mayor of the city.

But George wasn't as good, as appealing, as exciting as the city seemed to be. I had been there before, but I really *hadn't* been there before. It was as if I had seen New York across some crowded room, caught her eye, but never got the chance to talk to her. Now I was talking to her, *feeling* her. Being seduced by her.

I was easy prey.

We finally got to his brownstone in the East Sixties. It was huge but it wasn't homey. It was gorgeous but stark. Cold. He told me this was home base when he was in New York. There was an indoor pool, which was impressive. But it didn't feel like a home to me.

We went up to the top floor, just the two of us, and we got down to the crunch. We started to talk about money.

I said, "You know that Gary and I want three million."

Right away, George said, "I can't pay you that much. It will screw up my salary structure."

I'd grin when I thought back on that one later on. I have a feeling the last time George worried about a salary structure was in the third grade, running a lemonade stand.

"What exactly are you offering?" I asked.

He said, "Two million. Five years."

I laughed right back at him, a friendly laugh, and said, "Guess I'll be on my way. We can't do business together."

A few days later, George Steinbrenner flew to Chicago where Gary and I had set up headquarters in the Hyatt to take the final bids and listen to any eleventh-hour offers. And we made our deal.

George agreed to pay $2.96 million over five years. The $60,000 there at the end was for the Rolls. It was all written out on a hotel napkin.

At the bottom of that Hyatt napkin I wrote to George, "I will not let you down. Reginald M. Jackson."

I was a New York Yankee.

Let the games begin.

9
NEW YORK, NEW YORK

When Dave Winfield signed with the Yankees, he said, "I'm no country bumpkin."

I was.

I know, I know. I'd said that if I ever played in New York, they'd name a candy bar after me. I had played on those three championship teams in Oakland. I'd hit a whole bunch of home runs. *Sports Illustrated* had labeled me a "Superduperstar." On the cover.

What I'm trying to get across is this: By the time I signed with the Yankees, I had already put some numbers in the books. I had already made a name for myself.

So I thought I'd be welcomed in New York. I didn't think they were going to give me the keys to the city or put out the red carpet or anything. But I did think the prevailing attitude would be, "Nice to have you aboard, big guy." Remember, when I became a free agent after the 1976 season, Montreal offered me the best deal by far. Gary Walker had begged me to sign with the Expos.

Sounds a little hokey in the telling, but one of the reasons I didn't sign with the Expos was that I felt I should play in the United States. I felt I should be here, that I was more a natural resource of this country.

The bigger reason was that I really wanted to play in New York. I told Steven, I told Matt Merola, and I told Gary that on top of everything else, the fans of New York knew baseball better than anyone. I felt I would be appreciated more in New York than any other place I could play. The Yankees had made the World Series in '76, but then they'd gotten blown away by Cincinnati in four straight. I thought I could be the extra something that could make the difference for them.

Not the straw that stirs the drink, thank you.

Maybe the salt in the soup.

I'm not saying I was the only baseball player in the world who could have meant the difference for the New York Yankees in 1977, though just about every comment I made that year and since was construed that way. That's the way I was painted, but that's not the way I thought coming in. I think a hitter like Ken Singleton could have made the difference for the Yankees in '77. A Reggie Smith. Someone who could put some heat in the middle of the lineup, hit the ball over the wall and knock in 100 or so runs. It just worked out that I was the last piece to the puzzle because I was a free agent —the one George Steinbrenner courted and signed.

That's the way it happens in baseball. In the playoffs against the Brewers in 1982, the Angels didn't have that missing piece to the puzzle. I wasn't it. We were up two games to none, but we couldn't slam the door, step on their necks. In the end, we needed just one out pitch from a reliever, and we couldn't get it. It could've been Goose Gossage. Or Dan Quisenberry. Or whoever. We needed just that little touch to get over the hump. It wasn't there.

When I got to New York, that's the way I thought people would look at Reggie Jackson. I figured New York would say, "Hey, here's a guy who's won, who's been on winning teams. The Yanks were almost there last year. They're a great team, and they just need that little bit of spice. That's what Reggie can be, and aren't we lucky to have him?" Hmmm. Nice thought, anyway.

Didn't work out that way.

I wasn't ready for New York.

And New York wasn't ready for me.

They don't care about your credentials in New York. They'll

skim your portfolio, but they don't want to read it too closely. New Yorkers expect you to work, and you'd better be ready to prove yourself. It's as if there's this big electric fence surrounding the city of New York, and they want it to be tough for you to get over that fence. You've got to show you've got some balls. You've got to work your way into the fabric of life in the city. They want to laugh at you when you start to climb over the first time. You want to become one of us in New York? Fine. But get ready for the shock, Jack. I don't mean this as a negative, because I came to like and appreciate the city. It's just the way things are.

When you do make it in New York, a man looks you in the eye and says, "That sonofabitch is tough; he's as tough as me." It doesn't matter whether you're a businessman or a lawyer or a doctor or a writer or a model or a truck driver or a street cleaner.

When someone who's good in a particular field says he's moving to New York, New Yorkers say, "Great choice. Great decision. Take your best shot."

But as soon as you walk away, they grin and shake their heads and say, "He's got no idea. That poor SOB has got *no idea* what it's going to be like trying to make it here."

I had no idea.

I'd never been to the theater in my life when I moved to New York. I'd never heard of Fashion Avenue. Upper East Side? Upper West Side? I didn't know what people were talking about. The Upper East Side could have been New England as far as I was concerned. The Upper West Side was Montana, Oregon, and Washington. Wall Street? Where was that? Did it run past the Great Wall of China? A woman I was going out with then used to make fun of me all the time because I'd never heard of Cartier until I moved to New York. I didn't wear cowboy boots because they were fashionable at the time; I wore them because people wore them in Oakland. Gucci? What was that?

I thought fur coats were for sissies.

I learned about fur coats. I also learned about public relations at the same time because a furrier, Ben Kahn, approached Matt Merola and gave me a $15,000 coat. *Gave* me. Just because they wanted Reggie Jackson to wear their coat for publicity purposes. That's the way things are done in New York. I learned about a lot of things, on the field and off. But I couldn't possibly have been more unprepared for life in New York. Call it culture shock, and then take it to the nth degree.

Ralph Dastino, the president of Cartier, took me to see my first play, *They're Playing Our Song,* starring Lucie Arnez and Robert Klein. Ralph thought it would be good for me; he thought I was an okay guy who really could use a good dose of class. Afterward we went to Sardi's for a late supper because Ralph wanted to show me that that was the way things were done. He also fixed me up that night with one of my first New York models. She was a very sleek date, tall, thin, hair pulled back, very sophisticated. She looked like *opera,* if you know what I mean. I knew I didn't belong, but I was ridin' so I just sat back and enjoyed the ride.

Ralph later introduced me to the heiress to the Cartier fortune. I remember her well because she was the first woman I'd ever seen who smoked cigars. I guess that was classy. By this time I was getting confused. He also took me to my first black-tie event.

One other person I have to mention again is Tony Rolfe. He's affiliated with Sulzberger and Rolfe, a real estate management firm on Madison Avenue. I met Tony at "21"—he hung around with Steinbrenner and the Fischer brothers.

Tony personally went out with me to help me find an apartment. He was exactly what I expected of New York: Jewish, good-looking, perfect gray temples, a top coat, the watch with the black band. He went to "21" for lunch, had cocktails at 5:30, knew everyone. He was even shaved by a barber!

Tony Rolfe was one of George's boys, but we immediately gravitated toward each other as friends. He became a real confidante. When George and I began to have our problems after my first three years with the team, Tony became somewhat of an orphan, the black sheep of the Steinbrenner crowd because of his allegiance to me.

I like Tony and admire him. When I "grow up," I'd like his personality and wherewithal.

I am more comfortable now in this sophisticated world. I do pretty well, if I do say so myself. But it's still not me. I don't like to ride in limos. I'll do it if I have to, but I'm really not comfortable. I never got used to buying retail. When I bought my first expensive piece of jewelry in New York, I went to the discount diamond district on Forty-seventh Street. I wouldn't comprehend buying the same thing at Tiffany's for twice the price. My father raised me with the words, "Make a good deal for yourself." I still try to follow those words.

I found out that the city was a close-knit fraternity, same as the Yankees. Before I came to the Yankees, I'd always thought of myself as a fun-loving guy. I could coin a phrase. I could bullshit with the best. I could raise some hell. That all changed in New York. I couldn't say things off the cuff. I couldn't put you on. Every sentence, every paragraph was looked on as the potential for a Headline. Where people had always thought of me as being smart, now it was different. Now I was a smart *ass*.

Let me put it to you this way: I didn't know I was such a raging egomaniac until they told me in New York.

I found out very, very quickly that my teammates hated the fact that I had a good rapport with the press, for example. They got offended that the media was always around me. It upset them. Behind my back, they made snide comments about how I was always seeking out the attention. Graig Nettles used to say that if a reporter tried to get past my locker without talking to me, I'd trip him to get his attention.

That was all bullshit.

For the last ten years or so, I've probably been one of the most interviewed men in sports. During the baseball season, a day hasn't gone by when I haven't been interviewed by somebody about something. And in all those years, I've *asked* to be interviewed maybe a half-dozen times. Tops. I'm talking about times when I went to a reporter and said, "I'd like for this to be said," or "I'd like to clarify that in a story."

It was never perceived that way, not from my first day with the Yankees, even before the team came north to New York.

To this day, I can't quite figure why my coming to New York and the Yankees was laced with such blatant bitterness. But it was. I don't know why the clubhouse atmosphere was so strained. The Oakland clubhouse had been a frat house. No cliques. No racism. Blacks and whites together. Boys being boys and not taking anything personally. One of the first things I noticed in Fort Lauderdale that first spring with the Yankees was that the blacks all lockered in one section of the room. Randolph. White. Carlos May. Mickey Rivers. Now me. That section wasn't all black, however. There were a couple of whites mixed in.

I remember one March day in '77 when Ken Holtzman was running his laps in the outfield. I was at the bat rack in the dugout. Martin, Munson, Nettles, Sparky Lyle and Dick Tidrow were in a giggly group at the other end, pointing at Holtzman.

I sidled down to listen.

They were making Jewish jokes about Holtzman. Crude, juvenile stuff. I shook my head, walked away and wondered what they thought of me. It just hadn't been done in Oakland. It felt strange. Disturbing.

I should have seen it coming. I'd met Sparky Lyle and Graig Nettles in Hawaii during the off-season when they and some of the other Yankees were there for ABC's "Superstars" show. Lyle was one of the Superteam captains. They had been cool and standoffish for no reason that I could discern. I remembered what it had been like when I went over to Baltimore, when Brooks Robinson and Mark Belanger and Lee May went out of their way to make me feel at home. There was none of that in Hawaii. I'd been signed in November so I was already a Yankee. But those guys didn't say, "Hey, let's have dinner, let's shoot the breeze. Glad to have you aboard." Those guys hung out as a team over there—ate together, went swimming together. I was never invited to be a participant.

Their attitude was the first warning signal that things would be very different in New York.

I wasn't one of *them.*

The year 1977 would turn out to be the worst of my life. It ended with the three home runs against the Dodgers and the championship of the world, but I could've hit 300 home runs that year and I still would look back on the experience as being a sick one for me. I went three years without talking about it. I didn't want to even *think* about it. Unless you're talking about a serious illness, I can't imagine another experience I could ever have that would be as mentally and emotionally debilitating. To this day, there are some things that I'm sure I've forgotten about, blocked out of my mind. I think that God has given us a device for forgetting our most excruciatingly painful experiences.

I'm not whining here. I'm not looking for sympathy. I did my job. We won. I got through it. Maybe it made me a better man. But I would never want to go through anything like it ever again. I wouldn't want *anybody* to go through it. There were times in '77 when I would look in the mirror and be embarrassed because of all the shit I had to take. I was ashamed that I just didn't grab some-body and punch the living daylights out of them.

There was a night in Kansas City, a night I will tell more about, when Sparky Lyle berated me in front of the team in the dugout for an error I'd made.

"Get your head out of your ass," Lyle said. "Don't you know we're in a pennant race?"

Sparky Lyle, right? Here's a guy who's in the second pennant race of his life, and I'd already been on three World Series winners, and he's going to tell me about getting my head out of my ass because we're in a race.

I wanted to fight him right there, but that would've meant giving in. It was humiliating to do nothing, but it would've been more humiliating to give a person like Lyle—a crude, self-serving, person—the satisfaction.

It was that kind of season. I never felt more alone in my life. I had one girlfriend—Dayna, who'd moved from California to live with me. We either ate dinner together or with Matt. I didn't even know where to go when I wanted to go out. I wasn't into culinary adventures; I wanted places where the owner would protect me. As soon as I found a place where I felt safe, I stayed there. I had breakfast at the same coffee shop every day. I would eat dinner just about every night at Jim McMullen's, a restaurant on Third Ave-nue. It was like living by rote. I had swordfish so many times at McMullen's I should have grown gills.

There was an African gentleman who lived next door to me. He didn't know anything about what was going on with the Yan-kees. He couldn't have cared less about the Yankees. But he was always coming by to ask me how I was. I guess I looked sick to him.

My apartment is on Fifth Avenue and overlooks Central Park. There was an afternoon in the middle of the season when I sat on the terrace for five hours, just staring at the park, not moving, not saying anything. It was like I was in a catatonic state. Dayna thought I'd finally cracked up, lost it. About four in the afternoon, she just came over to me, tapped me on the shoulder, and quietly said, "Shouldn't you think about getting to the park soon?"

I just turned and looked at her. I didn't know how long I had been sitting there.

I got changed, went down and got my car out of the garage, drove to Yankee Stadium, and cried all the way. We were fighting

for a pennant. I was in the middle of this crazy passion play that
had so little to do with baseball, that starred me and George and
Billy and Thurman and the press and New York. And there I was
sitting in my car crying, because I knew what would be waiting for
me at the Stadium, because it was waiting for me every night. It got
to the point where writers would walk toward my locker with this
pained expression on their faces, like they were thinking, "I don't
even want to ask this poor bastard these questions."

But they'd ask.

I got two hits that night. It was that kind of season. People
always ask me if the three home runs in the Series are what I
remember about 1977. I might tell them yes, but what I really
remember best was that afternoon on the terrace. People ask me if
1981 was my toughest season because I didn't get a new contract
with the Yankees, because of the strike and the physical examination George made me take, because of what happened in the World
Series, which we blew to the Dodgers.

'81 was a picnic compared to '77. A day at the beach. By 1981,
I had done it. You want to say I stink? Fine, I stink. But I've still
got 400 homers. You still want to say I stink? Okay, you're right.
But I've been in six World Series already. You want to say I can't
play? Terrific. But I've had a great career. That's the way I felt in
1981. They couldn't lay a glove on me by then.

All I wanted to do in 1977 was survive. Because up until
August (when Billy and George finally put me at cleanup and the
team started to roll) I thought I was going nuts.

When I tell you this, I tell you the truth: If I'd had any idea
what it was going to be like in New York, I never would've signed.
To this day, with all I accomplished on the field in New York—
and off the field—I wouldn't have signed with them in a million
years. Not a chance.

I would've gone to Montreal or San Diego. Or I would've gone
to the Dodgers. The week I shook hands with George Steinbrenner,
Maury Wills called me on behalf of the Dodgers, asking me if I was
still available. They were willing to match any offers I'd received.
I really wanted to be a Dodger. They had the history, they had a
class organization. And they were in California, close to home. I
told Maury that technically I was free, but that I'd given Steinbrenner my word, and that was that.

I'll always wonder what it would have been like with the

Dodgers. They had all those right-handed hitters: Steve Garvey, Ron Cey, Dusty Baker, Bill Russell, Davey Lopes, Reggie Smith. I showed how much I loved hitting in Dodger Stadium every time I played a World Series game there.

At the end of two World Series against them, two World Series the Yankees won, I looked over at their dugout and thought, "It could've been you guys if you'd only contacted me sooner."

I wish I had worn Dodger blue. But I decided to wear pinstripes instead.

The rest, as they say, is history.

Read all about it.

10

"THE STRAW THAT STIRS THE DRINK..."

The writer's name was Robert Ward. He had dark hair and was sort of nondescript and harmless-looking. He showed up in Fort Lauderdale the first week of spring training, smiled at me, put out his hand, and told me he wanted to do a nice, upbeat story about me coming to the Yankees and all the implications of that. Said the story was for *Sport* magazine.

I smiled right back and told Robert Ward I really didn't want to cooperate with *Sport* because I felt I'd been burned by them in the past, that there had been times when I felt they sensationalized stories about me.

I had only been in the Yankee clubhouse for a couple of days, but I already sensed enough trouble with my new teammates. I didn't need any help from *Sport*. There was nothing specific yet, no overt hostile acts. It was all little things, and a general, vague feeling that I wasn't wanted. For instance, if I didn't initiate a locker room conversation, I wasn't involved in a conversation.

So when Ward broached the subject of the story to me, I told him, "I'm very tentative about doing anything for *Sport*. I'm afraid they're looking for something from me that would make a splash and do me harm. I just don't want to get involved."

I told Ward this same thing more than once in as many different—and polite—ways as I could. He'd show up before workouts. He'd show up after workouts. I'd tell him I wasn't interested. He'd tell me he wasn't out to rip me or hurt me or write a controversial story.

"I'm not out to get you," Ward said at one point. "The story will be in a positive light."

I thought, *Right.*

Again, this went on for several days. And after a while, I actually started to feel sorry for the guy. He seemed decent enough. He also seemed to be a big baseball fan. He kept telling me it wasn't going to look very good for him if he went back without a story (for once, I'd like a writer to tell me something different). So when he showed up at the Banana Boat Bar in Fort Lauderdale late one afternoon, I basically said, What the hell.

I told him to sit down and have a beer.

What I should have done was run for my car.

Because of all the damaging things that happened to me in 1977—particularly in the way I related to the Yankees and they related to me—the most damaging of all turned out to be the story Ward ended up doing for *Sport.*

I'd been worried about them sensationalizing, and that is exactly what I got.

I used to go to the Banana Boat, a dark, cozy bar that looks almost like a still life in the afternoon, because it was the only place I really knew in Fort Lauderdale, and also because Mickey Mantle used to hang out there. Mickey would come down to the Yankee camp in the spring, put on No. 7, and do some coaching, just as an honorary sort of thing, and most days after workouts, he and Whitey Ford and Billy Martin would head over to the Banana Boat. Mickey would have a couple of beers, laugh a lot, play backgammon. He was fun to be around. I didn't go there and try to force myself on him. But I was a Mantle fan. Always have been. It was a thrill for me to sit around with him and talk about hitting and baseball and the Yankees.

Mickey also seemed to be a Reggie fan. We once did a favor for George. A friend of his had opened up a fish-and-chips store in Ocala and George flew us in to sign autographs. A writer came over and tried to get Mickey to give a quote about me. Mickey said, "Why don't you get away from us. You just want me to knock Reggie and I won't do it."

Another time, Mickey was telling Hopalong Cassidy, the ex-football player, about a time he, Mantle, had hit a ball out of Tampa Stadium. The way Mickey told it, the ball had gone at least half a mile. He kept looking at me, asking me to validate his story. Of course, I swore that every word was true. We had Hopalong Cassidy believing it. It was more difficult to keep Mickey from bursting out laughing. Right from the start, I had a good relationship with Mickey Mantle. I wished he could've been a teammate.

This particular day Mantle and Ford were there playing backgammon. I was kind of tired and sitting by myself, sipping a beer. Ward came over and asked if he could sit down. I'd had a couple of beers. I said, "Sure."

We just started talking about baseball, myself, and the Yankees, just shooting the bull in a bar situation. It was something I'd enjoyed doing when I was with other teams. And I thought I'd made myself clear enough to Ward about not wanting him to do a story. So we talked. I told him about meeting Graig Nettles during the off-season in Hawaii. I told Ward I thought Nettles had been a little standoffish toward me. I joked about Thurman being sort of gruff and grumpy, but how I was looking forward to playing with him because I always thought he was such a hell of a competitor when we were on opposite sides.

Understand this: I had barely relaxed for a minute since I arrived in camp and saw what the attitude toward me was like.

I don't enjoy the drills and drudgery of spring training anyway. There is so much tedium to it—for me anyway—because I am never out of shape. I work out all the time. Don't get fat. Don't need to work off the winter the way many others do. I just want to get my swings and get ready for Opening Day. I'm impatient. Spring training is like a holding area for me. Now it was more drudgery, more wearing on my disposition than usual, because of this sense, this smothering feeling, that I was not wanted. There was no overt hostility from Martin. Not yet. There hadn't been any problems with Thurman. None at all. I just had my guard up. I had spent the first part of my life with it up. Then I let it down in Oakland. Now I had the right hand high again.

So it seemed fun to be drinking beer with someone in a quiet setting and shooting the breeze about baseball. Naively, I assumed we were "just talking." In sports, at least for an athlete, that generally means off-the-record, especially when both guys are having a drink.

Ward seemed to understand that. He never asked a leading question.

He never took a note.

After we'd been chatting for a couple of hours, he asked me what I thought I could mean to the Yankees in the '77 season.

I said, "Well, everywhere I've been, I've been lucky enough to be the center of influence on the club offensively. I'm the kind of guy, the kind of power hitter, who fits the last piece into some puzzles. I can be the kind of guy who can put a team over the top."

I didn't think that was a particularly earth-shattering statement since the Yankees *had* made it to the World Series the year before.

Then I held up a glass and compared the Yankees to one of those complicated drinks a bartender can mix. A Planter's Punch, something like that. I talked about Munson and Rivers and Catfish and Nettles and Chambliss and Lyle and Randolph, about what they all could contribute.

And I said, "Maybe I've got the kind of personality that can jump into a drink like that and stir things up and get it all going."

At least that's the way I remember it. Ward remembered it differently. Maybe you heard. It was in all the papers.

Here was the fateful—or fatal—quote from the story in *Sport:*

"You know, this team . . . it all flows from me. I've got to keep it all going. I'm the straw that stirs the drink. It all comes back to me. Maybe I should say me and Munson . . . but really he doesn't enter into it. He's being so damned insecure about the whole thing."

Later there was this quote: "Munson thinks he can be the straw that stirs the drink, but he can only stir it bad."

I could have lived with "the straw that stirs the drink" quote. Ward had obviously taken a thought that took me a paragraph to articulate and compressed it into a sentence. But at least I'd said something like it.

I have no idea where he got the quote about Munson because I never said anything like that. Not anything even close to it, mostly because I hadn't been around Thurman enough to get any kind of reading on him. But those quotes about him hurt me more than anything, and follow me around to this day. They hurt me with Thurman. They hurt me with teammates who hadn't been all that warm or open-minded to begin with. The story seemed to confirm their worst suspicions about me, feed a bitterness that was there before I ever put on a Yankee uniform. I was never really close with Chris Chambliss, for instance. After the *Sport* story came out, Chambliss never loosened up at all with me, only spoke to me when necessary. It's too bad because I always thought he was a decent guy.

I could never read how it affected my relationship with Billy, whether or not it had anything to do with things that happened later on, because Billy and I didn't have a good relationship from the start, at least in his mind.

I've gone over this in my mind again and again, wondering if I could have made things smoother. I've gone back and forth. But the bottom line is probably this: There was nothing to be done, I just don't think Billy Martin liked me.

There's this old joke about poor, pitiful Pearl. She's this bag lady, and she's walking down the street one day, carrying all her belongings in a brown shopping bag, and she's screaming to the heavens.

"Why me?" Pearl screams. "My house has burned down, my kids have forgotten I'm alive. Why did this happen? Why to me? Why, why, why?"

Suddenly there is a thunderclap and Pearl hears the voice of God.

"I don't know, Pearl," He says. "There's just something about you that has always pissed me off."

There was something about me that always pissed Billy Martin off.

To this day, I don't think I've lived down the things Ward had me saying in that story. When the story finally came out and I read it, I had two reactions: One, he shouldn't have been quoting me in the first place, and two, he quoted me incorrectly. I really had thought there were rules between athletes and writers about bar conversations. I never would've talked to him if I thought those rules didn't apply. Now I understand sensationalism.

My ignorance about that was my fault. I never should have let my guard down. Hell, I never should have invited him to sit down in the first place.

All in all, it was the worst screwing I ever got from the press. And I've had a few in my day. The only good thing that came out of it was that I became a lot more careful after that. I've become more acutely aware of who to trust and who not to trust. There have been times in the past few years when I've wanted to say something to a writer, wanted to get something off my chest, and I've just stopped myself cold because I haven't forgotten the Banana Boat.

Call it maturity if you want to. I wish I'd had a couple of orders of maturity in front of me at the Banana Boat.

I never saw Robert Ward again after that day. I never heard from, never heard about, never heard *anything* of him. Until a couple of years ago I was sitting next to a man on a plane, a novelist, and he asked me if I'd ever heard of Robert Ward. My first reaction was to say no because once you start talking to a stranger like that on a plane, they've got a way of holding you hostage the rest of the flight. But I was sort of interested that he would bring up Ward's name, so I told him about the story and what it had done to me.

The man listened, and then he told me this: "Ward's a friend of mine. I know him fairly well, and you ought to know that after he wrote that story, he regretted it for a long time."

The fact that he felt sorry didn't help me a whole lot when the story came out at the end of May.

The Supreme Court couldn't have helped me when the story came out at the end of May.

The story came out on May 23. We were playing at home against the Red Sox, and it was the first time the Yankees and Red Sox had played that season. That's always a splashy event for both teams and their fans.

Little did I know that the Yankees versus the Red Sox would only provide a backdrop to the festivities of the late afternoon and evening.

Little did I know that the animosity between the Yankees and Reggie that had been building in March, April, and the early weeks of May would come to a full boil in front of 30,000 people at the Stadium.

The season was just six weeks old, and still I felt no less an outcast, an intruder, than I had the first day of spring training. I still felt like it was twenty players against, maybe three undecided —Bucky Dent, Willie Randolph, Ron Guidry—and one—Fran Healy—for me. There had been a few isolated instances when I felt a thaw. A very few. A couple of weeks before, in Milwaukee, Thurman had come out to the outfield during batting practice and stood next to me. Nothing momentous was said. We just talked about the team, how it hadn't jelled yet, and how it would be up to the two of us to see that that changed. I thought it was a nice gesture on his part, especially in full view of the team. A lot had been made in the newspaper about George having "betrayed" Thurman by giving me all that money; he'd promised Thurman he'd always be the highest paid regular. Munson had also made some jokes in the paper about George having given me the Rolls-Royce. Thurman had said, "I sure wish George would buy me a car."

So even this minor, friendly chat became a major event for the press, a crucial summit conference. Thurman extends hand of friendship to Reggie! The smallest gesture became the biggest headline. That's what the soap opera had already evolved into. Every movement, every word, had to be analyzed, placed under the microscope. I thought it was sick.

There were already stories about problems between George and Billy, Gabe Paul and Billy, George and Gabe. I'd hurt my arm early in spring training, throwing a ball, and it was still sore. I was making mistakes in the outfield. I wasn't hitting. I'd been to the plate about 150 times and had as many strike outs as hits. We were hanging around the top of the American League East, staying in the vicinity of second or third, but by no stretch of the imagination were we playing the kind of baseball of which we were capable. The kind of baseball George had paid all the money for.

Billy had been fined $2,500 by Steinbrenner in Anaheim for complaining too long and too loud that he needed a player named Elrod Hendricks to be called up from our Syracuse farm team to back up Thurman and Fran Healy at catcher.

I jokingly offered to pay Billy's fine for him.

That became big news, too. Billy didn't think I was so funny as a standup comedian.

If I'd had any doubts leaving Lauderdale, it was now becoming more and more apparent to me that Billy Martin didn't think very much of Reggie Jackson's skills as a baseball player. He didn't want me to bat cleanup. I mentioned to some writers one day that my arm was still bothering me, and Billy blew his top. It was as though I'd leaked some top-secret document to the press. My sore arm was the Pentagon Papers. That was in Milwaukee in April. The next night my name wasn't on the lineup card when I checked it in the dugout.

We were both sitting in the dugout while that night's regulars took batting practice. I heard Billy say to a couple of the beat writers, "Reggie's arm must be bothering him. That's what he told the press anyway."

I was just staring at the field. I heard him. He knew I heard him. It was for my benefit.

"A couple of days off will probably do him a world of good," Billy said. "Isn't that right, Mr. Jackson?"

I held my tongue, just kept staring at the field. As much as I wanted to speak out, as I've always spoken out to any of my managers, I was the new kid in class—and I truly didn't want to antagonize the teacher.

"Right," I said.

There were chances for me to pinchhit that night in both the eighth and the ninth innings. We were behind and a dinger could have tied the score, but Billy never called for me. We lost to the Brewers. It was becoming crystal clear to me that it was as important—maybe more important—for Billy to show me who was in charge as it was for the Yankees to win baseball games. Sometimes when he's managing he gets on this dizzying power trip and can't see past his own ego. It's hurt him—professionally and personally —and his teams. This time, it also hurt *me*.

When we went into Oakland the first time, Billy sat me down against Vida Blue, a left-hander. Even though I was slumping, I desperately wanted to be in there against Blue and the A's. And Billy knew it. I still have a home in Oakland. A lot of my friends were at the game. I had the glory years with the A's in the early '70s. I sat.

Even when the game got to the fifteenth inning, Billy wouldn't let me hit. He sent up a kid named Dell Alston, who'd just been called up from the minors.

Things were no better with my teammates. I sat alone on airplanes. If I didn't go out to dinner with Fran Healy when we were on the road, I ate in my room. I spent most of my free time on the phone. Talking to Matt Merola. Talking to Steven Kay or Gary Walker. They all tried to give me pep talks, tried to tell me things would get better, tried to tell me I'd hit soon. I'd listen. But I wouldn't believe it.

I just wanted out.

Again, the season was all of six weeks old.

After the first few weeks, I'd go into Gabe Paul's office every homestand and ask to be traded. When I'd signed with the Yankees, George Steinbrenner told me that anytime I wanted out, he'd accommodate me. I asked him if we should put all that in writing. He said there was no need.

"Anybody who doesn't want to be here, I don't want to be here," George said.

The amazing thing is that I believed him. I made that mistake a lot with old George.

So I'd march into Gabe's office and say, "Gabe, trade me. The Yankees are right for a lot of people, but not for me. It's a good team, but I'm just not right for it, haven't been from the first day. Anybody can see that. Trade me please. I want out. George said if I wanted out, you'd take care of it."

And Gabe would lean back in his chair, smile placidly at me, and say, "Reggie, don't look at the hole in the donut. Look at the whole donut."

Every conversation.

Don't look at the hole in the donut. Look at the whole donut.

I'd just nod and say, Uh-huh, and leave. I'm going off my rocker, I'd think. On certain days I'd really feel that I'd gone nuts, and Gabe would give me the same aphorism, and that would be that. I'd go back to the clubhouse and put on No. 44.

Looking back, of course, I would've done the same thing Gabe did, handled it the same. What he was really saying to me was, "Jack, I don't care if you become a total raving psycho, as long as you don't rob a bank or kill somebody. You're going to hit because you always have. We're going to be in the race. We're selling tickets wherever we go. We're getting the kind of press no team has ever gotten. Just go out and play."

Oh . . . well.

So that is what it was like in the early days of '77. Arm's sore.
Can't hit. Booed wherever we went, including Yankee Stadium.
Hitting third, fifth, sixth, everywhere but where I should have—
fourth.

Every stop we made, the questions were the same.

Reporter: "You're not batting cleanup."

Me: "Oh, yeah, well, I know."

Reporter: "Why not?"

Me: "Ask Billy. He's the manager."

Reporter: "Haven't you always batted cleanup?"

Me: "Well, uh, yeah."

Reporter: "So why not here?"

Me: "I guess I'm just an overpaid, mediocre ballplayer like
everybody says I am."

Not one of my teammates, other than Healy, ever came over
to me and put an arm around my shoulder and said things would
get better. Which would have been nice, considering we were all
trying to win a pennant and a World Series together. I'm not saying
I needed to be stroked constantly, or coddled, or told I was loved
madly by all the guys I was playing with. It just would have been
nice if there'd been *some* contact, some communication. Never once
all season did either Catfish Hunter or Ken Holtzman do that for
me. I'm talking here about guys I'd been to war with in Oakland,
guys I'd fought side by side with on the way to three straight world
championships. Catfish Hunter and I would end up with five World
Series—three from Oakland, two from New York—and never once
did he give me any support in 1977 when I needed it the most.

Maybe I did come into the Yankee situation too brash, too
cocky, too full of myself. Hell, I was thirty years old and had been
pretty damn successful. My head could have been a little swelled.
It would have been nice if old Cat would have come over and said,
"Key down, man. They don't like that stuff so much. Talk with the
bat." I would've listened. He never said a world.

Looking back, I realize that the whole Yankee situation bred
one instinct above all: self-preservation first. It wasn't something
you thought about, did consciously, but somehow it happened. I
guess Cat was just maintaining his own island—private and separate. I was hoping he'd be able to build a big enough arc to save
me but that was probably impractical. Maybe even impossible. I

certainly don't think he meant to leave me drowning. But the good old boy in Cat never had a chance to surface while he was a Yankee. In fact, I think if it wasn't for the pressure, the way New York and the media and the Yankees seemed to consume human beings, Cat would have pitched a couple of more years than he did.

This was the setting, the atmosphere for the breaking of the Robert Ward story. There had been hints of the quotes for a couple of days in the newspapers. I guess some advance copies had gotten around. At least I was prepared that it was going to be bad.

I didn't know how bad until I got to the clubhouse, late afternoon, May 23, 1977.

All around the room there were players in groups of threes and fours, reading, muttering, occasionally glaring at me. Very pleasant. Like a picnic—with sharks. Thurman walked by with the magazine sticking out of the back pocket of his uniform slacks. No one, not even the players with lockers next to mine, came anywhere near me.

A little later, something took place in another area of the clubhouse that, at the time, I wasn't aware of. Fran Healy was at his locker and the assistant trainer, Herm Schneider, came by and said, "Thurman's in the doctor's room. He'd like to talk to you." The doctor's room was connected to the trainer's room. When Fran got there, Thurman was concentrating on the *Sport* article. He saw Fran, and asked him, "Did you read this?" Fran said he hadn't (and hasn't to this day). Thurman began to read it out loud for Fran's benefit. He paused for a moment to catch his breath.

"Maybe he was quoted out of context," Fran said.

Thurman then uttered what some people call a classic. "Quoted out of context for three fuckin' pages?!"

Fran laughed and went back to his locker. He had no idea of the impact the article was going to have. He thought it was no big deal.

He was wrong.

For now the show, the New York circus, was off and running in full stride.

It was official now. It was in black and white, everything they'd wanted to believe about me since the first day of spring training, and there wasn't going to be any court of appeals. I thought I was better than they were.

I was the straw that stirred the drink, at least in my own mind.

I wish I could have corrected the impression. That night, I went to eat at Harper's, two blocks from Jim McMullen's (it used to be managed by Jim). I ate with Fran Healy, Lou Piniella and Matt Merola.

At dinner, I suggested an apology. Fran said he didn't think it would work but to try it anyway.

He was right. I tried—walked up to Thurman the next day in the locker room and tried to explain—but he'd have none of it. He refused to say a word or listen to a word. He just walked away.

The situation on the team deteriorated rapidly after that. Things became much more polarized.

The next day, Carlos May and Mickey Rivers moved their lockers away from mine. Two days later I showed up for a double-header with the Texas Rangers, and in the back of my uniform slacks I found a note that said, "Suck my ass," left there by one of my teammates.

Anyway, I got into my uniform as quickly as I could before the Red Sox game and headed for the field. When I got into the cage for batting practice, the Yankees who were standing there just drifted away. Batting practice has always been a big show for me, for my teammates, for the other team, for the media, for the people who come early to the ballpark. I plunked some balls into the seats, but it was as if I were hitting in an empty ballpark at noon. Like I said, it was in the open now. I was the alien.

In the seventh inning, I sort of let everyone know that I was accepting the nomination.

I had doubled in the second off Bill Lee and scored on an error. The Red Sox got a couple of runs later on, so it was 2–1 when the seventh inning rolled around. It was then that I just laid on a fastball from Lee, hit one out of sight to right field. I knew it was gone the minute I hit it. I stood at home plate and admired it, the way I always do when I know for sure it's a dinger. The home run tied the score. We'd eventually lose the game, partly because I misplayed a ball in the outfield, an error that seemed to fit perfectly into the whole bizarre scheme of the afternoon and evening.

I didn't plan what I was going to do next, just did it after I crossed home plate.

As I approached the dugout and saw everyone crowded at the corner, waiting for me with their hands out, I decided I'd had enough. I flashed on everything that had happened, the way I'd been treated. I thought about what the clubhouse had been like before the game, about batting practice.

And now we were going to have this traditional, phony ceremony of camaraderie?

The hell we were.

I made a sharp left and headed to the other end of the dugout. Didn't shake a hand. Didn't look at anybody. Half the ballpark saw it clear as day. I'm sure the television audience had a terrific picture of the whole thing. I didn't care. I wasn't one of them? They didn't want me around? I was an outcast? Fine, I at least wanted them all to know that I didn't have to have a picture drawn for me anymore.

After the game I didn't want to talk to anybody. A writer asked me why I hadn't shaken hands, and I snapped something about having a bad hand and left. The next day someone told me that Thurman had called me a "fucking liar" again, which I thought tied up the evening with a neat ribbon.

In the papers the next day, Billy said something sarcastic about me being mad at him because he'd been benching me against left-handers. Then there was a quote from him about the ball I'd misplayed in the outfield and how I always seemed to forget about things like that.

I didn't think the situation could possibly get any worse.

I found out differently in the dugout at Fenway Park three weeks later.

11

THE DUGOUT AT FENWAY: NOT A BOSTON TEA PARTY

Billy Martin is one of the most complex people I've ever met in my life.

You want more, right? Well, we start there. With complex. If there's a bottom line to all of the stuff that went on between us, that's it.

People think I hate Billy Martin. I don't. I hate some of the things he did. And I will say I don't understand him.

I didn't understand him in 1977. I didn't understand him in 1978 or 1979. And I don't really understand him today.

Billy really is a funny guy. He's nice, he's mean. He's good and bad. He's kind and he's cruel. He's done some intelligent things and he's done some dumb things. He would be an absolutely fascinating character study for someone who knows a lot more about psychology than I do. There were times when he was as nice to me as a man could be, and there were times when he went as far out of his way as possible to hurt me as a ballplayer and as a man. He's said complimentary things about me. He's said a ton of negative things. The many faces of Billy.

But one thing was always obvious. He did not want Reggie
Jackson to be a Yankee in 1977. That part I do understand. Understood it then. Understand it now. I think it always bothered him
that he wasn't consulted about me signing with the Yankees. In
Billy's eyes, I was always "George's boy." That was his pet expression for Yankee free agents. George's boys. He was sitting around
with some of the Yankees when it was announced I was going to
sign with New York instead of Montreal, and Billy said, "I'm going
to show him who's boss around here. One of George's boys isn't
going to come in and run the show." I hadn't even met the man yet.
This was January 1977.

We kind of went from there.

It always bothered Billy that George likes to be close to his
players. Maybe it was some misplaced jealousy. I'm not sure.
Maybe Billy wanted to be George's best buddy with the Yankees.
Maybe he saw it as a threat to his authority. But it really ate at him
that George likes to have allegiances with certain players. No one
will ever get as close to George as a player he likes. In my early days
with the Yankees, it was me and Thurman. The last few years it's
been Lou Piniella.

I didn't know a lot about Billy when I came to the Yankees.
He was a fiery little guy who'd managed other teams and done a
good job wherever he went before he'd manage to get himself fired.
I didn't know that much about his ups and downs, what was good
or bad about him, other than what I'd read or heard from other
ballplayers. He was the first manager to ever put a shift on me,
when he was with Minnesota and I was with the A's. He had the
third baseman play behind second, the shortstop play second base,
and the second baseman, Rod Carew, play short right field. It didn't
work, but you can't fault the guy for trying.

But I never saw him in action, saw his entire act, until I came
to the Yankees.

And on a Saturday afternoon in 1977 at Fenway Park—on
national television, of course—Billy and I became about as famous
as a player and his manager can be.

We had been on the road for a while, and we had finally started to
play. I had started to hit, finally. When we came into Boston on the
seventeenth of June—one of those June weekends in Boston where

you can't imagine a more perfect setting for baseball than the little green emerald of a ballpark on Lansdowne Street by Kenmore Square.

We were in first place. In the Friday night game, the Red Sox beat up on us pretty good, but going into Saturday's game, we were still a half-game in front.

Things had eased up slightly between Thurman and me. Not much. A little. We weren't going to the movies or anything, but we were at least shaking hands after one of us would hit a home run, which the press seemed to think showed tremendous progress. But we still weren't speaking in the clubhouse.

Things had not improved at all between Mr. Martin and Mr. Jackson, however. There was still no open hostility, no face-to-face confrontations, but the tension was always there. It would only take the least little incident, one tiny moment, to set him off. Billy has lived his whole life that way, I gather, smiling one minute, cocking his fist the next.

One little example: Before that Saturday afternoon game, Billy and Bucky Dent were sitting in the dugout talking. The night before, Billy had had Bucky squeeze bunt early in the game, and afterward you could see that Bucky was upset about it; he'd wanted to hit away. Bucky Dent is a nice, sensitive human being, and you have to be aware of that. Billy had already taken to pinchhitting for him late in games and replacing him in the infield with Fred Stanley. All of it was starting to chip away at Bucky's confidence. Again, Bucky was one of George's boys taking Fred's job. And Billy didn't particularly like that.

It was also beginning to affect his play, and it was easy to see.

While they sat there in the dugout, Billy was trying to explain to Bucky why he had him bunt the night before. In the middle of it, Billy turned to me of all people and said, "It was the right move at the time, wasn't it, Reggie?"

Billy and I weren't exactly in the habit of thrashing strategy around together, but I guess he wanted me to rubber stamp his position.

I didn't.

I said, "Skip, if you're asking me for my honest opinion, I wouldn't have had him bunt. It's only June. It was early in the game when you had him do it. Something like that might affect Bucky's confidence later in the year when you'll probably have him hitting away in that situation. You're going to need him then. It's too early in the pennant race for that kind of stuff. So, anyway, no, I wouldn't have bunted him."

"I disagree with you," Billy said, obviously pissed off. "I do things my way." Then he went back to talking to Bucky and I started talking to someone else.

I thought that was the end of it. I really thought it was just a mild disagreement about strategy. I thought we were bullshitting in the dugout before a game. I would find out differently a few hours later. That little exchange would be the final spark that touched off the explosion between Billy and me, an explosion that came about because of a little Texas League double by Jim Rice.

Billy would say later that I had been "second-guessing him in front of other players for weeks."

The double from Rice came during a game we would end up losing 10–4. Mike Torrez was pitching for us when it happened. I was in right. Rice took a big swing, and when the ball came off the bat, at first I froze on it because of the way he swung. Rice can hit them over the moon, but not this time. When I realized he hadn't gotten all of it, I started in. For a moment, I thought Willie Randolph might be able to get to the ball from his second base position. When I saw he couldn't, I came harder. But at the end, I knew the ball was going to fall in front of me. I slowed up. I didn't want it skipping past me or some such thing.

Maybe if I had been playing the outfield more confidently at the time, I would have played the ball more aggressively. But I had been slightly tentative all season, and now I was tentative again. Rice had the play in front of him the whole time. When he saw my hesitation, he took off for second and beat my throw.

I could have played the ball better, no doubt about it. To this day, I'm sure Billy thinks I didn't hustle after the ball. To this day, he's wrong. Hustle had nothing to do with it. It wasn't the greatest play I've ever made in the outfield, but I was giving it 100 percent, even if it didn't look that way to Billy.

The show started then.

Billy came out to the mound, ready to replace Torrez with Sparky Lyle. When he took the ball from Torrez he said, "I'm going to get that sonofabitch for not hustling."

I found that out later. He meant me.

I didn't know any of that was going on. Waiting for Sparky

to come in from the bullpen, I walked back to the outfield wall, leaned over, and chatted with Fran Healy, who was in our bullpen.

I had my back to the field. Healy saw what was happening before I did. He said, "You better turn around, Reggie."

I grinned at him.

"Why?"

"Because I think Billy wants you."

I turned around. That's when I saw Paul Blair, one of our backup outfielders, running straight for me.

I jogged back to where I'd normally take my position. It still didn't get through to me what was happening. I've played baseball all my life, and to this day I've never seen a player get yanked defensively in the middle of an inning quite this way.

Blair got up to me and I said, "You here for me?"

He just nodded.

I said, "What the hell is going on?"

Blair just put his head down and said, "You've got to ask Billy that."

It's funny now, looking back on it, because as I ran toward the dugout, I must have been the only person in Fenway Park who didn't see what Billy was trying to do. This was Billy the Kid doing his macho routine to the extreme, showing me up to my team, the other team, the fans, even a national television audience. He wanted me to take a big fall.

Maybe he'd wanted that from the start.

When I got to the top step of the dugout, I could see there was a fury about him, and it was all directed toward me. When Billy starts to lose it, the veins in his neck become very prominent. Now they were standing at attention.

I started down the steps toward the other corner of the dugout from where he was. He screamed over to me.

"What the fuck do you think you're doing out there?"

I put my glove down and took my glasses off. I put the glasses down on top of my glove. Afterward, everybody read that as a sign that I was getting myself ready to fight him. I wasn't. At the time, I was just taking my glasses off, which I often do when I come off the field.

I looked at him.

I said, "What do you mean? What are you talking about?"

He started down the dugout toward me.

"You know what the fuck I'm talking about!" he said. "You want to show me up by loafing on me? Fine. Then I'm going to show your ass up. Anyone who doesn't hustle doesn't play for me."

Considering the fact that Billy was in the process of going around the bend at this point, I was relatively calm, almost placid.

"I wasn't loafing, Billy," I said. "But I'm sure that doesn't matter to you. Nothing I could ever do would please you. You never wanted me on this team in the first place. You don't want me now. Why don't you just admit it?"

The distance between us had shortened considerably. Elston Howard was trying to get between us. Yogi was there, and Jimmy Wynn.

Billy was still screaming.

"I ought to kick your fucking ass!" was the next thing I heard.

And then I'd had enough. I figured just about everybody in the dugout *wanted* him to kick my ass. Or at least try. Other than Healy and maybe a couple of others, I didn't have an ally on the team. Before the game, I'd tried to make peace—again—with Thurman, put out my hand in the clubhouse, and he'd walked away from me. I'd been holding myself back all season, and now this forty-nine-year-old man was telling me he was going to whip me in a fistfight.

Right.

I stopped being placid then.

"Who the fuck do you think you're talking to, old man?" I snapped, just about spitting out the words.

"What?" Billy yelled. "Who's an old man? Who are you call-ing an old man?"

I guess in Billy's mind he's still twenty-five years old and the toughest kid on the street corner. He came for me. Elston and Yogi grabbed him. Jimmy Wynn grabbed me from behind.

"You're an old man," I said. "You're forty-nine years old and you weigh 160. I'm thirty and weigh 210. Let me tell you some-thing: You aren't going to do shit. What you are is plain crazy."

I'd find this out later, but by now NBC was having some show. They had one camera trained on us from the end of the dugout and another from across the field. Ray Negron, a kid Billy had hired in spring training and who had become a friend and aide-de-camp to me, went over and threw a towel over the camera in the dugout finally.

Yogi still had Billy in a bear hug, which was lucky for Billy.

I was livid, but I wasn't going to fight him in the dugout. I walked past everybody into the tunnel and headed for the clubhouse. I could still hear Billy screaming from behind me. I just shook my head and thought, The man has totally lost it.

I also thought this: When the game is over, I'm going to give him his chance to fight me.

When I got into the clubhouse, Bucky Dent was in front of his locker in street clothes. Billy had taken him out of another game, and Bucky had had enough. He had called his wife and told her he was leaving the team and to meet him at the airport in New York. He wasn't going to play for Billy Martin anymore.

When Bucky saw me come into the clubhouse and realized something big had just happened in the dugout, he started to change his mind. He was figuring it might be the wrong day for him to do something like that, what with World War III breaking out all around him.

Torrez was in the training room, icing his arm. Fran Healy had come running down from the bullpen. My locker was right next to Billy's office. I took my uniform jersey off, but left my t-shirt and my spikes on. I wanted good footing on the carpet because when Billy got back, I was going to fight him.

I said to Healy, "He's wanted this fight all season. Hell, even before the season, from the day I signed the damn contract. It's time I gave the little sonofabitch his chance."

Healy was having none of that. It's not Fran's style, which was always a lucky thing for me. He sometimes had to have enough common sense for the two of us.

"Listen," he said. "I knew something like this was going to happen. *You* should've known something like this was bound to happen."

I was pacing around in front of my locker.

"I did not loaf on that ball, Fran."

He said, "That doesn't matter now. The best thing for you to do is get a shower and get the hell out of here. If you stay, the only thing that can happen is that you'll make things worse than they are already."

"I'm going to stand right here by his office and wait for him," I told Fran. "He thinks he can whip my ass? Let's see him do it."

Torrez had come out of the trainer's room. Bucky was just standing in front of his own locker with his mouth open.

Fran just kept telling me over and over, in different ways, to leave. Then he went over to talk to Bucky. Fran always did have a lot of Henry Kissinger in him. He was always a calming influence for everyone, and he always did it on his own. He is a very decent man. And whatever he said to Bucky must have gotten through to him, too, because by the time Torrez and I had gone back into the trainer's room to talk, Bucky was getting back into his uniform.

Mike Torrez had come to the Yankees after the season started in a trade from Oakland. We weren't tremendously close, but he had been supportive of me lately. We had the same advisor, Gary Walker. We both spoke Spanish. Torrez basically told me the same things Fran had.

"Get out of here," he said. "You'll be a lot better off. There's absolutely no way you can win if you stay around here. If you fight and win, you're the bad guy. If you fight and lose, you're a fool. Go on home. Go back to the hotel, have a beer and cool down. That might not make as much sense to you right now as fighting, but it will later."

So I showered and dressed. One of the clubhouse guys offered to get me a cab. So did Ray Negron, who'd come back to see how I was. I told them both I'd rather walk.

Torrez told me he'd meet me later in my hotel room. Fran, who lives in western Massachusetts, told me he was driving home for the night and would see me in the morning at the ballpark.

He also told me not to say or do anything before then that I'd regret.

"The man's crazy," I said once more to Fran. "This whole situation has been crazy from the start." Then I left the clubhouse and made the long walk back to the Sheraton-Boston.

Of course, it wasn't over yet.

12

How I Helped Billy Keep His Job and Other Interesting Tales

The phone started ringing as soon as I got back to the Sheraton. People I knew from all over the country called to tell me what they saw, what the whole thing looked like on television, what the replays of Rice's ball showed, what the announcers were saying.

The show had gone national is what it had done.

For the first time, I realized this wasn't just a New York story anymore, wasn't just the Yankees, wasn't just Reggie and Billy acting up a little for the folks back in the city. Now we were making headlines everywhere. I wondered if Gabe thought this would be good for box office, too. We were being used by everyone and didn't even know it.

I didn't know what the hell to do. I didn't know whether to stay with the team in Boston or to get myself on the first flight heading West and home.

I ordered some room service finally, and some wine, and then I got a surprising telephone call from the Reverend Jesse Jackson.

Although I've since become friendly with Jesse and have come to respect him a great deal, I didn't know him when I got the phone call. He sought me out as a result of all the instant publicity—he felt I'd need someone to talk to.

Jesse is an interesting guy. He is interested in the community of poverty, not just the black community. He is interested in the *cause,* not just himself. Interaction between the wealthy and the poor is very rare, too rare. There is enormous wealth is the United States and obviously there is more poverty than there should be. Jesse Jackson can help to bridge that communication gap between the rich and poor.

Anyway, I sure was happy to hear from him while I was sitting in my Boston hotel room. I was having a communication gap of my own that needed bridging.

I told Jesse all of what had happened, the things I was feeling. I told him that I'd had it, that I was considering jumping the team, bailing out on the whole miserable experience once and for all.

I asked him what he thought I should do.

Jesse said, "Be cool. You cannot allow these people to take your talent away from you. You can't allow them to take your money-making ability from you. Most of all, don't let them take your character from you. Hey, this is the real world, Reggie. This is the way things are. You don't fold up the tent because things haven't turned out the way you hoped, because you're seeing the dark side of things. You stay and fight them with your God-given skills."

I talked to Jesse for a long time. It was almost like going to confession. I told him I wasn't at all prepared for what New York was like. Even with my successes, even with the publicity, even with the money and the magazine covers and the cars and the rest, I had come to New York from a different world.

"I've said this to my friends and my family all along," I told Jesse Jackson. "I just didn't have a clue. Rude awakening doesn't even begin to describe what I've been through since I put that uniform on. It should have been a suit of armor."

"It's the world, Reggie," he repeated. "You're in this situation now. Nobody's going to feel sorry for you if you quit. So you can't quit. Maybe a lot of this has happened because you are a wealthy, successful man and you're black. That's all the more reason to see it through. You've got to be a man about this. Realize what you mean to poor, underprivileged people, especially black people. You can't let them down—they need you."

I felt better after talking to Jesse. I wasn't exactly ready to go out dancing, but he helped me put things in perspective. I occasionally forget the values I grew up with in Wyncote; I sometimes forget how a man is suppose to act. Sometimes it takes a Jesse Jackson— or my dad—to set me straight. In fact, that night Jesse sounded like an echo of my dad, who was always saying that I had to disregard my personal feelings when situations like this arose. I had to disregard them because, as Jesse said on the phone, "You stand for hope. It might not be said out loud to you but that's the reality. That's the way it *is*. And you've got to face that. And deal with it properly."

Steinbrenner called and told me not to do anything rash—I was starting to get the message that perhaps I shouldn't do anything rash—and said he would be joining the team in Detroit, our next stop on the road trip. Gabe Paul called and told me there would be a meeting the next morning in his suite to straighten the whole mess out.

That sounded fairly ambitious on Gabe's part.

The meeting would be me, Gabe and Billy.

Torrez came by the room after a while, and we opened the bottle of wine. I'm usually a beer drinker. Wine is for special occasions. Technically, I guess this particular Saturday qualified as a special occasion. Steve Jacobson of *Newsday* called from the lobby and asked if he could come up. I told him to come on up. Phil Pepe of the *Daily News* and Paul Montgomery of the *Times* came with him. The more the merrier.

I rambled on for a long time that night, getting things off my chest that had been building all season. I was part preacher and part defendant in a trial. I told the writers I was just a rich nigger to most of my teammates, that they'd never accept a black man making the kind of money I was making. I thought that at the time and felt that at the time because it was my only answer. I simply couldn't think of anything else. You have to remember and understand what was happening to me that season. Constantly.

I was the first really high-paid free agent. (Catfish's situation was different: He'd become a free agent as a result of a legal loophole in his Oakland contract.) Add that to the fact that I was black, articulate, and a pretty successful businessman. I also had a bravado that seemed to offend. My attitude was: Thanks very much for the money and the acclaim, I truly appreciate it, but I do deserve it. I paid my dues, I put the numbers on the board, *I earned it.*

I was a threat. A symbol to the whole country. And not a popular one. They were not ready for all of this or for me. I was booed everywhere I went. I mean *everywhere.*

I remember going out to right field in our first spring training game in Fort Lauderdale. There was a chorus of boos. I looked around and couldn't imagine what was going on. When the inning was over there were more boos as I ran off the field. I was running with Mickey Rivers and I said to Mickey, "What the hell's everyone booing for?" I thought they might even be booing him. I had no idea what was happening until I went up to hit. And I mean I was *booed.* I didn't know what hit me. I was stunned, flabbergasted.

The boos were there for every at bat, every single place I went, for everything I did. I was even booed when I returned to Oakland —and I almost burst into tears. This was home.

I remember being in Orlando, playing the Minnesota Twins in another spring training game. It was a sell-out crowd. I made every spring training trip and played every game. I came up to bat and there was the normal chorus of boos. I took a big swing, fouled a ball off, and then for some reason the stadium got quiet. Real quiet. And some guy in the stands hollered out, "You overpaid nigger!"

I stepped out of the batter's box and the umpire looked at me and Butch Wynegar, the Twins' catcher, looked at me. I just said, "God, I don't have to listen to that, do I?" But I did. So I got back in the box and hit.

We went to Texas once. The game was on national television. I hit two home runs against Doyle Alexander. There was a sign that stretched from center field all the way to the right-field foul line. It said: REGGIE JACKSON IS A BOZO. This sign had to have been a hundred yards long. I was staggered that someone would've taken the time to do something that negative against another human being they knew nothing about. But I had such a negative image that it was in vogue, it was fashionable to be down on Reggie Jackson.

It was mind-boggling. This was not a baseball phenomenon. This was a social phenomenon. There were other free agents making big money. But I was the one singled out.

So I blew up that night in my hotel room. It all exploded and I lashed out.

Sparky was unhappy with his contract, I said, so he bitched

about mine. Nettles and Munson, as well. It was as if what I had accomplished in Oakland had never happened, as if I had fabricated my resumé. Well, I'd played out my option, which I felt took some courage. Many other players had the same right but didn't choose to take that path. If they wanted the spoils they should have fought the war. I told the reporters that Steinbrenner was the only one in the Yankee hierarchy who'd treated me like a man since the start. Told them my close relationship with Steinbrenner made my teammates jealous, made Billy jealous. Told them I didn't give a damn about any of that anymore.

But I told them I wasn't going anywhere, at least for now. I was going to play right field when they told me, DH when they told me to do that, and hit wherever the hell they wanted me to in the batting order.

"I'm not going to fight anybody," I said. "I'm going to play the best I can for the rest of the year, help this team win if I can, and then I'm going to get my ass out of here."

Everyone left finally. I made a few more phone calls—Gary, Matt, Dayna, my dad—and went to bed.

I had the meeting with Billy in the morning. I assumed it wasn't going to much resemble a church service.

The meeting was at nine o'clock. When I got off the elevator at Gabe's floor, Billy was standing there. He was wearing a tan suit and a white shirt without a tie. He looked terrible, like he'd been up all night.

He looked at me.

I looked at him.

Neither one of us said a word to each other. I walked down the hall toward Gabe's suite with Billy a couple of steps behind me. The walk seemed about as long as the Boston Marathon.

Billy did most of the talking for the first ten minutes. I just sat there and listened. The monologue was a little incoherent at times. I wondered where in the hell he was coming from. I know we'd both had a tough night, but this guy was really off the wall. In the middle of his rambling, though, he made a statement that got right to the heart of his position on Reggie Jackson.

"We won without him last year," he said to Gabe as though

it were only the two of them in the room. "We can win without him this season."

Then he gave his version of the Rice play from Saturday's game.

"He didn't hustle, Gabe. He was trying to show me up. That's what he does with the team, tries to show me up. The only thing I could do was show him up."

It was then my turn to talk. I said to Gabe, "I did not loaf on that ball."

Even I was getting exhausted hearing my own voice say those words.

I guess Billy must have been tired of hearing it, too. Because he snapped out again and jumped up out of his chair. Billy's boiling point was obviously room temperature at that moment.

"You're a fucking liar!" he yelled at me. "Get up, boy. I'm going to kick the shit out of you right here!"

I didn't move. We had already played this scene once, the afternoon before. I didn't think we had to rehearse it again. I stayed where I was and looked over at Gabe. I was trembling with rage.

"Hey, Gabe," I said calmly, "you're a smart guy. Why don't you tell me what you think he meant when he said 'Get up, *boy*'?" You expect me to understand something like that? You expect me to deal with something like that? You tell me what to do, okay, Gabe? I'm all ears."

Billy was still strutting around the room. He headed for the door to leave. Gabe firmly told him to *sit down.*

" 'Boy' is just an expression," Billy said. "I'm from the South. I live in Arlington, Texas. It's just something that's said."

I had to stop myself from smiling. Billy'd grown up in Berkeley, grown up poor. But I guess if you grew up in Berkeley and played most of your career in New York, *then* managed in Detroit and Minnesota, *then* moved to Texas, it was perfectly acceptable in the year 1977 to call a black man "boy."

I said, "Really now, Gabe. How do you feel about all of this?"

Gabe, of course, was being Gabe. When he wasn't telling you to look at the whole donut, he had other Paulisms at the ready. If you went up to Gabe and said, "Do you think it will stop raining?" he had a standard answer.

"Always does."

Now he looked at me and said, "Well, Reggie, I just don't know."

Perfect.

Absolutely perfect. At least Gabe was staying in character.

I had come to the meeting with good intentions. But my good intentions were wearing off quickly. I had gone to Gabe's suite ready to tell both of them that I was going to play out the year, do whatever it took to win, and now Billy wanted to fight again.

Old Gabe? He, well, he just didn't know.

"What do you guys think I am?" I said to Gabe and Billy. "Gabe, we've gone over this a thousand times already. George Steinbrenner, your boss, told me that if at any point I didn't want to be a Yankee, then I didn't have to be a damn Yankee. Listen, the uniform is great to wear. The Yankees are Babe Ruth and Mickey Mantle and Whitey Ford and Lou Gehrig and Joe Di-Maggio. But what you both don't seem to understand is that it's the guys who wear the uniform who make the Yankees. It isn't the other way around. This uniform didn't make Reggie Jackson. I appreciate that I got to wear it once in my life just to see what it feels like. But you know I don't want to be in it once this season is over. I don't want to be a Yankee, I don't want to be in New York, I really don't want to play for a man like this."

I pointed to Billy when I said the last part.

"I actually came here to try and make peace with Billy," I continued. "Maybe that's impossible. What is also impossible is for me to play baseball the way I can with him treating me the way he does, trying to show me up, trying to break me down. I just want you to know where I am. I'm not going to demand anything. I know you're not going to send me anywhere because you would have done that already. I assume Billy is going to stay. I'm going to stay. There's not a damn thing I can do about it. The only recourse I have, as a man, is to bust my ass for Billy regardless of what he tries to do to me, and take it from there. And that's all I have to say."

We all just sat there. Billy looked like he was sick.

Gabe finally said, "I'll remember everything you said, Reggie. I'm going to talk to George, explain the way you feel, the way Billy feels. Just remember: There's no substitute for talent. Things will work out somehow."

I was pretty sure I'd heard that before.

I got up and walked toward the door. I didn't shake anybody's hand. I just left Gabe and Billy sitting where they were. As I opened the door, Gabe had one last thing to say.

"Don't look at the hole in the donut, Reggie. Look at the whole donut."

Honest to God.

Our wonderful weekend in Boston ended, well, wonderfully.

The Red Sox beat us 11–1, falling on Ed Figueroa like a building.

I had a fourteen-game hitting streak stopped, though I did hit a couple of balls pretty good.

On the flight to Detroit, I sat by myself in the back of the plane.

It was nothing anyone could have described as an upset.

There may have been busier days in the history of the lobby of the Ponchartrain Hotel in Detroit, but I seriously doubt whether any of them rivaled the kind of show the elegant old lobby saw from Yankee players and Yankee writers and even the Yankee owner on the morning and afternoon of June 20, 1977. George Steinbrenner had flown in from Cleveland to join the team in Detroit. George had been watching on television Saturday afternoon when Billy and I had danced our dugout dance.

The scuttlebutt was that George had not exactly enjoyed the show.

By noon on that Monday, no one had any fix on what was going on. Everyone was just hanging around the lobby, trying to sort out the rumors from the facts, trying to figure out what facts were really facts. One writer said that George had flown in to fire Billy for sure. No questions asked. No court of appeals. Billy was gone by the end of the day. Someone else said that Milton Richman of UPI had written a story saying Billy had already been fired and that Yogi Berra had been named as his replacement. Milton was right; he was just seven years early. That kind of day. Writers were interviewing players. Players were interviewing writers. The lobby of the Ponchartrain sort of looks like a movie set anyway. Now we were putting on a movie of our own.

Like something out of the Marx Brothers.

But maybe somebody was going to die in the end.

All I knew for sure was that if Billy did get executed by Steinbrenner, I didn't want to be part of the firing squad. If Steinbrenner wanted to fire him because the team wasn't doing well enough, if being swept by the Red Sox was the last straw, that was his business. It was his team. He paid the bills. If he was unhappy with Billy's work habits, that was his business, too. But I did not want to be the reason the man got fired. My problems weren't just with Billy. They were with an entire negative situation on the ballclub, and I already had enough troubles there without being blamed for costing the manager his job.

However, if Billy got the boot, who do you think the public was going to believe? Twenty-four other Yankees or me?

You don't have to be a computer whiz to figure that one out.

And there was one other thing I couldn't get out of my mind: I still thought that Billy Martin should have been the kind of manager I could relate to. He was tough. He didn't give a shit. He was his own man (even if that man did want to pick a fight with me). He was a winner, a plus as a manager. He gave you the feeling that when he was calling the shots in the dugout, you had a definite advantage. He would tell you to go to hell at any second. He was an individual, same as me. I really could relate to so much of what he was about. He was even born in May, same as me. He liked women. He liked to have a good time. He was from a broken home. He didn't give a damn if you were late as long as you did your job. It seemed to me that despite all the garbage and nonsense that had gone on between us, there should have been some foundation between us for something or other.

If he would just leave me alone and let me play ball the way I always had.

When I ran into Steinbrenner in the Ponchartrain lobby early that afternoon, I told him all of that. My mood obviously had improved a bit since Boston. Then again it had nowhere to go but up.

I said, "George, this may sound crazy, but we can still win this thing. We can win it with Billy as manager. I don't want you firing him because of me. This club is ready to split wide open as it is. If you fire Billy because of what happened Saturday, you might as well kiss off the season."

George said nothing while I laid out my cards for him. When

I finished, he said, "I appreciate you talking to me this candidly, and I'll think about everything you said, but my decision has already been made."

I took that to mean that Billy was history, which meant that R. Jackson was going to be Public Enemy No. 1 forever, or for as long as he was a Yankee anyway. There would be no getting around that.

Fran Healy came over to chat with George then, and I headed back to my room to read the Bible. I had been doing that more and more.

I read the Bible for support and for strength. I think everyone is similar—they will contact God in times of great need. I was the same way. I was a little more fortunate than most people because I'd met Gary Walker in Arizona, and Gary is a devout Christian who gave me a kind of constant nudging toward theological matters. He constantly urged me to get close to God, close to Christ. He urged me to read the Bible for my own information, my own welfare. Gary introduced me to Christianity in 1966, then I was reintroduced to it by Alvin Dark when he was the manager of the A's in 1974. But I never took the time, until I really needed it, when I felt alone in New York.

I feel I'm fortunate because I think black people are naturally close to the earth and close to God. There are everyday sayings in the black culture, like: "Lord have mercy" and "The Lord is willin' if the creek don't rise" and "If the Lord be willin' we'll eat tonight." The old gospel songs like "Swing Low Sweet Chariot" also give black people a reference, an association. No matter how vague the picture, you're raised with a picture of God.

I also think if you're close to poverty, you're automatically blessed with being closer to the Lord.

I believe in God. I believe that when you die, your spirit goes to heaven. I believe that just the way when I go out and turn the keys to my car I expect it to start. I believe that the way I reach for a cold glass of milk and I expect it to taste good. I don't check the cow, read the label, or look at the truck it arrived in. It's not something I think about. It's something that just *is*.

I need milk to live. I need God to live.

So I read the Bible that day and took support and comfort from it.

I figured that by the time we all got to the ballpark that night, the Yankees would have another manager—Yogi or Dick Howser, another one of our coaches, *somebody*. ABC was telecasting the game nationally, as part of its Monday Night Baseball series. I assumed that Howard Cosell and everyone else was going to have a field day with me. I like Howard now and respect him as a journalist. But then I felt about him the way most people felt about him—he was *Howard Cosell* and I didn't know what was going to come out of his mouth next. Of all the people I've met and worked with in television, Howard's been one of the most supportive. I believe I've learned a lot about being a broadcaster just from working with him, watching him. No one can do what Howard does. His only drawback, as far as I can see, is that he's so damn intimidating. Most athletes are afraid of the guy, of the way he can shoot from the hip and razzle-dazzle you with his use of the English language. But he's a good, honest journalist and I don't think he gets as much credit as he deserves. He's said he really believes I can be the first athlete-turned-commentator to get out of sports and be a legitimate news personality.

Anyway, to this day I don't know precisely how much I had to do with Billy Martin keeping his job that Monday afternoon in Detroit. See, there was always so much backstage intrigue with the Yankees, even among the players. There were so few times when anyone ever got the whole truth or the whole story, especially face-to-face. Face-to-face, man-to-man, that wasn't the Yankee way. It's one of the reasons why the Reggie-Billy confrontation in Boston was so startling to me.

So I don't know whether or not I tipped the vote in Billy's favor, or Fran did, or some of the other players did. I never asked Steinbrenner, and he never volunteered the information to me. I don't even know if there was a vote.

I don't know if George came to Detroit with any intention of firing Billy Martin.

But about four o'clock, George called and asked me to stop by his room. When I got there, Billy was sitting with George. And this was a different Billy from the one in Gabe Paul's suite just one day before. He was just like a whipped dog. It was the first indication I had that when backed into a corner, he'd do anything it took to remain manager of the Yankees. Whatever the two of them had been talking about, they'd had a meeting of the minds and Billy didn't call me "boy" this time.

He also didn't want to fight me.

The conversation wasn't a very long one because it was getting to the time when both Billy and I had to go out to the ballpark. We were more or less conciliatory toward each other. George seemed to want a one-for-all-and-all-for-one type of chorus.

"Hey, we might as well work this thing out," I said. I can't say I was 100 percent sincere, but I do have a fairly powerful self-preservation instinct of my own. "We've still got a good club here and there's still enough time to move in a positive direction. All the yelling and fighting in the world isn't going to change that. What the hell, let's put this behind us and make a run for it."

Steinbrenner asked, "Can you play for Billy Martin?"

I said, "Sure."

He turned to Billy.

"Can you get along with Reggie?"

Billy didn't look up, but he didn't hesitate. "Yes."

Steinbrenner said, "Then you two meet in the lobby downstairs in a little while and ride out to the ballpark together and go beat the Tigers."

He always did like giving his pep talks.

We did what we were told. If you want to know what it was like playing for George Steinbrenner and the Yankees in 1977, just remember those forty-eight hours:

1. Scene in the dugout at Fenway.
2. Scene in Gabe's hotel suite.
3. George playing Mr. Fix-it.
4. Billy and I riding out to Tiger Stadium in the same taxicab.

There was never a season anything like this one.

The conversation in the cab was pretty much the same as it had been in George's room. We basically talked about turning things around and winning the division. There was no mention of what had happened in Boston. Billy didn't apologize for replacing me with Paul Blair in the outfield. He didn't apologize for wanting to fight me. Didn't mention anything about any misunderstandings.

Billy has never apologized to me for anything as a matter of fact.

We had promised George we'd try to get along. We didn't promise we'd go steady. It was obvious that we needed to have a very long conversation.

We showed up together, which sort of stunned everyone. But then a lot of my Yankee teammates were easily entertained. Most of them didn't expect Billy to show up at all, much less with me. George showed up much later to give another of his inspirational (or at least he thought so) sermons. He said Billy was going to be around for the rest of the season. He said he was tired of us embarrassing him. He said he was sick of all the backbiting among the players.

He said he wanted us to get our asses in gear and win.

It would be a terrific story if I could say that we all pulled together like professionals and beat the Tigers that night with me hitting the game-winning home run. But remember, this was a Marx Brothers movie from the start. It had to end like a Marx Brothers movie. We were the Yankees. We were making things up as we went along. I heard once that the movie *Casablanca* was written day to day, that the actors would show up at the set and be given that day's dialogue.

Here's looking at you, kid. We did it the same way.

We lost to the Tigers that night. I misplayed a fly ball because of the lights—Tiger Stadium has the worst lights in the American League for an outfielder, at least they did that night—and cost us the game.

Billy defended me afterward, saying the loss wasn't really my fault, that the lights were indeed bad, that it could have happened to anyone, that I had hustled on the play.

I guess some would call that progress.

13

ON STAYIN' ALIVE IN THE CLUBHOUSE, BATTING CLEANUP, AND WINNING THE DIVISION: NOT ALTOGETHER UNRELATED EVENTS

The clubhouse never changed. A funny thing happened in July —I started to hit like hell—but the mood in the clubhouse, the tense atmosphere, the silences when I would walk in every afternoon, all that remained a constant into October. In the clubhouse, there was this crazy show going on, populated with heroes and villains and comics, all part of the crazy Yankee quilt. On the field I was one of the lead actors. In the clubhouse I had a front-row seat but wasn't really a part of the show. In that room I was like an off-screen character who created all the crises in a movie. I was a presence—you just never saw me.

There's a quote from 1977 that has followed me around a little bit. It's not up in lights like the one about the straw and the drink, but people seem to remember it. It goes like this: "I go to pieces in turmoil, but I thrive on pressure."

Didn't say it.

First of all, if I went to pieces in turmoil, I would have ended up in a rest home by June. The nice men in the white suits would have come and taken me away to a place with a name like Happy

Valley; every once in a while they would have let me sit in the shade and listen to a Yankee game on the radio. No, I had my chances to go to pieces—many chances—and didn't.

Secondly, I don't think any man, or athlete, *thrives* on pressure. You *survive* pressure and rise above it, even conquer it if you're good enough. But for everything that I've accomplished in my career in big stakes situations, I don't think of myself as thriving on pressure. I thrive on my automobile hobby. I thrive on my friends and my family. I thrive on playing the game of baseball.

I survived the pressure of my first season with the Yankees, survived the greatest test I've had in my baseball career or in my life. And the biggest pressure for me was in that clubhouse, day in and day out.

Every day was the first day of school.

When I went to the Angels in '82, I remember thinking one day in the spring, *Hey, I can go wherever I want to in this clubhouse.* I didn't have to worry about walking past Rod Carew's locker, or Don Baylor's, or Doug DeCinces's, or Brian Dowling's, or Bob Boone's. There were no restricted zones, no No Trespassing signs. I would make a joke if I wanted to, take a joke. I could playfully give a teammate some shit and not worry about making a headline. It sounds like such a simple thing, unless you were the Yankee wearing No. 44 in '77.

You sort of had to be there.

Except you wouldn't have wanted to be there.

From March until October, a ballplayer spends more of his waking hours around the clubhouse than he does around his own home. You get there three, four hours before a game, you play the game, you stick around for a couple of hours afterward. You're supposed to feel safe there. The clubhouse is one of the seductions of baseball; it is a place where you don't have to grow up. You eat there, you watch television there, you spend your time in the training room if you're not in the frame of mind to talk to reporters, you can even sleep there. For a lot of players, it's a nice, much-needed hiding place—from the media and from the real world in general. It's like a college frat house only more important somehow, because the people in there are supposed to be united in a common goal. You're not supposed to dread walking in there. You're supposed to be part of the fraternity.

That house was never my home in 1977.

It looked great though. Lush carpet. Lush buffet table in the middle of the room toward the back. Table filled with boxes of balls for us to autograph. Lounge area off to the right in back with soft sofas and chairs and a color television set.

But every day I'd walk in, and it would be like there were these imaginary arrows showing me the way to my locker. Or footprints that I was supposed to follow without deviating. If I could connect the dots, there wouldn't be any trouble. Walk to the middle of the room, stop before I got to the buffet table, take a sharp military left turn, sit down, start getting dressed. Talk to Fran Healy if he was around. If not, keep the mouth shut. Don't go near Nettles. Don't want to mess with Nettles; it would be like betting against the house. Don't go near Lyle. Don't go near Munson. Just get the t-shirts out, get the sweatshirt, get the wristbands, get the batting gloves, get the bats, get the spikes. Get dressed. Get ready to go out and try to take it all out on a pitcher.

As they say in show business, it was a tough room to work.

I would be drawn into clubhouse banter only indirectly and then in a half-hearted way. I would always be hearing from the writers about some new remark that Nettles had made that was getting a big play in the papers. Nettles has been a great third baseman for the Yankees, one of the elegant fielders ever to play that position. He's spent a career in New York turning doubles into double plays. And he has the justified reputation for being one of baseball's masters of the one-liner.

I always found Graig Nettles to be a man who was uncomfortable with himself. He was certainly uncomfortable with me. For reasons I could never fathom, there is something that seems to eat at Graig. I certainly was never privy to his past, to the events that shaped him, so I never got to know him well enough to discover what that thing is or why it's there. I do think, however, that it's the basis for his humor, which is razor-sharp, hard-edged, at times bitter. One thing that may have eaten at him over the years is that until the '78 World Series he never really got the credit he should have as a ballplayer. He was either in Brooks Robinson's shadow or in the shadow of one of the higher-paid Yankees. Come to think of it, money may have been the cause of some of his bitterness, too. He was never paid what he should have been paid as a key member of those championship teams.

One of the things about writing a book like this is that you're committing thoughts and words to paper, and committing them to something that is, hopefully, permanent. I have a hunch a lot of athletes and entertainers don't really think about the consequences of putting things down in print. They don't think ahead. That's why you'll so often hear about retractions, about mysterious changes of opinion.

Well, I've thought a lot about this next story and a few of the stories that follow. I've decided to tell them and I've decided to let them stand up and speak for themselves. This story has also been told in the press.

One day in the spring of 1979 we were in Saint Petersburg, Florida, to play the Mets. Nettles took out after Henry Hecht, a gifted baseball writer for the *New York Post* who happens to be Jewish. Some of the Yankees had been caught breaking curfew a couple of nights before (one of George's silly games at that time), and Hecht put their names in the paper. Nettles apparently thought this was some breach of newspaper etiquette. Hecht came to the visitors' clubhouse at Al Lang Field that day, and Nettles was waiting for him.

Nettles tore into Hecht, real verbal abuse. And in the middle of his outburst, Nettles screamed, "You know what you are, Hecht? You're nothing but a back-stabbing Jew cocksucker!" Hecht didn't even dignify it with an answer; he just turned and walked away.

I was dumbfounded. Not because Nettles said it. I was used to that—it was the way he thought. I heard it at various times in the clubhouse when Nettles would have an outburst about one of the writers covering the team. But I was shocked that he would blow his cover that way in front of outsiders. Maybe this sounds fairly obvious, but remember I'm listening to all this as a black man, and I can't help but be wondering what the thoughts are about *me*.

Nettles and I played together for five years in New York. I always had the feeling he was behind me, ready to turn the knife with an eminently quotable Nettles remark:

"The best thing about being a Yankee is getting to watch Reggie Jackson play every day. The worst thing about being a Yankee? Getting to watch Reggie Jackson play every day."

"If Babe Ruth were around today, he wouldn't be able to bat cleanup. He didn't strike out enough. I guess *I* don't get to bat cleanup because *I* don't strike out enough."

Ah, yes. It was definitely a diverse group, the Yankees of '77. You had Nettles, who was close to Munson, who was close to Lyle. That was the strongest clique on the team, a clique that Billy was very fond of. I never tried to break that clique. Couldn't have done it if I wanted to. Didn't want to anyway. I did get close to Thurman before his death. That just happened naturally. Eventually we each came to see what the other could do and a mutual respect grew out of this. We had similar passions—business and flying. Besides, things got so crazy between Reggie and Billy and George that people stopped paying attention to Reggie and Thurman. That helped as much as anything.

I wouldn't have wanted to be close to Sparky Lyle. I didn't have much respect for him. It bothered me that he went out of his way to make me the villain in his book, *The Bronx Zoo,* for no reason at all. He really slammed me. I barely knew Sparky, had very little contact with him. I never even had a social drink with him during the time he was there. It always seemed like some sort of cop-out or sensationalistic way to try and sell his book. That's one of the reasons I'm finally writing this one.

It was in Kansas City in July that Lyle and I had our "get your head out of your ass" incident. It was all pure Lyle. Hal McRae crushed a ball into the corner in right during a game we'd end up losing 5–1. The ballpark in Kansas City has one of the slickest artificial surfaces in the world; Peter Gammons, a baseball writer for the *Boston Globe,* once described watching balls roll around on it as being like watching marbles moving around in a bathtub. I didn't do too well with the marbles. I dribbled McRae's ball around like Magic Johnson at his very best, and by the time I got the ball back to the infield, McRae had scored.

Bad play.

When I got back to the dugout after the half-inning, Lyle was waiting for me. I had bad luck in dugouts in 1977.

"Get your head out of your ass," Lyle snapped at me.

I knew he was talking to me, but I mumbled something catchy like, "What?"

He was on the top step of the dugout, about eight to ten feet from me.

Lyle knew he was dealing from strength. If I hadn't popped anybody yet, I wasn't going to do it now. He was speaking for the whole team, and we were both fully aware of that.

He said, louder this time, "Get your head out of your ass. Don't you know we're in a fucking pennant race?"

I didn't say another word. It was the same as it had been with Billy in Boston. I'd have loved to have fought right there, but that would've only made things even more impossible than they already were. So I held my tongue. If holding my tongue was an Olympic event, I would have won a gold medal in 1977.

Lyle probably expected me to thank him for pointing out that stuff about us being in a pennant race.

When Rich Gossage came over to the Yankees the next season, Lyle, who was supposed to have this wonderful reputation as a gutty gamer, pouted all season long. Didn't want to pitch long relief. Didn't want to take a backseat to the Goose. Sometimes he didn't want to pitch at all. Said he had a hernia and couldn't pitch in the World Series that year. Not many players, including me, thought he was hurt at all. I even think our manager doubted it. In my opinion, Sparky just gave up.

Oh, well, maybe if Sparky could have gotten his head out of his ass, he might have figured out that we were in a World Series.

Lou Piniella was unique. He was the master politician of the team. He's dark and good-looking and can be extremely affable. Lou got along with everybody. It was funny, but he was friends with me, with Thurman, with Billy. That's just his personality.

Piniella adapted and adjusted to New York better than anybody on the team. He could handle the city, the pressure, the media. He could handle Steinbrenner. I think Lou can pretty much handle anything at any time. Very few ballplayers are like that.

Lou was a hell of a hitter and a hell of an outfielder. He didn't have great speed or a terrific arm, but he sure got the job done. When he *didn't* get the job done, Lou also had a hell of a temper. He could yell and scream, get pissed off, destroy everything in sight, act selfishly when he made an out—only it wasn't taken to be selfish. Or if it *was* taken that way it didn't make any difference. That was just Lou. If I kicked a water cooler or threw a bat, it was offensive. No matter what Lou did, it wasn't offensive. I always liked Lou and I guess everybody did. Above all his other traits, it's just plain likeableness that stands out for Piniella.

He took care of himself above all, made sure he preserved Lou Piniella. But hell, that was the only way to cope with being a Yankee. Couldn't blame him, couldn't dislike him for it. Now he clearly seems to be one of Steinbrenner's fair-haired boys. More power to him. My guess is he'll be in the Yankee organization for many years to come.

My favorite image of Lou Piniella is of him packing for a road trip. The guy was 100 percent pure mess. He never took his clothes home until June, when his family came to New York for the summer. To prepare for a road trip, he'd simply take his clothes out of his locker, ball them up, and cram them into his suitcase. When we'd get to the next town, say on a Sunday evening, he'd send his clothes out to be cleaned on Monday morning and have them back in the afternoon. Then he'd be lookin' sharp as a tack. If he didn't have the right shoes, he'd buy a pair. When he ran out of clean shirts, he'd just buy another one. I never saw a guy buy so many clothes yet never have *any* clothes. He'd buy six shirts, several pairs of pants, a dozen socks, two or three pairs of shoes—and he'd do this four or five times a year. Not because he liked them. He *needed* them because he'd have *lost* the last batch of stuff he'd bought. I'm sure he had a wardrobe in the back of his car, a wardrobe at the ballpark, a wardrobe in his cubicle at spring training. Lou left clothes all over the league.

We had quiet men, too, like Roy White. He was a sweet guy. A super guy and a good family man. I hope he stays in baseball because the game needs people like him. Roy was getting toward the end of his playing career in '77 and didn't want to ruffle any feathers. (It didn't help; he would end up his career playing in Japan anyway.) Besides, he was an old Yankee guy, and old-fashioned Yankee *black* guys were taught to be seen and not heard. That's just the way it had always been. Elston Howard, a coach with us, had been the same way as a player, and he'd won the damn MVP award once.

But every so often, after I'd gotten up on my soap box about the situation with the team, about not being accepted because I was black, White would sidle up to me at the batting cage and quietly say, "It's about time somebody said something like that around here." Roy had just been conditioned differently. He didn't want to say the things publicly that needed to be said.

Willie Randolph was the same way when he came up. Didn't say boo. But eventually I felt he was rooting for me. He didn't make a production out of it with the team or with the press, but he'd tell me, "Say what you think, Jack. You're right. Speak your mind 'cause you're speaking for a lot of the black guys around here."

In my later New York years I would come to like Willie Randolph enormously. He's a good man. Very sensitive. Very aware of who he is, both on and off the field. Willie is very family-oriented; his family always comes first. Even at the beginning, you could see it bothered him that he never got enough credit for being an integral part of the ballclub. He always had the feeling that Steinbrenner didn't think he was good enough, and yet in Willie's heart (in all the players' hearts as well) he knew he was a hell of a ballplayer.

He didn't feel Steinbrenner ever gave him credit for being able to play hurt, when actually Willie was playing with small hurts all the time. His legs are susceptible to pulls, the same way mine are. Willie hasn't forgotten that. I don't think he's forgotten to this day. As long as he remains a Yankee, he'll carry the scars from those early years. He never felt like a member of the so-called Yankee family. Maybe he does now. But Willie Randolph can play the game. He'd probably be better off someplace else.

Bucky Dent could play, too. He was the perfect shortstop for that Yankee team. All we needed was a guy who could make all the plays, and that's exactly what Bucky did. He wasn't flashy the way Nettles was, but he could make the routine plays all the time and the great plays often enough. He never missed a ball right at him. Never. If there was a double-play ball, we would get the double play. He got his bunts down. He drove in fifty runs a year. He was one of those players outstanding at doing a necessary, if unappreciated, job. You hear a lot in baseball about guys giving "110 percent," or some such nonsensical thing. I don't want guys giving me 110 percent because that means they're trying to do things they can't do, especially when the pressure is on. Give me a team of players who know what they can do, know what they can contribute, and give me just that. These are pros who understand their limitations and their capabilities and play within them. In specific situations, at bat or in the field, I don't want guys trying too hard. I want them doing what is necessary.

Bucky Dent was like that. When he hit the famous three-run homer off Mike Torrez in the 1978 playoff game against the Red Sox, all he was trying to do was hit a single.

He really is a sweetheart of a man, Bucky. He just wants to win, even if he knows he's not going to the Hall of Fame or even to the All-Star Game. He was right for the Yankees, though Steinbrenner forgot that later on when he traded him to Texas. Bucky is good-looking, and the girls always loved him. He put a lot of young fans in the stands. He fit the Yankee image fine. He mixed in nicely with the rest of the chemical solution that somehow made the team so successful in the end.

Bucky was one of the undecideds who ended up a big supporter of mine by the time the '77 season was over. He came up to me one day in September, shook my hand and said, "I'm glad I got the chance to play with you. I don't know if I could have taken everything you had to take and still survived."

Curious team. Crazy chemistry. Ship of Fools one day, sleek luxury liner the next. Perhaps the most interesting character of all on the team was Mickey Rivers, who played so brilliantly in '77 when he wasn't hurt. The Yankees haven't had an offensive catalyst like him since they let him go in 1979. He was a comic figure on the field, always looking like he had a limp, full of nerves and twitches, twirling his bat like a baton when he'd take a big swing and miss. Mickey could play. He was difficult to understand a lot of the time because he spoke in a sort of frantic mumble. Some players made fun of him and delighted in telling Rivers stories to the press, which got him the reputation of being a Step'n' Fetchit–like character.

However he was by no means dumb. He was a street-smart kid from Miami with a terrific sense of humor and a distinctive way with words. It was almost as if he reveled in everybody playing him for the fool.

There was a very subtle form of racism at work here, another way for people to deal with a talented black star. Okay, Rivers has a lot of talent. Okay, he makes good money. Okay, he dresses well. Okay, no one on this team can do what he does physically. But let's not forget that he's not bright and he's black. That seemed to make everything else palatable. That was Mickey Rivers's image, and it bothered the hell out of me that he didn't fight it at all.

He didn't care about the way he sounded with the press. He allowed himself to be branded a nonsensical character when he really wasn't. He let his problems off the field make him into something of a caricature for the newspaper guys. This kind of thing happens in sports sometimes. I'm not saying it's deliberately done; often it's done subconsciously. But it's something else blacks have to be aware of. Let's just say we have more p's and q's to watch.

It was done with Mickey Rivers. It's being done now to other black athletes in every sport.

They never tried to make me sound stupid. With me, it was arrogance.

"Well, Reggie is smart and wealthy and a great athlete. He *has* done it under pressure. He did hit those three home runs in the Series, and he does have all those championship rings. Too bad he's such an arrogant, self-serving sonofabitch."

At times I was told I was a credit to my race. I always wanted to tell a white guy he was a credit to *his* race.

It's just another form of prejudice. I've always been aware of it. I saw it even more clearly when I came to the Yankees. They dealt with me one way and with Rivers another. We just didn't fit the mold, at least on that ball club.

But then George had smashed the mold all to hell when he put the team together. He wasn't really interested in sociology lessons or human relationships.

Just the all-important loss column, as we say in baseball.

History might not note the following fact, but I will: I started batting cleanup on a full-time basis the tenth of August. We were five games behind the Red Sox at the time. I don't think Billy had any choice. There was some talk afterward that there had been a meeting between Billy and Gabe Paul, with Gabe acting under orders from Steinbrenner and telling Billy to quit screwing around and to write my name down in the fourth spot every day. The season was starting to get away from us.

I didn't care why he did it. In the immortal words of Thurman Munson, I was just happy to be there.

For the month before that, I had felt my engines starting at the plate. I've always been a streak hitter. I was having good batting practices every day, and I wasn't losing the good feeling between batting practice and the time the game would start. At that point, Chambliss was still batting cleanup most of the time, but I was averaging an RBI a game in back of him. On the tenth, Billy finally made the move. I was where I belonged in the order, and I didn't have to answer any more questions about why I *wasn't* there.

Q. Why do you want to hit cleanup, Reggie?

A. 'Cause I always have.

Before the tenth of August, I had batted cleanup ten times all year.

When the regular season was over and we'd won the American League East, Steve Jacobson of *Newsday,* a writer I'd liked and admired even before I came to the Yankees, gave me these statistics: Between August 10 and September 28, when we clinched a tie for the division, the Yankees played forty-nine games with me hitting fourth. We won thirty-nine of those games. I had forty-eight RBI in those games. I hit thirteen home runs.

All of that pretty much ended the Martin-Jackson debate about the batting order with a flourish, I thought. When Billy put me fourth, he was quoted as saying, "As long as he keeps swinging the bat good, he'll stay there." I swung good. So I stayed there. When we clinched that tie on September 28, I hit a grand slam in the first inning against the Indians.

There is one game in the stretch that I remember best because it turned out to be a coming attraction for all of my personal fireworks in the World Series, even if I couldn't have known the Series fireworks were in my future. It came during a three-game series with the Red Sox in New York in the middle of September. We'd gotten into first place by then.

In the first game of the series, Guidry mowed through the Sox to put us two and a half in front. I didn't do anything to help him. It was a big oh-for-four is what it was. Afterward, I was not exactly doing cartwheels. This was the Series that was going to decide the division, everyone sensed that, and all the hitting I'd been doing was going to be swept away if I couldn't deliver against the Red Sox. This was my type of situation, a Reggie Situation if there ever was one. If we were going to step on the necks of the Sox, slam the door, turn out the lights—pick an image—I wanted to be a part of it.

I went straight home after the Tuesday game. About midnight, the phone rang. It was Steinbrenner calling from P.J. Clarke's, a legendary saloon on Third Avenue.

This was 1977 remember. George and I were still sort of going steady.

He said, "Get your ass down here."

I didn't feel much like a party, but when the boss calls and wants you to hoist a few, you go hoist a few with the boss.

When I got to the back room at Clarke's—a dark room with wooden tables and a couple of chalkboard menus—George and a bunch of his friends were sitting at a big table. He excused himself, and we went to a corner table by ourselves.

"Forget about tonight," he said.

I told him that was not the easiest thing in the world to do at that particular time, all things considered.

George said, "All we needed tonight was Guidry. We didn't need you. We are going to need you tomorrow, and I'm telling you right now that you're going to win the game for me."

I grinned, more at his bravado than anything else. One thing George has never had is a confidence problem. Except it would be me in the batter's box the next night, not him.

"Is that so?" I asked.

"Trust me," he said, grinning right back. "Have I ever lied to you?"

I thought it would be bad form at the moment to bring up his promise about trading me if I ever wanted to leave. Didn't seem appropriate. And this was George at his best, turning on the charm, being supportive at the same time. George can be very good at that when he wants to be. Get at a table with George one-on-one, get in a room with him, and the man can sell you an oasis in the arctic circle.

He doesn't always pick the right spots for his pep talks. But this was the right spot, at least for me. I believed him because I wanted to believe him, which was the point of the exercise. We sat there at Clarke's, a New York place that can seem so dark and comfortable and safe late at night, and we shot the bull about this and that. He finally went back to his table and I went home.

The next night we won the game. And I had a big night.

Hey, you take your omens where you find them.

It was one of those special Yankee Stadium evenings, the kind that is part Broadway opening, part Fourth of July fireworks in Central Park, part heavyweight championship fight. Yankees versus Red Sox. Two and a half games between us in the standings. Division on the line. From the first time you step on the field you know this one, this night, is something special. The atmosphere around the cage snaps and crackles and pops. The players feel it. The writers feel it. The crowd that's shown up early feels it.

This, I think, is what old Ernie Banks had in mind the first time he said, "Let's play two."

But it was New York and the Stadium and a big, big game, so you knew that one would do.

It was a crackerjack of a baseball game in front of 55,000 people. Both teams kept threatening all night long. I twice stopped the Red Sox from scoring with great catches in the outfield. If I do say so myself, not bad defense for a guy who couldn't field Jim Rice's Texas Leaguer properly in June.

I jumped up at the wall in right for one off the bat of George Scott. And dove on the grass to catch a sinking flare hit by Dwight Evans. By the time the ninth inning rolled around, it was still 0–0. Ed Figueroa against Boston's Reggie Cleveland.

Cleveland, a guy who just spit sliders at you, had been pitching beautifully for the Red Sox, keeping the ball down, not giving any of us anything over the meat of the plate.

Thurman led off the ninth.

While Cleveland finished his warmup pitches, Thurman and I stood in the on-deck circle together. Now this wasn't about *Sport* magazine anymore. This wasn't about all the anger that had passed between us during the season, all the bitterness and misunderstandings. This was the No. 3 hitter and the No. 4 hitter talking about winning a division.

This was the way it always should have been if each of us hadn't brought so many of our own insecurities into the 1977 season.

Thurman stared out at Cleveland and said, "I'm going to single between short and third."

I said, "Huh?"

Thurman was still looking at Cleveland.

"I'm going to single between short and third, and then you get me home."

I said, "Deal."

Thurman singled between short and third.

Usually, I don't hear the crowd. That's part of me getting with the program. I'm able to tune the crowd out and just focus on the pitcher and the situation. This time I couldn't help but hear the crowd. It was a deafening, wonderful stadium sound. I began to wonder just how far a man can hit a baseball if he really tries.

But as I stepped into the box, a funny thing happened. Dick Howser, the third base coach, walked halfway down the line toward home plate and signaled for me to come meet him. Thinking back, this was fairly amusing since it would be a bunt sign relayed from Billy to Howser one year later, in 1978, that would touch off World War III between Billy and me. That, of course, is another story. Now Howser wanted to have a chat about the bunt sign.

Repeat: the bunt sign.

First, he wanted to make sure I *knew* the bunt sign.

"We may have you bunt," Howser said. "But watch me after every pitch 'cause Billy might change his mind, depending on the count."

"Let me get this straight," I said. "You guys want me to *bunt*?"

"I just give the signs, Reggie," Howser said. "Where's the best place for you to lay one down?"

"I have no idea."

Howser grinned at that.

"When was the last time you bunted?"

I had to think about that one for a second.

"1972," I said.

Howser put on the bunt sign with the count one and one. The last thing on earth I wanted to do at that moment was bunt, but I squared around like a good scout. Cleveland was so shocked he threw me a ball. He looked at me like I'd dropped my pants.

Two and one. Billy took the bunt off here.

I took a strike.

Two and two.

Cleveland missed again.

Full count. Bottom of the ninth. Nothing–nothing. Thurman on first. Yankee Stadium was not quiet.

Reggie Cleveland threw me a fastball down. I mean, *down.* Everyone said later it would have been ball four easy, it was so low. A dirt duster. We'll never know for sure. Because I went down and got it like a golfer hitting a sand shot and hit it about 430 feet into the bleachers in right center. I hit it as hard as I've ever hit a ball in my life, then I dropped my bat and watched it go. I felt this explosion of noise in my belly and, for the first time all season, felt the Yankee Stadium crowd come to me.

Yankees 2, Red Sox 0.

Ballgame.

As I circled the bases, running hard, shoulders hunched, maybe against the noise, I felt like there was a big hand behind me, pushing me, making me run harder. I wanted to have a microphone in my hands to say to the people, "*This* is why I came here. *This* is why they paid me the money. You might not love me all the time. You might have to hate me and respect me as long as I play here. But *this* is what I can do for you when the chips are down and blue. Put me under the gun on a night like this, and I'll deliver for you. Tonight I'm giving you your first big dividend."

When I got to the plate, Thurman was the first to grab my hand.

"You done good, you sonofabitch!" he yelled.

"Just following orders," I yelled at him.

We were three and a half in front, and there was still a lot of baseball to play, but I knew then that we'd win the division. And we did.

I had survived the pressure. But it was only regular season pressure.

Little did I know that the fun was only beginning.

14

How to Go from Mr. Pinchhitter to Mr. October

So here is how it all ended in 1977.

Billy Martin benched me in the fifth game of the playoffs against the Kansas City Royals. That was October 9.

On October 18, there was that business of me hitting three home runs on three swings in the sixth game of the Series against the Dodgers. It was called the greatest game a hitter ever had in a World Series. I can live with that. (Smile.)

But I almost didn't get the swings because we almost didn't get out of Kansas City because Mr. Martin had to slap me one last time, with the whole world watching.

The ending of 1977 wasn't any easier than anything else had been. I almost didn't get the chance to become Mr. October.

I finished the regular season with thirty-two home runs, 110 RBI, a .286 batting average, ninety-three runs, thirty-nine doubles and —miraculously—my sanity. Then I promptly went one-for-four-

teen in the first four games of the playoffs against the Royals and
left myself wide open for Billy to get his last parting shot on a
Sunday night in Kansas City with the American League Championship series tied 2–all and a pennant hanging in the balance.

I couldn't believe that after my heroics in September—I won't
say I carried the team because so many others played well, but if
that September was a tug-of-war, I was the anchor man at the back
of the line—that it could all end in a nightmare.

But as we got ready to face lefty Paul Splittorff in the fifth
game, I knew I was all dressed up to be the scapegoat. All season
long Billy had been telling people that the Yankees had made it to
the World Series in '76 without me. Now there was a chance that
the Yankees weren't going to make it to the Series with me.

It wasn't exactly the last chapter that I had planned. Still, I
had one last chance to come through. I had played in do-or-die
games before with the A's. I had busted my hamstring scoring the
tying run in the fifth game in '72. I had homered in the seventh
game against the Mets when we won the '73 Series. Nobody was
calling me Mr. O in those years, but I did have a way of showing
up when the table was set.

Then I got to the clubhouse at Royals Stadium and found there
was no seat for me at the table.

Now you have to understand something: When I get to the
ballpark, I don't rush out to the dugout and check the lineup card.
Fringe players do that. Platoon players do that. Reggie Jackson
doesn't do that. Jim Rice doesn't do that. George Brett doesn't do
that. Munson didn't do it. You don't worry about the lineup card.
You just get dressed and get the mind right and get ready to go out
and take batting practice with the regulars.

I should have checked the card.

It was Fran Healy who gave me the word. Can you believe that
one! I was sitting in front of my locker. Fran pulled a stool next to
mine, and his face looked like there had been a death in the family.

"We need to talk," he said. "You're not playing."

At first I thought he was kidding. So I told him that and
smiled. But then Fran dropped his voice. I peered around the room.
When I did that, my teammates stopped looking at me.

Fran said, "Billy's got Blair in right. He decided to sit you
down against Splittorff. He asked me to tell you."

"Since when are you guys such fuckin' buddies?" I tried to joke but I felt sick. No one had to tell me I was one-for-fourteen. *But this was the money game.*

"Fran," I said, almost pleading, "he can't do this to me. He can't."

I started to get up. I wanted to go find Billy. I knew what Martin thought of me; that much had been made abundantly clear since March. I had a pretty solid fix on what I thought of him. But I felt I'd help carry his team down the stretch, and outside of Catfish, I had been in more big baseball games than anybody in the damn room. Splittorff was a lefty? Big deal. That was going to be Billy's explanation, though, and I knew it.

I couldn't understand what was going on. This, to me, was vindictive on Billy's part. He was actually willing to risk blowing a pennant just to show me and everyone else once and for all who was in charge.

Unbelievable.

"There are things Billy wanted me to tell you," Fran said quietly. "If we win, he says he'll go out of his way to say how good you were, what a pro you were."

"If we win," I said to Fran. "Well, that is just dandy."

We just sat there. I was numb. It was the same sort of numbness I'd experienced that afternoon in my apartment when I sat and stared out at the park and didn't know if I could go on. Billy Martin was sitting me down in the fifth game, and there wasn't a thing I could do about it. He couldn't even bring himself to tell me. Billy didn't want to be around me. He didn't give a shit about me. He didn't give a shit about the team obviously.

This was simply get-even day for Martin with Jackson, and fuck the consequences.

Fran got me through it, one more time. If I live to be 100, I could never repay Fran Healy for his friendship and his kindness that season, for being a constant pillar. He's a big, sensitive, sandy-haired Irishman, and he looks a little like Clint Eastwood. He spent his whole career being a pretty good catcher in places like San Francisco and Kansas City and New York, and he was always storing up insights and observations that now make him such an excellent broadcaster of the Mets games for Sports Channel. To this day, I am overwhelmed by the reservoirs of compassion he showed me, almost from the first day. It was not a brilliant political posture around the Yankees to be Reggie Jackson's friend.

But he had been my friend, eating dinners with me on the road, sitting with me in my room, stopping me from fighting with Billy, talking common sense. He didn't talk a lot about himself, but once at a dinner someplace I tried to ask him why he'd done what he'd done for me.

Fran was embarrassed by the question. He said, "Reggie, our friendship transcends time and mileage. You befriend someone out of a gut feeling. And you've got to go with that gut feeling."

I couldn't possibly thank him enough. Or even truly understand why he went so far out on a limb for me, why he was the way he was. I got an inkling, though, when I later met his dad, who was a great old tough Irish Catholic. An old-time mailman with solid values who obviously raised his son to follow in his footsteps.

Now Fran sat in the clubhouse and gave me the right words to say to the press. He told me to go out of my way to say how tough a pitcher Splittorff was for me. He told me to say that it took guts for Billy to bench me, right or wrong. He told me to bowl everybody over with low-key grace. One way or another, he told me I was going to get a chance to play before the night was over—the chance to play and to prove myself.

"Billy doesn't deserve this," I said bitterly.

"If you get a chance tonight and we win," Fran Healy said, "you'll be glad. Everybody will say you're a team man, and they'll be right."

It happened just the way Fran said it would. Reluctantly, I delivered the lines he gave me. When I got onto the field, the writers came at me in waves and waves, and I honestly think I fooled them with the way I was handling the situation.

I would walk toward the batting cage, and the media crowd would move with me. I went down to talk to Howard Cosell. The crowd moved with me. I went to the dugout to get my glove, and the crowd waited for me at the top of the steps. I just kept holding it all in, as I had done so many times during the season. If there was one thing that 1977 taught me, it's that there are all kinds of ways to be a man.

I kept saying that at the very least, Billy had guts.

I said I hoped I'd get the chance to help out, hoped there'd be a place for me in the game before it was all over. I said that we hadn't come all this way to lose.

I hoped I was right.

Martin never came near me until we were losing 3–1 in the eighth inning.

My memories of the game are a jumble because I was so full of nerves sitting in the dugout, waiting for the game to come to me. Until then, the only thing I'd ever experienced like that fifth game was the '72 World Series, when I had to stand in the dugout on crutches because of the hamstring and watch the A's go about the work of winning the Series without me. This time there were no crutches and no bad leg, but there was the same feeling of being a spectator. A spectator, but also a leading man who had suddenly become a bit player in full view of the whole world. I could feel the ABC cameras boring holes right through me all night long.

I hated it.

There was a fight early in the game when Nettles thought George Brett slid too hard into third and responded by giving Brett a kick and a shove. Both dugouts cleared. All the players, including me, picked a partner and danced until order was finally restored.

Splittorff was good for the Royals, damn good, and pretty much had us under control. But in the eighth Willie Randolph singled. Whitey Herzog, the Royals manager, brought in Doug Bird, a right-hander, to pitch to Thurman. Piniella would be up after Thurman, and I could feel the blood start to pump. If just one of them could get a hit, Cliff Johnson, our right-handed hitting DH, was scheduled to bat fourth in the inning.

I couldn't guess what was going on in Billy's mind—who could ever guess what was going on in Billy's mind?—but I had to think that if we got a runner in scoring position, Billy would go lefty-righty against Bird.

And if he did go lefty-righty, the lefty had to be me, unless he'd gone totally off his rocker. I gave a quick look down to the end of the dugout. Billy was standing at the top step, glaring out at the field.

Bird struck out Thurman.

I felt like I'd been kicked in the gut.

But then Lou Piniella, bless his heart, singled. Billy just turned quickly and said, "Reggie, hit for Cliff."

He didn't have to call me twice.

I wanted a dinger, of course, when I stood in against Bird. I wanted a dinger more than I'd wanted anything in a long time. I wanted to hit one as hard as I had off Reggie Cleveland in September. But obviously the Lord didn't have me penciled in for my dinger until the next week.

I singled off Bird, and Willie scored.

3–2.

When you've hit nearly 500 home runs in your career, it's tough to pick out one and say, Yes, that was the biggest, that was the very best, that one meant the most to me. But there will always be a special place in my heart for that little run-scoring single against Doug Bird. I had come through like a man as Fran Healy said I would. I had kept my self-control and my self-respect. Martin had to call on me, and I had delivered. Not for him. For me. For *the team.*

Mr. Pinchhitter.

We scored three more runs in the ninth inning—Roy White knocked in the winning run—and we won the game 5–3 and won the pennant.

In the clubhouse, there was the normal celebration with champagne, but as I stood and talked to the writers, champagne dripping from me the same way it did everyone else, I was more drained than exhilarated. I talked about how much shit I'd had to eat all season, how I had been a winner my entire career and felt like a winner still; talked about how exhausting it had been to be in the eye of the storm so many times. I talked about my little single.

But I felt apart. No new experience. Two-for-sixteen, which is what I ended up with in the end, was not enough. The RBI single was not enough. It occurred to me that night that I might *never* be able to provide enough to be accepted by the Yankees. The only thing that made me feel elated that night in the visitors' clubhouse in Kansas City was the prospect of the World Series. I felt like I had been given a second chance, and I hoped to make the most of it. . . . We'd won—which is what fourteen teams set out to do in February.

I made sure to seek out two people in the clubhouse. George Steinbrenner was one of them. I half-shook his hand, half-embraced him, and thanked him for believing in me.

George said, "You showed me a lot tonight, Reggie."

I said, "George, I hope to show you a little more in the Series."

Then I made my way through the crowd and the cameras and found Fran Healy, his locker area a quiet oasis. He was grinning at the spectacle around us, holding onto a beer.

I said something I probably didn't say enough during the baseball season of 1977.

"Thank you. I never could have made it without you."

We shook hands.

"Yeah," Fran said. "You could have made it without me."

There were really two World Series that year against the Dodgers. First there was the one played over the first five games. We led 3–2 after that one. It was the Series, but there was nothing memorable or dramatic or startling about those games. The Dodgers were hitting the ball pretty well; we were hitting it better. We led 3–1 and had a chance to clinch in LA, but the Dodgers came back behind Don Sutton in Game Five. By then I had six hits and a couple of dingers, and the Kansas City Series seemed like it had happened a long time ago.

It goes that way. When you start to hit the ball well, when you're in one of those streaks where you just want the pitcher to hurry up and throw the damn ball, you wonder how you ever even spelled s-l-u-m-p. One-for-fourteen? Lordy, how could I ever do something like *that?*

My second home run of the Series came on my last swing in the fifth game, which we lost 10–4, and which moved everybody back across the country to New York to settle the thing. I had no way of knowing at the time that an eighth inning homer off Don Sutton in a 10–4 blowout was going to be part of a historic package.

Who could have known?

Who could have known that the "second" World Series of 1977, the one played in Game Six, was going to be mine?

People still want to know what I remember the best about the sixth game; people will probably always want to know. Was it the last home run, number three? Was it the unbelievable "REG-gie!" chant after that last one? Was it getting showered with confetti out in right field when I took my position in the ninth?

I remember *everything.*

I remember batting practice. The three dingers, off Burt Hooton, Elias Sosa and Charlie Hough. Running the bases after the last one, off Hough. The winning. The champagne. Finding out that only Babe Ruth had ever hit three home runs in a World Series game. Finding out that no one had ever hit five in a Series. Having the writers remind me that I had hit four homers on four consecutive swings, going back to Game Five.

Everything. Don Larsen had his perfect game in 1956. I had mine in '77. Three swings. Three dingers.

I should have known in batting practice. But batting practice can be tricky sometimes. You can hit ball after ball into the seats, feel like you're on top of the world, want the game to start *right now*. The next thing you're doing is sitting in front of your locker after the game, munching on a piece of chicken, and wondering where the oh-for-four came from. During the game you want to yell out to the pitcher, "Hey, there's gotta be some big mistake here. You can't be striking me out this way. Cannot be doing it. Didn't you see me in batting practice?" Then there are other times when your bones are creaking and your head is hurting and you can't even carry the ball out to deep right during BP, but before you know it, you've got three hits, two homers, four RBI.

Batting practice can confuse the hell out of you.

But BP on October 18 was something special. I cannot ever remember having one like it. The players around the batting cage were amazed, and so were the writers. The crowd, especially out in right field, was going crazy; people show up earlier for Series games, and the ones who did on this night got themselves a show. I hit maybe forty balls during my time in the cage. I must have hit twenty into the seats. Upper deck. Bullpen. Into the black in center. Didn't matter. The baseball looked like a volleyball to me.

Willie Randolph came up to me finally and said, "Would you do us all a favor and maybe *save* a little of that?"

I laughed. I knew I felt goooood.

"There's more where that came from," I said. Then I got back in there and hit a few more into the black. I've had great batting practices in the past; I got a standing ovation one time in Detroit when I finished. This was different. By the time I was done, it wasn't just the people out in right. Everyone in the ballpark was whooping and hollering. We were ready. The crowd was ready. And so was I.

Between BP and the game I went back into the clubhouse and told Fran, "I feel great."

Fran said, "I noticed. Have you heard about Pearl Harbor?"

By the time the game started, I hadn't spilled any of my adrenaline. Still had a full tank. Still felt pumped up. Even when Hooton walked me on four straight pitches, I wasn't deflated. I still felt *good.* I was going to be ready when he threw me a strike.

He threw me a strike in the fourth. First pitch to me. Nobody out. Thurman on first. I figured Hooton would try to pitch me up and in. That's always been the book on me. Get it up and in. Don't let me extend my arms. Well, Hooton got it up, but not in far enough. I got it. I got it a little on the end of the bat, but I got it. It was a line drive to right, and the only thing I was worried about was that it might not stay up long enough. It did. We were ahead 4–3.

One.

I was still in batting practice; that is exactly the way I felt. When I came up in the fifth, after we'd scored a couple more times, Hooton was out of the game and Elias Sosa, another right-hander, came in to pitch to me. I stood there next to the plate and watched him warm up and I was thinking, "Please, God, let him hurry up. Let him hurry up and finish warming up so I don't lose this feeling I have." When he was done, I purposely got into the batter's box late so he didn't see where I was standing. I didn't want him to see where I was standing and start thinking; I just wanted him to throw a strike on the first pitch, try to get ahead.

He threw me a fastball right down Broadway. I call them mattress pitches because if you're feeling right you can lay all over 'em. This was the hardest ball I hit that night, a screaming line drive into right. The one off Hooton worried me because I'd hit it on the end of the bat. The one off Sosa worried me because it was hit so hard I was afraid it might dip short of the stands.

It didn't.

Two.

The crowd really started to come alive then. "REG-gie! REG-gie!" they chanted. We were winning the game that could give us the first Yankee world championship since 1962. It was only the fifth inning. I had swung the bat just twice, and I already had two dingers. The people in the Stadium knew there was a chance to be some history.

"REG-gie! REG-gie!"

Finally it was the bottom of the eighth. We were ahead 7–4.

Tommy Lasorda, the Dodger manager, had brought Hough, a knuckleballer, in to pitch. I stood watching him warm up, and I wanted to yell over to Lasorda, who I like, and say, "Tommy, don't you know how I love to hit knucklers?"

On the first pitch if he got it anywhere near the plate, I knew I'd have a good pass at it. The crowd was insane with noise as I dug in. They were expecting a home run. They wanted a home run. They were chanting "REG-gie." Sometimes if you focus in on crowd noise too much it can be distracting. Didn't matter this night. A plane landing in center field wouldn't have mattered this night.

I just wanted Charlie Hough to throw me one damn knuckleball. I had nothing to lose. Even if I struck out, I had nothing to lose.

Hough threw me a knuckler. Didn't knuckle. I crushed it nearly 500 feet into the black, those beautiful empty black seats in dead center. I found out later that I was only the second man ever to do that in the new Yankee Stadium.

That wouldn't have mattered a whole lot to me if I'd known at the time. As I began to move around the bases, I felt so . . . vindicated. Completely vindicated. When I passed first, I smiled at Steve Garvey and he smiled back; he'd tell me later he was so excited for me he was pounding a fist inside his mitt so no one would see. I felt so light on my feet, floating on the noise. It was the happiest moment of my career. It *is* the happiest moment of my career. I had been on a ball and chain all year, at least in my mind. I had heard so many negatives about Reggie Jackson. I had been the villain. Couldn't do this. Couldn't do that. And now suddenly I didn't care what the manager or my teammates had said or what the media had written.

I had three. We were going to win it all. I know I ran hard around the bases, took them fast, but when I think back, the trip seems to have taken an hour. God, it was a great moment. A hundred million people had seen that Reggie Jackson was okay, no matter what they'd read, no matter what they'd heard.

I feel like God was with me as I ran the bases. I believe *He* was saying, This is a good man. He survived and triumphed. I don't feel silly or embarrassed saying that. I believe it is true.

I got back to the dugout, and everyone pumped my hand, pounded me on the back, and hugged. I had three. We were going to win. The crowd would not quiet down. For the first time that season, I ran back up the steps and took a curtain call on the field, waving my cap this way and that. But only after I had mouthed the famous and almost mandatory "Hi, Mom" at the camera. I hadn't wanted to go back out. As a matter of fact, I refused. But Ray Negron pushed me up the steps and I took my bow. That just ignited them more.

And when I went out to right in the top of the ninth, the people out there just showered me with paper and programs, anything they could get their hands on. It reminded me of a ticker-tape parade. The next morning the front page of the *Daily News* would show me waving to the crowd in right in the ninth. My back was to the camera. Underneath it just said,

    REG-gie.
        REG-gie.
            REG-gie.

There were not many bad moments that night, but one sticks out in my mind. It was in the clubhouse right after we won, and Bill White, who does both radio and television for the Yankees, was one of the first media people to get to me. He wanted to do a national TV interview. White and I had never gotten along, though I'd tried. He'd been a fine player in the '60s for the Cardinals and the Phillies, and I thought as an ex-player-turned-broadcaster he'd have respect for my ability. Never did. There was something about me that made White uncomfortable toward me. Maybe he's just an uncomfortable person. As long as I was with the Yankees, he belittled a lot of what I did.

So now I'd hit three home runs and we've won the World Series and everybody is having a party in the clubhouse. White sticks a microphone in my face.

White: "How do you feel?"

Jackson: "Great—but I'd like thank all the people who stuck by me the whole year, friends in New York and Arizona and Oakland. And I want to thank God for everything that happened tonight."

White: "Now come on, Reggie. Quit with the commercial and tell us how you really feel."

The sonofabitch.

Here was the greatest moment of my life, here I was trying to be sincere about the people who'd helped me get through the whole ordeal, and White gives me some dialogue about a commercial. I wanted to tell him to stick his mike up his ass, but I shut up about it. I'll never forget that, but I wasn't about to let him even put a dent in my night.

Tommy Lasorda and Don Sutton and Steve Garvey came over to congratulate me, which I thought showed real class. But then the Dodgers have always been a classy organization.

"That is the greatest performance I have ever seen," Lasorda said. "That is the greatest performance that anyone *will* ever see."

Sutton said, "I agree."

I even went into Martin's office after some champagne, put my arm around him and drank more with him; it seemed like a wet enough moment for us to act like Army buddies. Hell. We'd won the World Series.

It was over. I had made it to the top of the mountain after so many times during the season when I thought I never would. You can never know what the future will bring. I wasn't ready for Arizona when I left Wyncote, and I wasn't ready for Birmingham when I left Arizona. No one is ever ready for a Finley, and after you've had a Finley, who could be ready for a Steinbrenner or a Martin? But there was a sense that night that I had survived my test. I had survived 1977. They had tried to break me but couldn't. I had made mistakes—talking to Robert Ward—and survived them. I had seen a sign calling me a bozo in Texas and ended up hearing the cheers in New York on October 18. Billy hadn't thought I was good enough to hit cleanup for him until August, then I helped carry his team after that.

He'd benched me in Kansas City. I'd come back to hit three over the wall in the clincher.

I've had more than six years to think about those home runs, that night, the last chapter to '77. If I could have stood up in the clubhouse and grabbed a microphone and talked just to the Yankees, I would have kept it simple, but I would have been speaking from the heart.

"I'm really sorry for all the problems we had on the ballclub this season. I'm sorry my presence in this room caused so much inconvenience for everybody. But we won. We won the world championship, and we all contributed. You've earned my respect. I hope now that I've earned yours."

Of course, you never do things like that. Even in the moments of triumph, it's hard to express what's really in your heart, on your mind. I've never been able to do it enough with family, or anyone, and I've certainly never done it enough with teammates. I didn't do it that night. My dad and my sister were there, however, to share in the triumph. I remember staying in the clubhouse very late that night and hugging and hugging my dad.

I then went to Jim McMullen's, the same place I'd been going all year. Matt Merola was with me, and Ralph Dastino, the president of Cartier's. The restaurant had not yet caught on as an "in" spot. It hadn't been open very long. Jimmy McMullen came over to sit with us. He had a bottle of Dom Perignon sent over to our table. I'd never even *heard* of Dom Perignon. I was still a Ripple man in those days and the champagne tasted bitter to me. A man came in, walked over to our table and said, Hugh Carey is down at Rusty's and he'd like you to join him and his party. I said, "Well, I'm having a party here. He's very welcome to come here and join me and my friends, but I can't leave."

I didn't know who the hell Hugh Carey was.

So about a half hour later, limousines pull up in front of Jim McMullen's and *Governor* Carey came in with a crowd of fifteen or twenty people. Suddenly the place got jammed, packed. And McMullen's has been packed ever since. The party lasted all night. Then I went over to do the "Today" show with Dick Schaap and stayed for the big victory parade. I'd never *seen* so many people. It seemed like the whole city turned out to cheer us. The next day I was on the first thing smokin' and headin' west. I was going home to Oakland. I was going to drink some beer, drive my cars, look at pretty ladies and bullshit with my buddies. I felt like I'd been to war. As it turned out, I'd even decorated myself. *Sport* magazine gave me its MVP award for the Series—I was nine-for-twenty, five home runs, eight RBI—but I already had the only trophies I wanted.

Three dingers one night in October.

15
WHO WAS IT WHO SAID THE MORE THINGS CHANGE THE MORE THEY STAY THE SAME?

"**Y**ou better get your head on straight, boy!" George Steinbrenner shouted. He doesn't have a bass voice, but when he tries to be a tough guy, he drops it a few octaves.

He was standing in the middle of his office at Yankee Stadium looking, as usual, like your typical high-powered businessman. Blue blazer. Gray slacks (I've never seen George in a brown suit, by the way). Blue shirt. Red-and-blue-striped tie. Black shoes. His hair was combed the same way it always was in the five years I worked for him. In those entire five years, he had the same amount of gray hair. His face was contorted into a coach's grimace.

It was July 17, 1978. I was hitting around .260. We were in fourth place, a cool fourteen games behind the Red Sox. In a few hours we would be playing a game against the Kansas City Royals, who had just beaten us twice in a row.

"I mean it!" George reiterated. "You better get your head on straight, boy."

The boy in question was me.

Welcome to the 1978 season. Starting with that night in July,

here was all that happened over the final seventy-five games, including playoffs and World Series:

I got suspended for five games.

Billy had a few too many scotches and called George Steinbrenner "convicted" and me a "born liar," and also said we deserved
each other.

Billy said he resigned, but basically he got fired by George for
all the stuff about convicts and liars. Bob Lemon replaced him.

Five days later, before the Old-timers Game at Yankee Stadium, George rehired Billy. Not for the rest of the '78 season. Not
for '79. For 1980.

While all that was going on, we came from those fourteen
games behind the Red Sox, ended up tied with them on the last day
of the regular season, won the playoff game at Fenway Park—
possibly the most exciting game ever played—beat the Royals in the
American League Championship Series and won the World Series
after losing the first two games to the Dodgers.

That was about it.

I thought I had seen everything during the making of the
movie that was the '77 season. As it turned out, 1977 was only the
original, like *Star Wars.* The next season was the sequel. Call it
Billy and George Strike Back.

As far as I'm concerned, it all really started the night this boy
was told to get his head on straight.

I came into the '78 season like it was my sophomore year in college.
I had grown up a lot my freshman year. I'd survived all the hazing.
I ended up with good grades. At the very end, on the last day of
school, I made Dean's List. I figured sophomore year would be a
breeze.

It certainly was better in the clubhouse, at least for a while.

I would never feel totally at ease in the Yankee clubhouse—
I never feel at ease when I go back to the South either—but in the
spring and early summer of 1978, I no longer felt like it was an
armed camp. Thurman and I could actually sit and talk about a few
subjects that interested both of us: business and airplanes and baseball. Goose Gossage had come over from the Pirates in the free
agent draft, and he told me straight out he had always been a Reggie
fan. I felt that Bucky Dent, who would have great moments before

the season was over, and Willie Randolph had become friends. And Fran was still there. I don't think I could have run for class president and won, but the atmosphere was definitely more relaxed with my teammates.

Unfortunately, when the regular season began, I got off to a slow start. So did everyone else except Ron Guidry, who was brilliant from start to finish in '78 (he'd finish 25–3). Now I generally don't worry about slow starts, mostly because I always seem to have them. It sounds like a cliché, but I've always assumed that when the weather got warm, so would I. I also think a slow start is a natural by-product of a championship season for a team. You go into Opening Day thinking, We'll turn it on when we have to. That happened with the A's. It wasn't arrogance. Just confidence. One hundred and sixty-two games is a marathon; there's no need to break any records the first mile.

Problem was, these were the Yankees, not the A's. In George Steinbrenner's view of the Yankees, there is only one way for them to go:

George wants to win all 162.

It's just part of his makeup.

So George got mad about the slow start and, of course, didn't keep it to himself. He began showing up in the clubhouse, screaming that we were embarrassing him and embarrassing New York and that he would clean house and bring kids up from the minors if some of us didn't start producing. It was a familiar theme. And it became obvious that he was putting a lot of pressure on Billy, who when under pressure in those years usually did three things:

1. Got mad.
2. Went to the bar.
3. Went after me.

With Billy, we didn't get to see a lot of the actual drinking, only the results, meaning the hangovers. By July of '78, he was showing up later and later at the ballpark, looking shakier and shakier when he did, wearing his sunglasses more and more often for the afternoon games. Billy has always had bizarre work habits, especially in areas like preparation and being on time. Most managers will show up four and five hours before a game for meetings, to go over statistics about the various tendencies of hitters against the opposing team's pitcher, etc. Not Billy. Most managers have the batting order posted long before batting practice. Not Billy. As the Red Sox began to pull away from us, it was nothing for Billy to show up at 12:30 for a two o'clock game, and for us not to have a batting order posted as late as one o'clock.

When he did show up, sunglasses on, he wouldn't go near anybody.

Once again, he and I had no relationship at all, unless we happened to be in the same newspaper story. The only time Billy and I spoke was if we happened to be walking in the clubhouse door at the same time. Nothing at all had changed. I thought winning would give Billy and me at least some mutual respect and a common ground for being civil to each other. But winning had changed nothing. Everything had been so triumphant at the end of the '77 season, and now I felt I was being pulled back into the same sick environment that had so dominated '77.

As far as Billy and Reggie were concerned, it was the same old nightmare.

I began to read that Fred Stanley, our backup shortstop, was more of a Yankee than I was. Or so Billy said.

Billy began to attack my fielding again.

Billy began to DH me again. Sometimes he would DH me only against left-handers, which made no sense.

He began to sit me down when the spirit moved him. And it moved him with no regular pattern, with no real rhyme or reason.

Now understand, I was proud of what I had done the season before. I'm not sure any player ever went through quite what I did in a setting like we had with the Yankees. I had overcome it all with a flourish at the end. I came back not expecting things to be perfect, but I sure expected them to be better. I had made myself one promise during the off-season: I wasn't going to go through anything like 1977 ever again. So now, as the bullshit was reaching high tide again, I decided I really was going to get out.

For a month before July 17, I had been trying to set up a meeting with Steinbrenner, Martin, and Al Rosen, the great Indians third baseman who had replaced Gabe Paul as team president. Steinbrenner kept putting me off. I told him that I had done everything humanly possible to try to play for Martin, that I had helped win the World Series for the man, and still he was treating me like an old shoe. I was tired of him bad-mouthing me in the papers and behind my back just to work off his own demons. I didn't want to be a part-time DH or even a full-time DH; I still wanted to play the outfield, and I thought playing the outfield made me a better hitter.

"George, how much has to happen?" I said to him one day on the telephone. "When are you going to get it through your head that I can't play for this guy?"

"We'll get together soon," George said. But we didn't. This went on for a month.

Finally we met in his office. Rosen was there. Cedric Tallis, a Yankee vice-president, was there. Cedric is a dad-like man who was probably described as jolly before he went to work for George, but in my experience with Cedric, his friendly, fatherly face was screwed up into a perpetual grimace. George didn't treat him like a dog; it seemed George was the dog, Cedric was the fire hydrant. Matt Merola was there. I had repeatedly asked that Billy be present for this session, but he wasn't there, which didn't improve my disposition any since I knew nothing could be resolved without him.

I went through my litany of complaints. Told George I wanted to play the outfield; he told me Billy was right, I was a lousy outfielder. I reminded George about his pledge to trade me if I ever wanted to be traded. George said, "You're not going anywhere." You could feel tempers igniting as voices rose. I was getting more and more uncomfortable because until this night, I had thought of George Steinbrenner as an ally, maybe even a friend. I had definitely believed he'd been an ally in '77 when I was not exactly overloaded with those. It's hard in retrospect to visualize how beguiling George had been when he turned on the charm. Maybe it's his money, maybe it's his ruthlessness. Whatever it is, there's something about him that makes you feel a little like a teenager trying to earn your dad's respect. He disarms you—until he gets you vulnerable. Then, as you ponder on what's going to happen next . . . BOOM! Again, it's hard to imagine today, but until this meeting I actually thought of him as one of the people who'd helped pull me through the hellish '77 season, never truly realizing he was at least partly responsible for it. I was beginning to realize it, however, at this meeting. He wasn't listening to my problems. Worse, he wasn't even trying to understand them.

George has a spacious office located right behind his box of

seats at the press-box level of Yankee Stadium. George likes the size
of the office because it is a great place for him to entertain. As our
little meeting wore on, I began to sweat like hell and feel more and
more uncomfortable, like the room was closing in on me. I remember wearing a brown tattersall shirt that night; by the time I left the
office, I'd noticed I had sweated through it as though I'd been in
a sauna.

Everybody was seated around George's big desk, except
George. He was pacing. Matt was on my right. Rosen and Tallis
were on my left.

Nobody had said anything for a while when George wheeled
around in the middle of the room, pointed a finger at me, and came
up with his "boy" remark.

Twice.

I thought to myself, Well, screw it.

I yelled right back at him. "Who the hell do you think you're
talking to?"

Matt tried to put a hand on my arm, but I angrily yanked the
arm away.

George: "I'm talking to you!"

Me: "Well, let me tell you something. Don't you ever talk to
me like that again as long as you live."

I was really hot. "Boy" indeed. I expected that from some of
my teammates. I didn't expect it from George. But he'd picked the
wrong fellow on the wrong night.

We just stared at each other. Finally I turned to Rosen. Rosen
was in the Hall of Fame, he'd been an MVP for the Indians, he was
a good man. And he was Jewish. Al has white hair, and his face
was the color of his hair right then. I think he was of the mind that
George and I were going to go at it right there in the office.

I felt like I was back in Gabe Paul's suite in Boston. Only now
George was Billy and Al was Gabe.

"Al," I said "you're Jewish. How would you interpret that
part about 'boy'?"

Rosen looked at Steinbrenner, then back at me, then cleared
his throat.

Rosen said, "Reggie, I'm not sure George meant that the way
you're taking it. I think you should both cool down."

Steinbrenner erupted again.

"Cool down, *hell,* " he said. "Reggie, you get the hell out of my office!"

Well, there had been times when I'd seen him order Al Rosen around that way. There had been times when I'd seen him do it to Tallis. People who work in the Yankee offices have always had horror stories about the way George treats the hired help; it's probably one of the reasons why George goes through front-office people and p.r. men the way the rest of us go through pistachio nuts.

Maybe Rosen and Tallis liked their jobs enough to take that from him. I wasn't about to.

I looked straight at George and said, "I really don't feel like leaving, George. I kind of like it here. I'm staying."

Nobody moved. There may have been some breathing in the room, but not much. This was a bad moment for George, mainly because he knew he couldn't physically throw me out of the office and neither could anybody else. I don't know what kind of game the two of us were playing, but I was willing to see it all the way through.

I didn't have to. Steinbrenner, without another word, walked out of his office.

I stayed a few more minutes, then took the elevator down to the clubhouse level. It was 7:15 by then, and we had an eight o'clock game. Walking down the long corridor I came to the door that said, "Pete Sheehy's Clubhouse," in honor of the wonderful old man who'd been with the Yankees since Babe Ruth's time.

Everyone should have the opportunity in their lifetime to meet Pete Sheehy. He was history. He was the Yankees. He was experience. He was also kind and understanding. He used to come over to me after I'd had a bad day or been involved in some turmoil or one of those frequent storms had burst all around me, and he'd tell me, "Hey, do like Casey used to say. 'Just whistle Dixie and sing Tra-la-la-la-la.' " I'd come in after striking out three times and Pete'd say, "If you want to, tear off your uniform. What the hell, Mickey used to do it all the time. Or just have a couple of beers and forget about it—that's what Babe used to do. Or just sit at your locker and relax the way Joe D. used to." He once said to me, "I'm glad you wear number 44. Because Lou Gehrig was my favorite player and he was number 4." Pete told me that he was to Lou

Gehrig as Ray Negron was to me—he used to run errands for Gehrig, tend to his needs. Everyplace you go around the league has clubhouse dues—a set amount that each player pays the clubhouse man to make sure there's the right kind of tobacco, to pay for that autographed baseball you give to a friend's kid, to pay for whatever extras you care to have. Every clubhouse but Pete Sheehy's. He wouldn't hear of it. We were just told to pay him what we felt like. The nicest compliment Pete ever paid me was when he said that as long as he was around, he'd never give out number 44 to any other player.

As I reached the door to the clubhouse, I wished that George Steinbrenner had had a touch of Pete Sheehy in him. It occurred to me that George hadn't listened to anything I'd said before our argument. Not one word. He was so stubborn he couldn't see what Billy was doing with me, to me, once again at the expense of everyone.

I carried a sort of dull anger, like an ache, with me into the clubhouse. It was as if an old injury that I'd thought was healed was acting up again, worse than ever. I was frustrated, sad, disappointed. I must admit, I wanted George to understand what the hell was going on, to pay attention to all the stuff that was going down.

I managed to get George's attention a couple of hours later, in the tenth inning against the Royals.

Tenth inning. Al Hrabosky pitching for the Royals. Game tied. Billy had decided to bat me cleanup that night. Thurman, hitting third, led off with a single.

Then things happened. Boy, did they.

As I left the dugout, Billy said, "Can you bunt?"

I said, "Bunt? Yeah, I guess so!"

At that point, my mind was practically blank. I didn't care. If '77 was hell, I was back there again, and I never thought I'd be anywhere even close. With what happened next I was saying, I've had enough guys, okay? You've beaten me down again. You want me to say uncle? Okay, I'm saying it. Uncle. Call me boy. Ask me to bunt. I can't play every day anymore? Fine. I'm your cleanup hitter, and I have to bunt in a tie game in the ninth? Fine, I'll bunt.

You don't like me, Billy? Fine. I can't field? Terrific. I'm going to give you the team you've always wanted, one without me.

He wanted a bunt?

He was going to get his bunt.

Hrabosky threw me a ball up and in when I squared to bunt. Ball one. I didn't even look for a sign on the second pitch. I bunted and missed.

Count was one and one. Dick Howser called time at third base and waved me up the line. Same situation as the previous September against Reggie Cleveland, only there wasn't going to be a dinger this time.

Howser said, "Billy wants you to hit away."

"I was told to bunt—I'm bunting!"

Howser looked at me, sort of stunned. He couldn't believe what he was hearing. (You didn't bunt after the manager took the sign off.)

"Reggie, he wants you to hit away."

"Listen, Dick," I said, "nothing against you, but when I left the dugout he told me to bunt, and I'm going to bunt. I'm gonna get the runner over and Piniella will come up and knock the run in, and we'll win. I'm a real team guy, right?"

Howser just shook his head.

"I hope you know what you're doing," he said, and walked back to the third-base coaching box.

As a matter of fact, I didn't know what I was doing. I was on automatic pilot, not thinking, just reacting, angry and tired and whipped. Just plain sick of it.

I tried to bunt twice more, missed, and struck out.

A year ago, Martin had shown me up on the field by sending Paul Blair out to replace me. Now I was returning the favor. When I got back to the dugout no one said anything until Gene Michael, a coach who eventually became general manager and then manager a couple of times, came over to me. Even now Billy couldn't deal with a face-to-face confrontation. It still amazes me how little of that there was.

Michael said, "Billy wants you to go inside, and take a shower."

We were in the middle of the dugout, about twenty feet from Martin, who had his jaw set and was just staring at the field. The

Yankees in the dugout weren't moving and they weren't talking.

"If Billy wants to come over and tell me to go inside, then let him come over and tell me himself," I said.

I wanted to fight somebody. I thought I'd gone by all that. I thought I'd left that urge in another season, another life, but now I wanted to fight. I needed to fight. I took off my glasses and set them down. Ten, maybe twenty seconds went by, then I turned to Michael and said, "You said that real tough. What'd you mean by that?"

As a coach and manager, Gene liked to act tough. But he didn't have it in him, deep down, at least not that night.

"I'm just telling you what Billy said," was Michael's answer.

Martin never said a word. Never made a move for me. I sat and watched the game, and after a while I went into the clubhouse and took a shower. I was like a robot more than anything else. I was there physically, but mentally I was divorced from the situation. Desensitized. I didn't care what they did. I hoped they suspended me for the rest of the season.

When Billy got to the clubhouse—we lost the game in the eleventh—he didn't come near me. But as soon as his office door closed, all hell broke loose. You could hear glass breaking, you could hear things being thrown against the wall, you could hear him screaming. I thought I heard what sounded like a phone breaking (I was told later it was a clock radio). I didn't know if anyone was in there with him, but I hoped not.

I just kept getting dressed. The writers came over and I told them I thought I was supposed to bunt. Told them I didn't care anymore. Said if no one wanted to talk to me, there was no reason for me to care.

Someone asked where I was going.

I said, "Home."

"Oakland home or New York home?"

I just shrugged my shoulders and walked out the door.

It is a long walk from the clubhouse to the exit to the parking lot. I was by myself, walking slowly, in no hurry to go anywhere. Dick Young, then with the New York *Daily News,* caught up with me. Billy apparently had called Rosen, Rosen had met with Tallis and Steinbrenner, and I had been suspended indefinitely.

"How do you feel?" Young asked me.

"Dick," I said, "I'm going home. In the morning, I'm getting on the first thing smokin' and headin' west."

The writers had heard that line before. I was always telling them I was doing that, in good times and bad.

The next morning I was on a nine o'clock American Airlines flight to San Francisco. The movie on the plane was *Coming Home,* which I thought was perfect. When we got to San Francisco, they stopped the plane on the runway where my friend Everett Moss was waiting for me with a car. Someone at the airport had radioed the pilot about what the crowd of media people was like at the gate.

Everett took my bags and we drove off. He has been a friend for fifteen years, and he can read my moods as well as anyone. He's a tough, quiet, caring, barrel-chested man, who I always know is there for me. You go to war with men like Everett Moss. He lives in my house when I'm not there and takes care of my cars. He's a sweet guy and my best friend.

"You want to be done for the season, don't you?" Everett said.

I told Everett he had that right. "But you know what?" I said to him. "I ain't paying a fine. They can suspend me forever, but I'm not giving them a dime."

When we got to my house, there were three cars waiting in the driveway. They belonged to two sportswriters and a UPI photographer. They were just waiting for me to get home. We turned right around and drove to the nearest pay phone where I called Betsy, my girlfriend. We stayed out at her house in Oakland for the week.

And had a great time.

There was one small subplot the night of the missed bunts and the suspension, and it got lost. Sparky Lyle took himself out of the game, got dressed, and went home.

And nothing was ever done about it.

Lyle had been bitching since the day Steinbrenner signed Gossage. He had been whining about renegotiating his contract if he had to pitch long relief. He had been complaining almost every day about pitching long relief. And when Billy called on him that night, Lyle pitched the fourth and fifth innings, came into the dugout and said, "Fuck it. I'm no long reliever. I'm going home."

Which is exactly what he did. By the time he got home, I had already been suspended. Nobody ever said boo to Sparky Lyle for quitting in the middle of that game.

There were all sorts of rules around the Yankees. But they only seemed to apply to me. They sure didn't apply to Sparky. Maybe somebody should have told that boy to get his head on straight.

16

BILLY SAYS, "ONE IS A BORN LIAR, AND THE OTHER ONE IS CONVICTED." BILLY GETS FIRED. BILLY GETS REHIRED.

I got the official word.

The Yankees suspended me for five days without pay. I was hoping for thirty days, or the season, but you take what you can get. I did tell Gary Walker and Steven Kay to let them know that I wasn't ever coming back if they stuck to the fine. George and Gary and Steven went back and forth on that one for a couple of days while I hid out at Betsy's.

I didn't read the newspapers. I didn't watch television. I didn't listen to the radio. I just listened to music and tried to get myself into a workable frame of mind in case I did not go back to finish the season. I really was hoping that they'd kick me out for the rest of the year because I couldn't stomach the thought of being back in the same atmosphere. I was just never going to win with Billy Martin around. I was always going to be the uppity one; he was always going to be the darling of the fans, gutsy little No. 1, the feisty streetfighter, every single time there was a confrontation between us.

After three days or so, Gary and Steven and George worked

it out: If I didn't say anything about not paying the fine, I didn't
have to pay the fine. George said, "Just get him back in uniform."
He wanted to be Mr. Fixit—it's another one of George's favorite
roles. I sometimes think that when George shaves in the morning,
he looks in the mirror and sees six or seven faces staring back at
him. George the patriarch. George the sportsman. George the tycoon. Tough George. Fair George. And you can take it from me,
there *are* a lot of Georges. I just hope you get a nice one.

I was to rejoin the team in Chicago for the game on July 23.
To duck the press, I took a most interesting route: Oakland to Los
Angeles to Phoenix to Tucson to Chicago. I didn't want to open my
mouth and make things worse before I saw what the lay of the land
was with the team. I figured I was the biggest villain I had ever been
with the Yankees. The Robert Ward story? Forget about it. The
near-fight with Billy at Fenway? Ancient history, Jack. This was
bad. Baaaad.

I decided to take a cab to the ballpark, still trying to avoid the
media. While traveling the abandoned streets of Chicago, I realized
I was a beaten man. I was melancholy. Down. Depressed. If anyone
had asked me about my state of mind, and if I were to be candid
with them, I would only have been able to say, "I quit. I quit, I
quit!"

But I couldn't be candid. However I knew I had to, somehow,
deal with the unbearable situation at Comiskey Park, which was
now only five minutes away. The silence in the cab was interrupted
occasionally by the clicking of the meter measuring miles and
money. My thoughts shifted from quitting to how I was going to
deal with my teammates, who probably didn't care whether or not
I showed up. However, I owed them an apology and decided I
would give it to them as soon as I got to the park.

But what about Billy? My mind was involved in a tug-of-war
with my heart. My mind said, "Apologize to him. It'll help keep
the peace." Once again I thought I should play the role of the
contrite man who had unwittingly disrupted the peaceful norm. My
heart said, "Forget it. You've extended the olive branch too often.
Don't apologize to Billy. The situation with him isn't going to
change. Unless it deteriorates even more"—which was almost impossible. If the situation got any worse, it would mean a machine
gun in Billy's hand, one in mine, and the two of us dueling at
sunrise.

If only they had known that in my mind and body I could no longer fight. I no longer wanted to play. I truly believe that if Billy had known that, known that I was defeated, he wouldn't have uttered the remark that spelled his demise in 1978.

I got to the park late. In the clubhouse, I was surrounded by media. During the press conference, I felt tremendous anger inside about the whole circuslike situation. I did feel a certain amount of empathy for the guys in the media, however. They were just doing their jobs.

Because I was so tardy, my teammates were already drifting out to the field, to batting practice. So my apology would have to wait until the next night in Kansas City. Of course, I had no idea that my apology would be preempted by another rather earth-shaking event in Kansas City.

The Yanks had won four in a row without me so no one could lay a hand on Billy for not playing me that night. We won again with me on the bench, putting us ten games in back of the Sox, who were still showing no signs of folding.

In the dugout Billy never spoke to me, never looked at me. After the game, I showered, dressed, faced the media, answered some questions. Then I got onto the bus with everybody else and went to O'Hare airport.

I bought a couple of papers and magazines at the airport, then went to a refreshment stand with Fran to get a milkshake. While we were talking, Cedric Tallis came by in a frenzy. He paused momentarily to tell us—and anyone else who would listen—what Billy had just said.

Up to that moment, I truly didn't care about anything that had happened that entire day. Again, I was a beaten man.

But now my mood shifted abruptly, though if you had asked me then to define my feelings, I couldn't have. Was this a reprieve for me? I'd thought I was on my way to my career gallows. Now, out of the blue, it seemed I was not going to have to eat my last meal just yet.

Cedric was gone with as much haste as he'd arrived. Then came Henry Hecht of the *New York Post.* He explained to me exactly what had happened. He and Murray Chass of the *New York Times* had run into Billy, who was apparently enraged that I hadn't apologized to him. When the two reporters asked him about the situation, Billy'd said, "One's a born liar"—referring to me—"and the other's convicted"—referring to George's 1974 felony conviction for making illegal contributions to Richard Nixon.

Henry Hecht then said that they'd asked Billy if he wanted that statement printed. Billy said to go ahead and put it in the story.

At that moment I was still so depressed I didn't really care what Billy had said about me. The full impact of the line hadn't sunk in yet. As far as George was concerned, he was the furthest thing from my mind. However, as I began to walk toward the plane, it started to sink in. I realized the fatal possibilities of Billy's rash statement. I made an immediate decision to stay as quiet as possible on this subject. I wouldn't say anything. Wouldn't step back into the storm. I didn't need it. Couldn't handle it. For the first time in my career, I'd bite my tongue and shut up.

I wasn't on the plane two minutes and we hadn't even taken off when Murray Chass, who was sitting across the aisle from me, said he wanted to interview me, get my comments. I switched seats to move closer to Murray. In my mind, I heard an echo say, "No comment." And that's exactly what came out of my mouth.   •

I stayed on the sidelines and watched.

The next day in Kansas City, Billy held a press conference and tearfully told the world he was resigning. Every writer, every coach, every player knew differently.

George Steinbrenner had fired him.

Hot damn. I felt like I'd won the lottery. I'd get to feel that way for almost a whole week, until I lost my lottery ticket on Old-timers Day at Yankee Stadium the following Saturday.

I should have seen it coming in Kansas City as I watched Billy's press conference on television before we went to the ballpark that night.

I thought, Damn, what a great act. It was such a brilliant demonstration of public relations. It was almost sickening schmaltz, but it worked. There were the tears. There was his speech about the Yankee pinstripes. There was his statement about how he wouldn't answer any questions about his resignation (it was about as much a resignation as a man being pushed out of a speeding car) because he was a Yankee and "Yankees do not talk or throw rocks." I thought, in the words of Warner Wolf, *Give me a break!* I couldn't believe what was happening.

Anyway, it was an unforgettable performance. It concluded with Phil Rizzuto, a really sweet guy, an institution as a broadcaster, and an ex-Yankee shortstop, and Billy walking off into the sunset, arms around each other's shoulders. If I must say so myself, it was a tear-jerking picture. Martin and Rizzuto played together with the Yankees, Billy at second base, Scooter Rizzuto at short. Rizzuto has been a Yankee radio-TV announcer forever. If you're not from New York, it's difficult to explain the Rizzuto phenomenon. He was a great shortstop during his Yankee playing career, but didn't become a legend until he became the Yankee announcer. He's famous for his exuberance, for his distinctive Brooklyn accent, for his unabashed Yankee prejudice, and for yelling "Holy Cow!" every fifteen seconds or so. He's also short and just a lovable guy.

Rizzuto was a hard guy to get to know unless he liked you. Someone pretty much had to introduce you to him. The Scooter just doesn't seem to really be into baseball people. He's into his family, golf and having a good time. I know his wife's name is Cora because he talks about her on the radio almost as much as he talks about the Yankees.

He's probably the only guy in the Yankee organization that Steinbrenner could never fire. Scooter is very secure and basically does what he wants.

He does not like going to the West Coast games. His attitude is, "I'm sixty years old and that's too far to go." He *will* go, but if it gets below sixty degrees in Oakland, he'll do an inning or two and then go back to the hotel. It's too cold. If we're in the Kingdome in Seattle and it gets below seventy, forget about it. The Scooter's back in the hotel. No one ever says a word or dreams of questioning him.

If we're on a ten- or eleven-day road trip, he'll say, "Well, I'll go to Oakland, you guys go to Seattle. I'll meet you down in Anaheim for the last three games." If we have a late flight after a West Coast night game—which gets you home next week—the Scooter'll leave that morning. Never even *thinks* of going to the game. If, somehow, he does fly all night, we could be playing the sixth game of the World Series and he'll stay home to make sure he gets his rest. I love it.

In New York, he'll sometimes leave the Stadium after the

seventh inning of a game. "I'm goin' *home,*" he says. "Gotta beat this traffic!" So he just goes.

If Phil is on the air and doesn't understand something, he'll just pull out his trademark: He'll simply say, "Holy Cow!"

He's a friend and I'm crazy about him. I think he had fun being my friend, especially when it was so unfashionable.

But now I watched him in amazement. I watched the whole thing in amazement, this Yankee pinstriped charade, the little old comrades banding together in time of need. They didn't even seem friends. Why would Rizzuto do this? I think all old Yankees are alike—they believe the family stuff. Maybe I'll be the same way someday with some ex-teammate, no matter what he's done.

I watched and thought, Shit, Billy's turned the whole thing around. He's become the victim! He's the one who called me a liar. He's the one who called his boss convicted. Now he's coming on like he's got the Yankee's "NY" emblem tattooed on his heart, he's crying his eyes out, and he's going to walk away a hero. I'll be a son of a bitch.

Billy Martin is not an intellectual, but there is a cunningness to him that is something to behold. A lot is made of his ability to self-destruct, and rightly so. But he has always alternated that with an instinct for survival that is sometimes beyond belief.

Yankees don't talk or throw rocks.

I wanted to laugh. I didn't know, of course, that George and all Yankee fans everywhere were eating that shit up like it was ice cream.

Bob Lemon did replace Billy as manager. He showed up from his home in California the day after Billy didn't talk, did cry, didn't throw rocks and left.

Lem was exactly what we needed at the time, a tough old baseball veteran with an even disposition. He immediately seemed to throw a blanket of calm over all the smoldering fires that had been left behind. At our first meeting, Lem just said, "You guys won last year, which means you must have been doing something right. So what do you say you go out and play just like you did last year, and I'll try to stay out of the way."

Bob Lemon is a big barrel-chested man with a nose that looks like it should belong to Rudolph the Red-Nosed Reindeer. We were in a bus going to an airport later that year, after a night game in Detroit, and suddenly the bus pulled over and stopped. From the back, someone wanted to know what was going on.

"No problem," Nettles called out. "We're just stopping to get batteries for Lem's nose." The manager laughed as hard as anyone.

Lem had started his baseball career with the Indians as an outfielder, ended up as a pitcher, won twenty games seven times, and went to the Hall of Fame. He had a reputation for being a quiet guy, unless provoked. Then, word had it, Bob Lemon could bust up whatever was in the way.

He was also known to have a drink or two. Personality-wise, that was about the only similarity between Lem and Billy.

In fact, Lem's most-famous quote was a drinking quote: "I never took the game home with me. I always left it in a bar along the way."

His second-most-famous quote was, "I drink after wins, I drink after losses, and I drink after rain-outs."

He called everybody "Meat." It was an all-purpose nickname. "How you doing, Meat?" "Grab a bat, Meat." "Don't worry about taking a strike, Meat." Everybody liked Lem, who stayed out of the way as promised. It seemed that everybody just relaxed the minute he walked into the clubhouse.

Our first one-on-one meeting was a brief one.

"You're going to hit fourth every day," he said. "Sometimes you'll play right, sometimes you'll DH. You know what to do. Just go hit some over the wall."

I felt like I'd been let out of prison. I could hear the gates clanging shut behind me, it was a sunny day, and I was a free man. I had a clean uniform and a bat in my hands. Billy was gone. The day Lem showed up we were ten and a half games behind the Red Sox. We won that night and cut it to nine and a half. Maybe there was hope yet.

We played the Indians when we got back. No one was mad at anybody at this point. Too much had happened; we were all emotionally drained. I got a little heat from the Stadium crowd, but it wasn't too bad. There were five or six guys behind first base who kept chanting, "Bunt, Reggie, Bunt," every time I stepped out of the dugout, but security people finally removed them. The next night against the Indians we swept a doubleheader. I went three-for-four in one of the games and had a dinger.

I didn't know at the time that we were starting out on the road to a miracle.

I also wasn't aware that George and Billy were having secret meetings that week and that Billy had already been hired to manage the Yankees again for the 1980 season, at which time Lemon would be kicked upstairs to become general manager. I found out Saturday, right before the Old-timers Game.

Dick Young told me. Trying to get a reaction, I guess. Up until then, I didn't have a clue and neither did anyone else. We were in the clubhouse getting dressed. It was about the time all the past Yankee greats were being introduced on the field.

Young came over to my locker and very quietly said, "Billy's coming back."

There was something in his voice that said this was no joke. I just looked at him.

"Billy's . . . coming back? When? How?"

Young told me the story. He said the Yankee phones had been ringing off the hook since Billy resigned—or was resigned—in Kansas City. He said George really felt bad after hearing Billy's speech about the Yankees. Said George thought he might have made a mistake but could turn things around with this grand gesture on Old-timers Day.

Young left to go out to the field, and I just slowly walked into the lounge where there was a television and watched what to me was a horror movie. I heard Bob Sheppard, the p.a. announcer, saying ". . . the manager for 1980, and hopefully for many years to come . . . Number One . . . Billy Martin."

I saw Billy come running out onto the field, waving his cap. He was back.

Pick a word. I was shocked. Reeling. I felt like I'd been hit with a Frazier left hook. And then I started to think about Steinbrenner and how he'd just sold me out for the sake of public relations. One week earlier, Billy had called him a felon, and now George had hired him back. The implication, at least in my mind, was that I was the bad guy. If George could hire him back, obviously George and Billy had kissed and made up. But what about me? What about the liar part? For the first time, for the very first time, I understood that deep down Steinbrenner was a man with few principles, a man who would sell you out in a second, a man to whom real loyalty could never be very meaningful. I knew. This wasn't an argument in his office with ugly words being traded back and forth. This was a bold, cold, calculated maneuver at my expense. I felt like he'd left me on the hot seat. He had made it quite clear in the eyes of the fans who the real villain was.

Wasn't George.

Wasn't Billy.

It was No. 44.

I stayed in the lounge for a long time, not speaking to anyone. Almost everyone was as stunned as I was. Bucky was furious. "They'd better trade me," he said to me, "'cause I ain't playin' for him." Then I tried to get myself ready as best I could for that afternoon's game against the Texas Rangers. I wanted to be ready for the Rangers and for every single game down the stretch, because I knew that the only way I could survive the season was to hit. My only weapon now would be my bat.

I talked to my father on the telephone that night, and he said, "Don't worry about Billy, and don't worry about George. Just bow your neck and grit your teeth. And hit. And be a man."

I told him I would try like hell to do that. I also told my dad I would never again trust George Steinbrenner as long as I lived.

17

OH, YEAH, ABOUT THE MIRACLE . . .

L em wasn't one for making speeches or having meetings. Lem was a Californian who was laid back before anyone invented laid back. One day in August after we'd ripped off another four in a row, he said to me, "This is the way I like it. You guys play, and I sit in the dugout and enjoy."

We played. He enjoyed.

And suddenly we had the Red Sox in our sights.

It was, well, just one of those things. The way the Miracle Braves of 1914 were one of those things. The way the Giants catching the Dodgers in 1951 after being thirteen games back was one of those things. We just went after the Red Sox, playing the kind of hardball we should have been playing all along. By the first of September, we were in second place, just six and a half behind and on the move. We went into Fenway Park a week later three games behind, swept the Sox four straight, and when we left Boston we were in first place. We outscored them 42–9 in that series, with Thurman and Piniella in particular hitting the ball all over the tiny old ballpark.

I was sitting with Piniella in the clubhouse after we won 7–4 on Sunday, and I said, "Well, what do we do now? We're in first place now, you know?"

Piniella blew some cigarette smoke at me and grinned.

"I know we're in first," he said. "What I'm wondering is how the hell we got here."

We were ten and a half behind when Lemon showed up in Kansas City. We went 48–20 down the stretch. We won twelve of fifteen in one streak, we won twelve of fourteen in another, and once we got our nose in front of the Sox as we got to the head of the stretch, we kept it there until the last day of the regular season when we lost—with Catfish pitching—to the Indians at home while the Red Sox won up in Boston, forcing a one-game playoff for the American League East title.

Game No. 163 for the Yankees and the Red Sox in 1978 was something kind of special. But the comeback was really the thing. I don't think there has ever been one as good in the history of baseball. Not the Miracle Braves. Not the Giants. Not the Amazin' Mets in 1969. The Red Sox were a terrific team, for one thing. For another, there had been all that melodrama and craziness for us until nearly the first of August. Suspend Reggie for the bunt. Liars and convicts. Fire Billy. Rehire Billy.

And come from fourteen games behind, which is where we were a week before Lem showed up.

We did all of that. I would like to tell you that we were constantly aware of the history we were making, that it was one long exhilarating roller-coaster ride, that we all ran around like cheerleaders when we weren't taking turns getting bit hits.

Didn't happen that way. Close but not quite.

This was just a group of professionals clicking on all cylinders all the time, having to win ballgames and then winning them. This was a team sport done right, with no bullshit or neuroses or off-the-field antagonism being carried on the field with us. We made the plays we had to make in the field. Thurman would get the big hit, or Nettles would, or Piniella would, or I would. We'd win again, look at the scoreboard, and not really worry about what the Red Sox were doing. If they could keep pace with us, fine. If not, we knew we were taking our best shot. Collective best shot. Didn't matter that I didn't like Nettles and Nettles didn't like me. Didn't matter that Thurman and I had had problems in the past. We didn't have time to think about that. You don't have time to let your mind wander when you're gettin' with the program. Suddenly you're just riding the big train, and you want to tell people to get out of the way. You don't talk. You just *do.* The conversation I had with Piniella was rare; the subject of the comeback never came up much. Once we caught the Red Sox, it was an unspoken fact that we were going to pull the whole caper off. If we had forgotten about being the world champions early in the season, we damn well remembered by September.

Catfish came off the disabled list in July after a doctor somehow cured his bad shoulder, and he turned into the Catfish of Oakland, going 10–3 down the stretch. Ed Figueroa won his last eight in a row. Guidry, who had one of the greatest, gutsiest seasons I've ever seen a pitcher have, merely ended 25–3 with a 1.74 earned run average; he won ten out of his last eleven. If we scored a run in the first inning when Guidry was pitching, we felt we almost didn't even have to take the field. That game was as good as won. When any of them couldn't finish, Gossage would come out of the bullpen and turn off all the lights before locking all the doors to another win. Lyle, by this time, had gotten lost in the shuffle.

I had my best month of the season in September, hitting eight dingers and knocking in twenty-six runs. Thurman finished with a rush to hit nearly .300. Piniella hit .314. Willie Randolph got hurt in the middle of September and a kid named Brian Doyle came out of the bushes to play like hell; he'd end up hitting .438 in the World Series, and no one would have squawked if he'd been named Series MVP instead of Bucky Dent. Nettles was Nettles, chipping in dingers and catching everything from shortstop to the third-base line.

Everything broke our way, including a newspaper strike that hit New York's major papers in the middle of August.

Now I've always thought I had a pretty good relationship with the New York press overall. By the time the '78 season came around, I felt I'd finally learned enough, experienced enough in my career to handle the press with confidence in New York and thus everyplace else. It took me until I was thirty-one years old, but there it was. I treated the writers as people; for the most part, they treated me the same way. I was still going to get fried every now and again, but I had come to expect that. Robert Ward had, of course, done it to me in *Sport.* A guy named Murray Olderman had done the same thing in *Sport* back in 1974; Olderman decided that it was hypocritical to have a Bible and a girl in your house at the same time. Very enlightened thinking.

But basically I liked a hell of a lot more writers than I didn't like, which made it easier when personality conflicts did come up on the Yankee beat. Some I never got along with. Some never wanted to give me credit as a ballplayer. There were always a few who were going to take Martin's side or Steinbrenner's side if it came down to that. Part of the game. You could get yourself crazy if you tried to understand the mind set of every writer.

If someone could be wary and open at the same time, that's the way I was with the New York press. I can remember telling Matt Merola, "If they want to get you in New York, they *will* get you." That was my first year with the Yankees. I realized right away that it was a whole new game from the one I'd played as a visiting player. When you only came into New York twice a year, the writers would treat you like a visiting potentate. When you were around every day, you had to watch out that it didn't turn into a bad marriage.

I just decided the bottom line was this: The press couldn't stop me from playing well. And I've always believed that enough good days at work could turn around anyone's bad opinion.

Not everyone in pinstripes had this sort of attitude, however. On the whole, the relationship between the Yankees and the media was an adversary one, to the extreme. It was constant sparring and it was wearing. During my playing days Billy always promoted an adversary relationship between his players and the press. He told us never to trust them and who to talk to and who not to. The result was that the media didn't really help the situation with the Yankees in 1977 and 1978. Looking back, there was fault on both sides. There was just so much going on with us every day. It made the guys covering the beat on a regular basis become more and more competitive. They all wanted to deal with controversy, and the more they gave their editors, the more their editors seemed to want. Headlines became a drug. The writers were the dealers. The sports editors were the junkies.

If the *Daily News* got a big headline one day about George or Billy or me, then the *Post* wanted a bigger one the next day. And on and on. The press could soothe or inflame, depending on the day and the day's events. One player would find himself in a hot story, another player would respond, then whatever that hot story happened to be, it would take on a life of its own for three days, or four, or a week. Those stories get lost in my memory. I'm sure if I went through the back newspapers today, I'd be amazed at some of the things that were taken so seriously. What I remember best are headlines black as night and tall as the Empire State Building.

Right up until the strike.

Then they were gone. Even if we had been bringing a lot of the trouble on ourselves, we couldn't do it anymore without papers and headlines. See, controversy is a little like the tree falling in the forest: If no one can see it or hear it, hey, maybe it didn't happen. Maybe we would have won without a newspaper strike. Maybe Lemon's presence and the way we were playing ball would have kept us from slipping back into the "I-say-you-say" games.

But the fact is that the clubhouse was a more relaxed place after the strike (which would last through the World Series) than it had been before.

Obviously, it helped.

In the middle of the season, I told Tom Boswell of the *Washington Post* that if the Red Sox kept playing the way they were playing, we might need a hot rod to catch them.

But we caught them. We even managed to get ahead three and a half games with fourteen left. Then we slipped just enough for them to catch us in the 162nd game. So it would be Yankees–Red Sox in Fenway Park. Monday, October 2, 1978. One game. Winner take all. American League East. I loved it.

Afterward, some people would call the playoff the greatest game ever played. But that was for the writers and the fans. Ballplayers don't think that way. Just don't. It's like I said, You don't know you've made history until you read about it somewhere.

It was some baseball game, though.

The big question for us after we lost to the Indians on the last Sunday of the regular season was, Who pitches tomorrow? Guidry had pitched on Thursday night, and Guidry liked to pitch with four days' rest.

The big question didn't live long.

As we were all getting dressed and packed for the flight to Boston, Guidry walked into Lemon's office and said, "I'll take the

ball." That's all there was to it. I'll take the ball. It was like something out of an old war movie, Patton or somebody like that looking
around at the troops and basically saying, "Okay, boys, let's go."
It's the only way it could go. This thin little guy the writers called
"Lou'siana Lightnin' " had been the leader all season. When everything else had been falling apart, he just kept quiet and kept winning. Again, he was the truest Yankee of all. The next season, when
Gossage got hurt in the shower fight with Cliff Johnson, Guidry
went out to the bullpen by choice because he thought he could do
the team the most good there. He never got the credit he deserved
for that one. He is a winner, and he always managed to get the job
done with a quiet mixture of humility and pride.

Gimme the ball. Let me spit a little tobacco. Here come the
fastballs and sliders. Hell of a man . . . Ron Guidry.

The Red Sox–Yankee rivalry probably starts with the fact that
the Red Sox had Babe Ruth and all but gave him away to the
Yankees in 1920. There's the geographic proximity of the cities
added to the cultural differences, and there is also the jealousy
factor—the Yankees always won the World Series and the Red Sox
never won the World Series. The passions of the fans, in this case,
are definitely transmitted to the players. The Yankees and Red Sox
do not like each other. It's the closest thing in this generation to
the old New York Giants–Brooklyn Dodgers traditional rivalry.

Mike Torrez was pitching for the Red Sox, and we were glad.
Torrez, of course, had been with us the year before, then he played
out his contract as a free agent and went to the Red Sox, which was
the baseball equivalent of leaving the Hatfields to become a McCoy.
And when Torrez left, he hadn't had many good things to say about
any of us.

Anyway, we wanted to get him.

It took a while. It was a beautiful day in Boston, an Indian
summer day. Fenway was packed. Both teams had come in with 99
wins, and only one was going to leave with 100. I'd torn a fingernail
off a couple of days before, so I couldn't play the outfield. Piniella
was in right (that would be fairly important late in the game). I was
DHing. First time up, I hit a bullet to left-center, but the wind
helped keep it in the park. Long out. Next time up, I hit what I
thought was a rocket to right, but the wind got that one, too. I
started to think the day wasn't so beautiful after all. I thought to
myself, "Uh-oh, my shit ain't falling." Guidry was doing his thing,

dead on, but by the seventh we were losing 2–0. Torrez, who hadn't won a game in six weeks, was making us look bad.

There were two out and two on in the seventh when Bucky Dent came up. On the second pitch Torrez threw him, Bucky fouled one off his foot and went down. No one was saying much in the dugout while the trainer went out to spray some pain-killer on Bucky's foot. We were all watching Bucky. Except for Mickey Rivers.

He was staring out at Bucky's bat.

"He cracked his bat," Mickey said.

Someone, I forget who, said, "What?"

Rivers repeated, "He cracked his bat." Then he went down to the rack, got one of his own bats (Bucky had been using Mickey's bats), walked up the steps and gave it to the bat boy.

It was sort of significant.

Because on the next pitch, Torrez threw Bucky Dent a fastball down the middle, and Bucky hit this long fly ball to left that just happened to stay in the air long enough to land in the screen over the Green Monster; that just happened to become one of the most famous home runs in the history of baseball. It looked like a routine out for Carl Yastrzemski at first. He drifted toward the line, looking up the whole way. Then at the last second, Yastrzemski's legs buckled, like someone had hit him from behind with a bat. Mickey Rivers's bat maybe.

I said out loud, "That's it!"

3–2.

To this day, I remember how quiet Fenway Park got. Like a funeral home. Steinbrenner and a lot of his friends were seated in a box next to us, and I could hear them whooping and clapping as Bucky rounded the bases. That was all I could hear. They were the only ones moving in the whole park.

Damn.

3–2. The little guy had turned it all around with his borrowed bat. Rivers walked after that and Thurman doubled him home, and it was 4–2. By the eighth, Bob Stanley was pitching for the Sox. He threw me a fastball down in the middle, and I hit it into the seats in dead center: 5–2. Wind didn't get that one. A hurricane wasn't going to get that one. I called it a "Prudential homer" afterward. Insurance home run. Little did I know.

I was pretty excited after the homer. As I headed back to the dugout, I even slapped Steinbrenner five before I got to my team-mates.

I yelled, "Nice to be in the game!"

But it wasn't over yet. The Red Sox got two in the eighth off Gossage, who'd come in to replace Guidry, whose arm and heart had finally gotten tired. So it was 5–4 going into the ninth. It had come down to that. Gossage against Boston. One-run lead. Top of the order coming up for the Red Sox. Repeat, some baseball game. *Damn,* what a game!

Rick Burleson walked with one out in the bottom of the ninth. Jerry Remy was next, and he ripped one to right. When it came off the bat, it looked like a routine shot to Piniella. From the dugout, it looked like a routine shot the whole way, except in the dugout we didn't know this one very important thing.

Piniella had lost the ball in the sun.

In the clubhouse afterward, Piniella told me, "I didn't see the damn thing until it landed about ten feet in front of me."

But he played it like he had, standing his ground almost casually. We were all watching Piniella and so was Burleson, who had to hold up between first and second because Piniella looked for all the world like he was going to catch the damn thing. It was only when the ball hit that you could see he was in trouble. Lou put both arms out, like he was trying to stop traffic. He just wanted the ball to hit him somewhere so it wouldn't get by him. If it gets by him, it rolls to the wall, Remy and Burleson run all day, and we lose.

The ball hit Lou someplace. Right in the glove.

Who knows what would have happened if I'd been in right instead of Lou? Maybe I would have picked the ball out of the sun. And maybe I'd have lost it the same way Lou did. And if I had, the bounce would have come to me on my bare-handed side, instead of my glove side. If. And if. And if.

But Piniella was there and I was in the dugout and he caught the ball and Burleson had to stop at second. For two months, we had been doing everything right and now, even if accidentally, we were still doing things right in the bottom of the ninth of the biggest game of the year; the biggest game there had been in a long, long time.

Piniella in the clubhouse later, smoking a cigarette, sipping on a beer: "Hey, we're not the world champions for nothing, right?"

So it was first and second. One out. Jim Rice and Yastrzemski left for the Red Sox. Rice was the MVP of the American League that year. Yastrzemski was Yastrzemski. Fenway wasn't quiet anymore.

Gossage got Rice to fly deep to Piniella in right. Lou had this one all the way. Burleson tagged after the catch and went to third; if he'd gotten to third on Remy's hit, Rice's ball would have been a sacrifice fly, the game would have been tied, and we might still be playing.

If.

But Burleson was on third. Remy had stayed at first. So it had come down to this: Gossage against Yastrzemski. It was no time for mixed emotions because we were too close to pulling the whole thing off, but I had been a Yaz fan for a long time. He had played his whole career for the Red Sox, he had won the Triple Crown, he had been an MVP in '67, he had made all the plays in left. Hell, he *was* the Boston Red Sox. The only thing he'd never done was win a World Series. Now he had the chance to make one more run —one *last* run—if he could do something with a fastball from Goose.

Goose popped him up.

Nettles caught it on the third-base line.

As we came pouring out of the dugout, I could see Thurman running toward Gossage like he'd never had bad knees in his life, jumping into the Goose's arms.

We'd done it. We'd made one last pass with the dice after making pass after pass down the stretch. All during the race, all during September and into October, we'd thought we were the better team. We felt we would win. Did the Sox choke? Choking is a very strong word, especially when you try to apply it to a game as great as that one was. Dandy Don Meredith once described choking as "a cold rush to the heart." I don't know if the Red Sox felt the cold rush that day. You'd have to ask them. I know we didn't; it wasn't in our nature. I always thought we had that psychological edge. In the end, there wasn't that sense of elation or magic, because we really felt we'd done what we were supposed to do. We knew after a while that we were going to win. Guidry and Goose. Thurman and me. Bucky and Nettles and Piniella. And old Lem. You make your own destiny sometimes. We had gotten into the habit of doing it in Oakland. Now we had done it in New York.

Winning can be a habit just like anything else. I don't think we could have won in 1978 if we hadn't won in '77.

The Red Sox didn't know how.

Piniella was right in the end. We weren't the world champions for nothing.

The playoffs and then the World Series could have been anti-climaxes after the playoff game with the Red Sox. After all, it was the Royals again in the playoffs, followed by the Dodgers again in the Series. Replay of '77.

But after the comeback, we weren't about to leave the season with anything less than the big trophy. We took care of the Royals in four games, with Guidry—of course—getting the clincher at the Stadium.

There were no repeats of the '77 dramatics in the League Championship Series. I hit .462 with a couple of dingers and six RBI in the four games. One of the dingers just happened to be off a left-hander named Paul Splittorff.

Yup. Loved it.

The same Splittorff Billy just had to sit me down against twelve months before. Uh, good night, Billy, wherever you are.

The Series really turned in the third game, on Friday afternoon in New York. Catfish pitched a superb game for us except for one tiny detail: George Brett hit three home runs off him. It was the strangest thing. Cat was the Cat of old up and down the Royals lineup except for George Brett. Bam. Bam. Bam. It was one of those days when you wondered why Brett isn't the best baseball player in the world. He's got the sweetest stroke this side of Rod Carew, he can hit for average and for power, he's big and young and strong. In 1980 he hit .390, made the best run in years at .400, and ripped off the MVP award from me while playing in only 117 games.

We won the third game despite Brett's dingers, thanks to ol' No. 15, Thurman Munson. He hit one into the monument area in left-center off Doug Bird, one of the hardest shots I've ever seen from a right-handed hitter in the Stadium. It was a 450-footer easy, and it gave us a 6–5 victory.

Then came the Series. We took the Dodgers in six. Guidry got a win. Gossage got a win. Catfish got the win in the clincher. Brian Doyle hit his .438. Bucky hit .417 and won the MVP award for the

Series, though I think that was as much for the Fenway homer as for anything else. Mr. October wasn't too shabby either. I hit .391 with two dingers, and I was involved in three of the four most memorable events of the 1978 World Series.

Quick now. A World Series in four acts.

ACT ONE: We lost the first game to none other than Tommy John. In the second game I came up in the ninth with the tying run on second, the go-ahead run on first, and two out. I'd already had three RBI and a double. Pitching for the Dodgers was a big strong right-handed kid named Bob Welch, who'd come up from the minors in the middle of the season and won seven or eight games for the Dodgers down the stretch as a starter. He was in the bullpen for the Series, and our scouts had told us he could throw as hard as anybody, that he was one of the great prospects in the big leagues.

In memory, it seems like the battle between Welch and me took half an hour. He wasn't going to walk me. I was going to take the kid all the way downtown if I could, all the way down Sunset Boulevard. He was going to throw fastballs. I was going to take fastball cuts. It was strength against strength and I had my .44's loaded. It was the highest degree of intensity I've ever brought to a single confrontation.

At least a confrontation I lost.

There are moments that stand out in your career, moments that you don't have to be objective about, moments that you know are bigger than life. Sounds like a cliché, right? Bigger than life? That's what Jackson versus Welch was. The noise of the crowd at Dodger Stadium just drenched the two of us, and this from a baseball crowd that usually sits on its hands and waits for Vin Scully, the Dodger announcer, to tell them what they're seeing. The usual Dodger Stadium crowd is about 50,000 people and 40,000 transistor radios.

This was different. It was so clear, the battle. Welch was trying to throw fastballs to my weakness, up and in. I was trying to get a fastball down the middle, because I knew if I could get one, I was going to hit a ball so hard it would kill somebody in the stands. I was so tuned into the moment. I could *feel* how hard Welch was trying to throw. I could sense the fear in the Dodgers, who the previous October had seen me hit the three dingers on the last night and leave them all for dead.

At one-and-one, he got a fastball up and in, and I took a Reggie cut the likes of which you've seen, one of those roundhouse swings that nearly takes me down and ends up with me in a crouch, my face contorted. I've seen the films. Even I get excited. Even when I miss.

I missed this time.

I don't remember the crowd noise building; I just remember it being there, all over us, all the time. Total drama is what it was. I didn't look at Howser down at third. Didn't look for any signs. What kind of sign is there for moments like these? Thumbs up? This is what I lived for as a baseball player. This was the event. We were the event. So was the kid on the mound. Was I going to be Mr. October again? Was the kid going to gun me down?

He threw me two more fastballs, and I took two more huge swings and fouled both of them off.

He wasted a fastball away and it was two and two.

He got a fastball up again, and I fouled it off again.

Another ball. Full count.

Another foul, and another.

Another big cut. Another foul.

Then he beat me. No excuse here, but Bucky broke from second as Welch pitched, and I lost my concentration. It was the right thing with a full count, two outs, and us down a run. I should have been expecting it, but I wasn't. For the first time since I'd stepped into the batter's box, I stopped focusing on Welch. Just for that instant. It was as if I had been working on this complicated equation, coming closer to getting it bit by bit, then miscalculated at the very end.

I swung and missed. (Got beat.)

Strike three.

Ballgame.

Damn, I was frustrated. It was one of the few times I showed emotion on the field. After walking back to the dugout, I flung my bat against the wall. Lem yelled at me to knock it off and cool down. That brought me back to my senses.

In the clubhouse, I kept it simple. I said, "Give him credit. He beat me."

ACT TWO: Back in New York with a full day to think about being down oh-and-two, we came together. I remember walking back to my apartment on Tuesday, the day of Game Three, with

Tony Rolfe. It was after breakfast. I said, "Guidry's pitching tonight. Which means we'll win. And if we win tonight, I say we'll sweep four and win the World Series."

This night belonged to Graig Nettles. His incredible performance kept us from going down 3–0 in the World Series, after which extinction would have been only a matter of time.

Just as Piniella's glove was in the right place against Jerry Remy in the playoff game against the Sox, Nettles's glove was there again and again in Game Three. Nettles played the greatest game I've ever seen a third baseman play. The fact that it came with us down 0–2 in games made it that much more amazing. Nettles just kept diving toward the line or toward the shortstop hole and taking hits and runs away from the Dodgers. Ultimately he took away a win. We won the game 5–1, but it was estimated afterward that Nettles's glove cost the Dodgers at least three runs, maybe more. Maybe as many as seven. In Game Three in '78, Nettles did as much to get the Yankees another World Series as any of us ever did. Bucky. Brian Doyle. Me. Catfish. Any of us.

Lem pretty much summed things up afterward. "I don't think anyone has ever played third base any better than Graig did tonight," is what Lem said.

Nettles got a line drive from Davey Lopes. Diving.

He went to his knees to stop a shot from Reggie Smith, got up, threw him out.

He later kept a bullet from Smith in the infield and kept Smith from getting a double.

He zipped to his right on one from Steve Garvey, whirled around, his back to the plate, righted himself, and forced Smith at second.

The next inning—I think it was the next inning, although Nettles's plays seemed to happen one after another—he made another great stop against Lopes. Again the momentum of his body whipped him around toward the outfield. Again he got the force at second. And the Dodgers didn't score.

Never saw anything like it. Not from Brooks Robinson, and I always thought he was the best. Not from anybody. When Lopes came up to the plate for his last at-bat that night, he waved a white towel at Nettles, like a flag of surrender.

The Dodgers led 2–1 in games instead of 3–0, which would have put us in the archives. Nettles had broken their hearts with his play at third; the next day we beat them in extra innings to break their backs. I'll never nominate Nettles for the Nobel Prize, but the man could play third base with anybody. That game was the best display of defense I've ever seen. I mean, even Casper Weinberger would have been proud.

ACT THREE: The Dodgers scored first in Game Four when Reggie Smith hit a three-run dinger off Ed Figueroa. Lou Piniella finally won it for us in the tenth with a single off Bob Welch. In between, I got what the writers called the first Sacrifice Thigh in the history of what I call the Fall Classic.

Here's what happened.

It was the sixth inning, and I'd just knocked in Roy White with a single to make the score 3–1. Thurman was on second, I was on first, there was one out, Tommy John was pitching for the Dodgers, Lou Piniella was up. Lou hit a lazy liner toward Dodger shortstop Bill Russell. It looked for a second like Russell caught the ball on the fly, then dropped it. There was some question later that he might have dropped it on purpose. No matter. He picked it up, cut across the bag at second, and forced me.

Where was I? Halfway between first and second. I'd frozen when it looked like Russell caught the ball, because I didn't want to be doubled off first and take us out of the inning.

Anyway, here comes Bill Russell across the bag with the ball in his throwing hand about to get a double play anyway, because Lou Piniella runs like a dump truck.

Except that I was in Russell's way. The throw came dead down the imaginary baseline between second and first, which is where R. Jackson stood frozen. Now I didn't put the whole situation together in that instant, and I didn't know how everything would come out in the end, but instinct did tell me this: Right then it was better to get hit by Russell's throw than *not* to get hit by Russell's throw.

It's like I said, winning can get to be a habit. Habits breed good instincts. I'd brought all of that with me from Oakland where we made the right plays *all* the time just from sheer repetition. So I brought a little Oakland to the '78 Series.

I held my ground and my right hip deflected Russell's throw. Piniella made it to first safely, and we were still in the inning. Thurman, who'd slowed up at third, came home when the deflected throw from Russell got away from Steve Garvey. It was 3–2.

Contrary to popular belief, I never moved into the throw. Just a discreet little shift of the hip. Wasn't like a stripper's bump-and-grind. They would have called me for interference if it had been too obvious. More like someone gently pushing shut a kitchen drawer. The Dodgers saw it differently, of course. They saw cheating. Tommy Lasorda came out and went crazy. It was a funny bit—for everybody except Dodger fans—on that year's World Series film. Garvey got as mad as he can get, and so did Tommy John, a gentle man who is one of my good friends now. And the umpire stood fast and said it was just one of those funny baseball accidents—Sacrifice Thigh (only because Sacrifice Hip doesn't have quite the same ring to it).

I thought I explained it very well to the press after the game, which tied the Series at two games apiece.

"I was just walking down the street," I said, "and this baseball came up and bit me in the leg."

ACT FOUR: The last game of the season, the one that won us our second straight Series, was just like a lot of others down the stretch. Catfish started and got the win. Goose came in and mopped up. Bucky Dent and Brian Doyle? They went six-for-eight between them.

The last two runs came on a dinger from me.

Off Bob Welch.

Off a fastball.

We led Game Six from the second inning on, and by the time Goose came along to sit on a 5–2 lead, we knew the Dodgers weren't going to come back. There wasn't going to be a Game Seven at Dodger Stadium. When Welch came into the game, the last question of the baseball season was whether I was going to get even.

I didn't know whether I was, but I couldn't wait to get to the bat rack. My teammates couldn't wait for me to get into the batter's box.

Thurman: "Dues day, Jack."

Even Nettles: "Time to pay the kid back, Reggie."

Catfish, with a big smile on his face, using the old Oakland nickname: "Get him, Buck."

Business didn't take long. There'd been a gap of six days and nearly four games, and we'd turned the World Series upside-down, but I felt like it was just a continuation of the same at-bat from Game Two. I was just going to get a couple more swings. Didn't matter that the Series was nearly over. Welch knew it. I knew it.

This was between him and me. Me and him. The two of us. Everybody in Dodger Stadium knew it. On the first pitch, he threw me the fastball out over the plate that I'd wanted the previous Wednesday night. I hit it toward whatever those mountains are that form the backdrop at Dodger Stadium. When I crossed the plate, I gave a little wave of my cap to the Dodger fans.

I figured they must be getting sick of me. Two years in a row, I'd thrown the last bit of dirt on their team with a dinger.

Fourteen games behind. End up tied with the Red Sox anyway. One-game playoff at Fenway. Win it. Lost the first two games of the World Series. Win four straight after that, something no team had done before that. All the time going from win to win like the mailman, like each new win was part of our appointed rounds and winning the World Series was the last stop on the route.

And it came on the heels of 1977. It was like getting a twenty-minute coffee break between world wars, both of which you won.

Go back over the whole history of baseball. Think back on all the great stories. Miracle Braves. Amazin' Mets. Cardinals catching the Phillies in '64. Giants catching the Dodgers in '51. Throw in every great Yankee team from the past, and the A's, and the Big Red Machine. Chew on all of them for a while and then chew on this: There have never been back-to-back championships like the ones we won in New York in 1977 and 1978. Never has a team had to dress and undress in public the way we did. Never has there been such silliness and anger and talent thrown into 300-plus baseball games. The A's had been colorful, but compared to what we had in the Bronx my first two years with the Yankees, the A's had played in black and white. The Yankees were big screen and technicolor, mostly because it was New York. The A's were a better team, but their movie was shown on one of those little old TV sets like we had in Wyncote. Steinbrenner and Martin and Jackson. Nettles and Munson and Randolph. Guidry and Gossage. Dent and Doyle. Rivers and Cat and ol' Lem.

And two World Series in a row.

As for myself, I didn't feel the same sense of relief and redemption that I'd felt at the end of the '77 season. As bizarre as the early and middle parts of '78 were, as much as we all felt like we'd landed in the cuckoo's nest, the first one I'd flown over, nothing was ever going to compare with my first Yankee season if we're talking about ordeals here. But I did walk away from the '78 season with my personal credentials as Mr. October intact, and I did feel fairly certain that for the rest of my Yankee contract I'd be left alone to play and hit, because I'd shown them two years running the kind of playing and hitting I could do when left alone.

In the 1977 postseason, I was in eleven games. I hit .306 with five homers and nine RBI. In the World Series, I broke nine batting records and tied a bunch of others.

In the 1978 postseason, I was better. No brag. Fact. In eleven games, I hit .400. Hit four dingers. Drove in fourteen runs.

I was a lousy bunter and a born liar, but I had ten Yankee home runs in two Yankee Octobers. And I had two more World Series rings, which made it five for all of you at home keeping score.

18
THE REAL WORLD

The first tragedy of the '79 season came just ten days after we'd won the '78 World Series. While the rest of us were sitting back and smiling a lot, having a few beers, and letting the scope of what we'd accomplished sink in, Bob Lemon's youngest son Jerry was killed in a Jeep accident. It was said that Jerry was particularly close to Lem, a chip off the old block. I didn't know about that. I just know that when I called Lem on the telephone with my condolences, he sounded like a man whose heart had been cut out, and in the wake of a managing thrill that had to rank right up there with all his great accomplishments as a player.

Seasons can go wrong for so many different reasons, especially when a team is coming off two world championships and what people were calling the best comeback that had ever been. A season can go wrong because guys get hurt or get old, or because the big guns just don't produce. Sometimes another team comes along and is just plain better. Sometimes there's complacency, the we'll-turn-it-on-when-we-have-to syndrome. Sometimes it's a combination.

In 1979, here was the awful combination:

Jerry Lemon died, affecting Lem's spirit.

Goose Gossage ripped the ligaments in this thumb during a silly locker-room brawl with Cliff Johnson.

George decided to replace Lem with Billy ahead of the 1980 timetable.

Thurman Munson crashed his plane and died.

In retrospect, we were lucky to finish fourth. The final standings were the least important aspect of this 1979 season. With all the craziness off the field in '77 and '78, we always had baseball— the game—to bail us out. In a strange way, it was the game itself that was our reality, certainly our haven of sanity.

With Thurman's death, though, it seemed like there was no sanity left. Anywhere.

It was obvious in spring training that Lem was a changed man. At a time when we were all feeling fat and confident after '78, Lem just let us go along feeling fat and confident. His attitude seemed to be, "Hell, it doesn't matter that much anyway." He had been such a happy-go-lucky type the year before. Have a drink. Have a laugh. Make out the lineup card. Watch us win. Nothing bothered him much. But in Ft. Lauderdale there was a sadness about him. It should have been a good time for everyone as we tried to go for three in a row.

Except that Jerry Lemon had passed away, and with that something had died in his dad. . . . Understandable.

Up until '79, Lem had never tried to impress anybody with the fact that he was a big, strong, tough man. Still, you knew it was there. You knew Lem wasn't going to take any shit. That was it basically. He wouldn't get into arguments with you. He wouldn't battle you. He wouldn't raise his voice. If he had to lay a fine on someone, he did it quietly. Then it was over, but the guy who got the fine had the sense that he better not mess with Lem again. But as soon as he got to Lauderdale, I could see that Lem was in a difficult transition period, that winning and losing baseball games was not as important as it had been.

I remember sitting with him one day in his office, and Lem saying, "Meat, I just wonder if it's worth it anymore. It's different now. My heart's not in it."

With this awful sadness in his eyes.

What do you say? I told him to hang with us, maybe we could

give him something back for the way he'd saved us the previous summer.

I hoped that I would never have to go through what he was going through, especially starting a 162-game season.

We didn't give Lem anything back. The season was just eleven games old when we lost Goose. Lyle had been traded to Texas during the off-season so we all knew Goose had to be it in '79. That was no problem—we were positive—because it was clear that Goose was just the best relief pitcher in the game, a fire-breathing dragon with all the guts in the world and a fast-ball to match.

After a game with the Orioles, we were all sitting around, and I started kidding Cliff about not ever being able to hit Goose when they were both in the National League (Cliff had come to us from the Astros in '77). Cliff was known as Heathcliff, which seemed to fit him for some reason. He was a hell of a pinchhitter, a pretty good DH. He played some backup first base for us and some backup catcher, and it seemed like he was always running into someone— an umpire, a teammate, someone. In the clubhouse, Heathcliff was always up for a good time.

Goose had a win and a couple of saves, something like that, already in the season, and he looked even more overpowering than he had the season before.

So I said, "Cliff, you must be awful glad you don't have to hit against Goose anymore."

Joking.

Cliff was walking toward the bathroom at the time. He said, "Man, that is bullshit. I used to hit the big guy pretty good. *He's* lucky he don't have to face *me* anymore."

Piniella started hooting, and so did Thurman and I. This sort of thing goes on all the time in the clubhouse, by the way. Ballplayers always like to say that they were invincible against teammates who'd been opponents in the past.

"Hey, man, how'd you do against Nolan Ryan?"

"Ryan? Sheee-it. I used to *own* his ass."

Doesn't mean anything.

Gossage waited until Cliff left, then he said, "Shit. He couldn't touch me. I used to strike him out *all* the time."

We all hooted a little more. Everyone was laughing, so I decided to agitate a little more, never dreaming that I was lighting a match to a gasoline can. Cliff was in the shower—the whole thing would have been hilarious, considering the setting, if there had been no fight—and I said, "Cliff, Goose says you couldn't hit him with a broom."

Then I headed for the trainer's room.

The next thing I heard was a lot of shouting from the shower room. Apparently when Goose walked in, Cliff asked him what he said about his hitting, Goose repeated what he'd said, they had some words, they started shoving each other and pushing, and they both went down. Hardly out of the ordinary, at least from my own experiences in Oakland. Like I've said before, when there was a fight in Oakland—something that seemed to happen often enough —no one even looked up from their card games.

This time was different. Johnson is a huge 6'4", 230. Goose is a big man from Colorado who goes 6'3" and about 220. We're talking about superheavyweights here. And when heavies get to scuffling in the shower on a slick floor, bad things can happen.

A bad thing happened. Goose came out of there holding his right hand—his pitching hand—and swearing. The next day we found out that he'd torn ligaments around the thumb and that he'd be gone for about three months.

No Goose.

Three months. The season.

Shit.

It was natural for us to start this particular season at a leisurely pace, but now that leisurely pace began to leisurely work itself into a disaster, and we didn't have a manager who wanted to put up with it all. Lem was still mesmerized. We weren't playing all that well (we thought, hell, we'll get them when we have to!). Guidry, who'd had that unbelievable season in '78, offered to go to the bullpen to replace Goose, and Lem shrugged and said, "Whatever you say." We were still the champs, of course. Record books said so. But in April and May, we were pretty much a .500 ballclub, struggling just to stay in the race, moving from second place to third, back to second, back to third, occasionally into fourth.

Then on the second of June, I got hurt, too. It was the strangest injury of my career. We were playing the White Sox at home. It was the ninth inning, and I was just jogging off the field with Mickey Rivers. Suddenly I felt this pop in my calf. Like someone stuck a knife in there. Just jogging off the field. Wasn't trying to get from

third to home in a playoff game. Wasn't running into a wall or
trying to stretch a single into a double.

I'd be out nearly a month. So now I was gone, and Goose was
gone, and Guidry was in the bullpen, and the Orioles were playing
. . . well . . . Oriole baseball, which is always pretty damn good.

And Mr. Steinbrenner was getting antsy, as only he could. No
one knew at the time—early June—that George was having phone
conversations with Billy and secret meetings with Billy about him
coming back early to manage.

In the middle of June, we made a three-city road trip to Kansas
City, Minneapolis and Texas. Again, we were playing listless, mediocre baseball. George came on the trip to watch. On a Friday night
in Arlington, he sat in the stands and invited me to sit with him
since I was on the disabled list. I could see that George was being
his impatient self. By then the rumors about Billy had begun to
swirl in earnest, but none of us were paying all that much attention
to them. Even with all that had happened, all the injuries, none of
the players were ready to hit the panic button.

We'd come from fourteen back, Jack. We figured we could do
it again if we had to. Lem would pull up his bootstraps and we'd
start winning.

Ed Figueroa pitched for us that Friday night, the Rangers
racked him pretty good, and we lost. George sat in the stands and
criticized just about everyone during the game. There was a ball hit
to Randolph and Figueroa was late covering first; George went a
little batty.

"I can't believe what's happening with this team," he said.
"Mental mistakes, I won't tolerate mental mistakes."

I just looked at him and said, "George, the guy made a mistake. No big deal. Happens. It's early yet. We'll be all right."

"No, damnit," he said. "There's something very wrong with
this team. There has been from the beginning of the season."

I tried to explain the circumstances—I didn't think you had
to be a Rhodes scholar to understand the team's problems—and
how I really did think we'd be in the race later on once we got
healthy and got Goose back. He wasn't hearing any of it.

All of a sudden he turned to me and said, "Do you think I
should fire Lemon?"

The question wasn't a shock because of the rumors. But I was
a little rattled by the matter-of-fact way he put it to me.

I said, "Hell no, George. You can't do that to the man after what he did for you last year. You just can't. This is his last year anyway. You can't do that. Give him a little time. We've only played sixty damn games. Don't panic."

We watched the rest of the game. George mumbled and grumbled.

Never once did he mention Billy Martin.

But Billy was already back, for all intents and purposes. It was after midnight when the phone in my hotel room started ringing. Writers calling. "Billy's coming back early, Reggie. What do you think about that?"

I asked if it was fact.

They all said it was.

I called Lem's room and told him I wanted to talk to him.

In a tired voice, he said, "Come ahead, Meat. I think I know what you want to talk about."

He was wearing his pajamas when he opened the door. He didn't look defeated. He just didn't look like Lem.

I sat down and said, "Is it true?"

Lem just smiled at me. "It's true, Meat. They're kicking me upstairs. Except they're really sending me home. Maybe it's best for everyone."

He asked me if I wanted a drink. I said no. We sat there for a while. Here was this big, proud man, one of the most admired pitchers of his time, a manager whose skills were never really appreciated by George or anyone else, sitting in his funny pajamas in the middle of the night in a hotel room in Texas, drinking his drink and talking about going home to California where the memories would, unfortunately, be more bad than good. For a long time.

"Every whore has his price, Meat," he said quietly. "I guess I found mine. They're going to keep paying me, so I just take it like a man and keep my mouth shut."

Every whore has his price. I was starting to think that if I stuck around the Yankees and kept watching George write this crazy script again and again, maybe I had mine, too.

I went over and shook Lem's hand.

"I'm proud to have played for you," I said. "You're a hell of a man, and you deserved a hell of a lot better."

He sure as hell did.

I wanted to talk to George Steinbrenner. I went back to my room and called him in his. It was nearly three o'clock in the morning, but I thought, Screw him. I hope I wake his ass up.

I didn't mess around when I heard his voice on the other end. It was no time to observe boss-employee etiquette.

"Why the hell didn't you tell me?" I asked.

He asked, "What do you mean?"

"You know damn well what I mean, George. You sit with me the whole game, you ask me about Lem, and the whole fuckin' time you've got your mind made up to bring Billy back. Maybe it's your business what you do with your managers, the way you use them and throw them away and bring them back. And it is up to them if they let themselves get used that way. But you had to know what this news would do to me, and you couldn't even give me the courtesy of telling me yourself?"

George didn't mince any words either.

"I don't need any advice from you on how I run my ballclub!"

"Well, let me tell you something," I said, raising my own voice. "You better make another move right now. You better trade me because if you don't, I plan to be hurt all year long. 'Cause I've played for that man for the last time."

George: "When I want your advice about how to run my baseball team, I'll ask for it."

I told George I needed a few days off, that I needed to go home to get my head straight. He said no way. That if I left the team I'd be fined or suspended.

And he hung up on me.

I called Gary Walker and Steve Kay because I was determined to go home despite George's threats. But they convinced me to go on to New York.

I would have just liked for George to have told me what the hell was happening so I could have prepared myself mentally. After all, in '77 and '78 we were in everything together—at least while we were winning we were together.

I was getting tired of him stabbing me in the back, no matter what I did for him on the field, no matter how much we won, no matter how many attendance records we broke.

He'd stabbed me when he staged his grandstand play with Billy on Old-timers Day.

Now, by bringing him back early, he was just twisting the knife.

There is no great story to tell about the Jackson-Martin relationship over the rest of the 1979 season. When my leg healed, I came back and played. I talked it over with my dad, who laid it all out for me one day when he and I were visiting my brother Joe, who was stationed at Fort Dix in New Jersey at the time.

"You've got a contract. No one made you sign it. Play ball the best you can and live up to it."

That was that. When I came back, Billy and I had a reasonably cordial meeting and agreed that we'd both try to get along this time. He seemed all used up by then anyway. It seemed obvious to me, probably was obvious to him, that he was going to let George pull his strings any time George wanted to, because that's how much Billy wanted to be manager of the Yankees. George played the tune. Billy danced. It's still that way. It will always be that way. In that way, Lem was so right. Every whore has his price. Billy knows that best of all.

Al Rosen quit about a month after Billy came back. He was one who finally did have enough, and he decided to leave on his own terms. Bob Lemon was his friend, and Rosen couldn't stand what George did to Lem—after all Rosen had recommended Lem his long-time friend for the job—so Rosen just walked away from the job of being president, which around the Yankees isn't a job at all. There is only one president, one general manager, one p.r. man, one player personnel guy, one commander-in-chief around the Yankees, and that man is George. The people who hold the other titles are just punching bags. Rosen couldn't take that anymore. He was embarrassed about what had happened to Lem, humiliated. He had talked Lem into coming back to manage us in '78. He thought Lem deserved to be treated like a man. Al himself wanted to be treated like a man—not an unreasonable request. But when George just went ahead and brought Billy back early, it was clear to Al that in George's eyes he wasn't respected.

Al worked hard. He traveled with us when things weren't going well. We all knew what his credentials had been as a ballplayer. All he wanted was respect. All he wanted was to be treated

like the professional he was. George wouldn't do that. We'd all
heard about George berating him in public, the same way he
berated all the people who worked for him. George never gave him
an inch, never gave him any credit.

So after Billy came back, Al said, "Enough bullshit." And was
gone.

The writers asked me about Rosen leaving. I was quoted pretty
much as saying the things I've said here, about what kind of human
being Rosen was, and why he had to leave. Because of loyalty to
his friend.

George didn't like that much.

How did I know?

He sent Billy to tell me to cool it.

"I'm just carrying a message, Reggie," Billy said. "George
wants you to stop bad-mouthing him because Rosen left. He thinks
it makes everybody look bad. Now you and I are getting along fine,
but if you could just lay low for a while, I think it would help you
out, me out, everybody."

I told him I couldn't do that. People kept asking me about Al
Rosen, and I kept telling them what I thought about Al Rosen.

The game occasionally got rough. I picked up the *Daily News*
one day, and there was a column by Dick Young saying that I was
late with payments on a $250,000 loan that George had given me
as part of my original Yankee contract. According to Young, the
story came from "a source close to Steinbrenner."

The gist of the story was that I was not only late making the
payment, but that I was in all sorts of financial straits.

Wrong.

Under the original terms, I was technically late. But after both
the '77 and '78 World Series, George and Steven Kay had sat down
and reworked some of the terms of the contract, especially the ones
that had to do with bonuses and loans. The loan payments had been
stretched out over several more years. Verbally, George had basically told Steve, "No problem. Don't even worry about it."

I hit the roof. I didn't mind when George criticized me for
missing a cutoff man or striking out with the bases loaded or
dropping a ball in the field. It didn't make me deliriously happy,
but I understood it. You play a game, you mess up in the game,
someone is always calling you to task, whether in the papers or on

television or someplace else. But now someone was making a calculated effort to discredit my character, and I was having none of
it. I wanted the whole Steinbrenner gang to understand that I
wouldn't sit still for that.

I called Matt Merola and told him to call Fugazy. I told him
to tell Fugazy to relay this general message to George:

"George, I know how much you love your reputation for being
a pillar of the community and all that. But you and I hang around
a lot of the same uptown places, like Jim McMullen's and Oren and
Aretsky's and George Martin. I have seen you there when you and
your pals are having a boy's night out. We know a lot of the same
people. I know what goes on. I want whoever it is who's spreading
these phony stories about loans and me being all burned up with
money problems to stop, or I am going to start talking."

Get the picture?

Thought you might.

So did George. Matt called Fugazy, gave him the message, and
Fugazy hung up on him. But Matt painted the picture fairly well.

The stories stopped.

I just thought it was time Mr. Steinbrenner knew that *I* knew
that we were no longer operating under the Marquis of Queensbury
rules.

It all seems so trivial now, so juvenile, so meaningless. The
death of Jerry Lemon would turn out to be only a tragic portent
for the 1979 baseball season.

Thurman Munson died during the 1979 baseball season.

19

THURMAN

I woke up with the oxygen mask slapping me gently in the face, like Martinez telling me it was time for school. It wasn't a dream, though. I was in one of the passenger seats in Thurman Munson's baby, his twin-engine Cessna Citation. . . .

I'll back up.

Thurman had convinced Graig Nettles and me to fly with him from Seattle to Anaheim in the middle of our West Coast swing. It was July 12, 1979. Five days before the All-Star break.

God, he was proud of that plane. It had the Yankees "NY" logo on the side, and he'd been using it more and more frequently that season, flying to Canton whenever he'd get an off-day, having someone fly it in on the road so he could use it when he wanted to travel by himself from stop to stop. All season long he'd been urging me to fly with him. Our wars were behind us by then, and if we weren't best friends, I at least thought of us as battle-scarred comrades who'd finally achieved a warm measure of respect and formed a basis of understanding.

I guess he'd been bugging Nettles the same way. In Seattle we both said, Fine, let's do it. We had a three-game series with the Angels coming up. Then Thurman was going to head for Canton.

There were four of us: Thurman at the controls, a copilot, Nettles, me. Thurman made a big production out of telling me where to sit. He told me later that the joke was supposed to be on me. One of the oxygen masks wasn't working too well, and during the flight he'd planned on telling me to put it on.

Problem was, when the mask came down, it was for real. While I was dozing, its mechanism was triggered involuntarily. Having a mask slap you in the face at several thousand feet works just fine as a wake-up call, though I'd always preferred to have a pretty stewardess do that.

Still a little groggy, I heard Thurman say, "Nothing in this damn thing ever works completely right." I straightened up in my seat, the grogginess a thing of the past, and noticed that the instrument panel was lit up like a Christmas tree. There was a lot of blinking going on. I am no aeronautical expert, but I own a twin-engine, which I keep in California and use mostly to hop from one business meeting to another in the off-season. I was pretty sure that what I was seeing in Thurman's Cessna was a definite excess of blinking.

I said, "Anything the matter, Captain?"

He said, "The altimeter seems to be off. I think that's why the masks came down. I've got to get this whole thing checked out during the All-Star break."

Thurman and I had a running debate about his flying. I told him that it was terrific to have a plane of his own; a private plane is one of the best possible toys for the person who can afford it. It is one of the wonderful perks that comes with success in whatever business you're in. But I told him he didn't have to fly it.

"Get yourself an old World War II pilot," I said. "Make sure he's wearing a leather flight jacket. Buy him a white scarf. Just check him out first and make sure he's learned to fly everything since Wilbur and Orville."

Thurman would grin his gruff grin and shake his head from side to side.

"I like to fly myself," he said.

Our debate always ended the same way. I wish to hell now I'd been a better debater. You think about these kinds of things afterward. When it's too late.

So there we were. Nettles and I and Thurman (how about that for a threesome?) were watching the blinking, then Thurman told us that we were just a few miles from the Orange County Airport (now known as John Wayne Airport). He said that the fog had come in and visibility wasn't good, so we might have to make one pass at the airport before landing. I refastened the oxygen mask to the ceiling and told him to wake me when it was over.

He couldn't take it down first pass. The fog was really thick. I asked Thurman how low we'd gone.

"About six hundred feet," he said. "No problem."

A few minutes later we landed. I was dating a stewardess who lived down in Orange County at the time, and I'd arranged for her to pick me up. When we got to the car, she was white as a sheet.

"Who was flying that thing?" she asked.

I said, "Thurman. You knew that."

"Well, why did he buzz the field as close as he did?"

I looked at her.

"What are you talking about?" I said. "We were six hundred feet up."

She said, "Like hell you were. Try a hundred. When he took it down that first time, he scared the daylights out of everyone."

Three weeks later, on August 2, practicing touch-and-go landings at home in Canton, Ohio, Thurman crashed the Cessna and died. It was about three o'clock in the afternoon.

We played in Chicago the night before he died. Thurman had the plane at Midway Airport; he was leaving right after the game for Canton and Diane and the kids. There was the off-day, then we were playing the Orioles at home.

He wanted me to spend the day with him in Canton, then fly to New York. He tried to get Piniella and Bobby Murcer to go with him. He was excited about getting his captain's license.

Said he'd be practicing touch-and-go landings.

Said he wanted me to come watch.

Bobby, Lou and I all passed. I had to film a television commercial in Connecticut, then visit some old friends. Bobby and Lou had their own reasons, but I think the biggest was that both of them wanted to get Thurman to stop flying the plane himself. Bobby said that maybe if we all kept after him, we could get him to give up the flying thing once and for all.

"It doesn't make any sense," Murcer said.

I figured he had that straight after my own experience at the Orange County Airport.

My memory of his last game is a touching one, because for the first time since Thurman and I had been teammates, he had to take himself out of a game. His knees had become assassins after all the years of squatting behind the plate, all the games when he'd taken his squat body and hurled it at the game of baseball. There is no tougher position than catcher. Knee bends are lousy for you to begin with, and Thurman had done about a million of them across his career. Get up. Get down. Get up again. Get down. Come up throwing. Take the chest protector off. Take the shin guards off. Hit. Put them back on. Go back behind the plate and repeat the process. Catching just breaks a man down, inning by inning, game by game, year by year. Thurman was still only thirty-two in '79, but he had the knees of an old man. Had he lived, he would have finished out his career as a part-time catcher, part-time first baseman, part-time DH. Maybe he wouldn't have admitted it, and he never would complain, but there would have been no other way for him to go.

He was at first base that night against the White Sox. He was batting third, I was batting fourth, and I remember thinking as I watched him from the on-deck circle that he looked slow, bat tired, beat up trying to hit the ball. He was still hitting close to .300, but he was doing it more on heart and guile. He drew a walk first time up, and I homered behind him. Then he struck out. In the fifth, he went up to Billy—who'd come back to manage by then, replacing Lem—and said, "Skip, I'm done. Can't go anymore." Jim Spencer pinchhit for him, and Thurman limped back into the clubhouse.

Nobody said a word in the dugout.

Looking back, I don't think it was just the knees, bad as they were. I think Thurman had finally been beaten up by all the crap around the ballclub. Just beaten up mentally to go along with all his physical problems. It was difficult enough for him to simply drag the body out and play every day; he'd reached the point where he couldn't cope with the combination of his body betraying him plus the constant state of unrest in the clubhouse. He was tired. He was frustrated. He was talking, as he did periodically, about asking for a trade to the Indians so he could be closer to home.

So he didn't have to fly home on off-days.

"This isn't fun anymore," he said after the game that night. "Reggie, it hasn't been fun for a long time."

We lockered next to each other in the visitors' clubhouse at Comisky Park, and we talked for a long time after the game. He always looked nice when he was getting ready to go home. He wore a clean, pressed white shirt and a pair of gray slacks. Again, you remember things. He talked again about how excited he was about his new pilot's license. He even took it out of his wallet and showed it to me. I guess he talked about flying more to me than to some of the other guys because I owned a plane. He asked me again to change my mind and fly home with him.

I told him again about my commitments the next day.

After a while, he got up to go and told me he'd see me at the Stadium in a couple of days. Then he walked out of the clubhouse on the bad knees, hurting but looking sharp for the family.

Piniella came over to me and said, "He may be hurting, but he looks good tonight, doesn't he?"

I said, "Always does when he's on his way to Canton."

From the time I heard on the radio that he was dead, the next several days were this numb sort of blur. For everyone. It was as if we were all in suspended animation, locked in time and being forced to be a part of a nightmare. We were playing Baltimore at home, and before the game George came down and spoke to us in the clubhouse. He talked about Thurman and all he'd meant to the Yankees, how it took a tragic event like this to make all of us realize what was important in life. I remember he was wearing a blue suit, and he was standing back in the corner of the clubhouse, near Thurman's locker. Finally he just broke down completely. So did Lou, off to George's left. So did Billy. Sad, terrible time.

Strange time.

Thurman's mask was in his locker. His uniform. Everything. And no one wanted to look at any of it. You didn't want to be in the room. This was a baseball place. A place for games. People got hurt in baseball. They had slumps. They lost pennants. They yelled

at each other and got into fights. But there was always another day
to play. Another game. *People didn't die.* Thurman didn't die. He
was a grump sometimes and funny sometimes. He was a gamer. But
he was there. Alive. He'd been dressed in a white shirt and gray
slacks, and he was going home to Diane and the kids, and then he'd
be back Friday to go back behind the plate because the knees would
have had a couple of days of rest. We'd be shagging balls in the
outfield and he'd come over to me and poke me and say, "Million
dollar plane. Not bad for an old catcher, huh?"

It was so freaky to be in the room that night, so scary, so
uncomfortable. So *hard.* The locker was *alive,* man. Thurman's
gear was there.

Only he was dead.

I can't remember a silence like it in my life, not before or since.
We all moved around in a trance. Then we were on the field, and
the game was starting. A message that George had written about
Thurman appeared on the scoreboard. Then the people in the Stadium began this ovation that went on and on, an eerie ovation that
just would not stop. I was standing at my position in right field, and
I just broke down.

The message was about "our captain" and how he would
always be with us. The applause wouldn't stop. I couldn't stop
crying. And the only thing that went through my mind was that
at least I'd left him on good terms. No matter what had happened
between us early on, despite all the misunderstandings, the last year
had been good between us. Thurman hitting third, getting on base,
doing something, me coming up after him and getting him home.

The night in 1977 against Reggie Cleveland: "I'm going to
single between short and third."

The monstrous home run off Doug Bird in the playoffs in '78.

The look on his face, the hurt look, when he'd come back to
the dugout and slowly take the equipment off and rest the knees.

All the nights in the trainer's room, just the two of us, when
he'd ask me about finance and real estate and the market. Lord, he
loved to talk about real estate. He felt he'd been cheated out of the
big money for much of his career, but he was making the money
at the end; he was going to make so much that when he finally
limped away from baseball, he wasn't going to have to worry about
money ever again.

Thurman: smiling the gruff grin and talking about flying and that damned million-dollar airplane.

Thurman: He was the one who gave me the nickname "Mr. October," even if he did it sarcastically at the time. It was right at the start of the '77 World Series. I'd come off the terrible playoff against the Royals. Things were still rough between the two of us, and I'd said something about Billy pitching Catfish in the second game of the Series, knowing that Catfish's arm was burned out at the time. Billy'd gotten mad and said something back in the papers. Same old stuff. Someone asked Thurman about the latest tempest, and he said, "I guess Billy isn't aware that Reggie is Mr. October." Sarcastic because I'd hit so badly against the Royals.

Then I finished with the three dingers, and he came up to me afterward and said, "See, I knew what I was doing when I gave you the nickname, you big coon." Putting an arm around my shoulder. Maybe things started to turn around for us right then.

It could have been better between us, of course, so much better. But at least it had ended so much better than it had begun.

On Monday, we all flew to Canton for the funeral, even though we had another game with the Orioles that night. (Bobby Murcer, who'd been closer to Thurman than anyone, knocked in all our runs and won the game for us.) This was the worst day of all. Painful. Emotional. I remember Bobby and Lou gave eulogies, and Diane Munson requested that a telegram I'd sent to her be read during the service, which meant a lot to me. I told Diane that if I ever made the Hall of Fame, I'd take their son Mike with me, because he would have gotten to make the trip one day with his dad.

Some last words about Thurman.

To this day, he has never been replaced on the Yankees. Had he lived, I believe we would have won two more World Series in New York, both in 1980 and in 1981. We would have gotten by Kansas City somehow in the '80 playoffs; no way could they have swept us if Thurman had been around. And we definitely would have won the '81 Series against the Dodgers. Rick Cerone came over in '80 from Toronto. He's a good kid and he played like hell, but he wasn't Thurman as a catcher, as a hitter or as a leader.

Very few people have been.

Thurman could contribute in so many different places in the lineup. He could hit second, third, fourth or fifth. In all those spots, you have to be able to do different things with the bat. Hitting second, you've got to be able to move the ball around, advance runners, hit the ball to the opposite field, hit for average, be smart on the basepaths. Hit third and you've got to be the most versatile hitter on the team, producing average, runs, power, clutch RBI. Thurman could do all that. He could have hit cleanup, too. And he could have batted fifth, because fifth is an RBI spot pure and simple. He was one of the few guys I ever played with who could have done all that, hit anywhere from second to fifth, and I've played with some hitters.

In '80 and '81, he could have been our missing link.

The legs were bad. The body was old. But Thurman would have figured out a way to get it all done, because Thurman seemed to be able to do anything he had to. He was bitter and upset at the end, he was tired of all the bullshit. But he would have started making a million a year, and that would have made up some for all the years when he thought he'd been wronged by George, when he felt George didn't hold up his end of the salary bargain.

George was always bickering with Thurman when he should have been soothing. When I came over and Thurman was so upset about the money I was making and Catfish was making, George should have pulled him aside and said, "Hey, I know I owe you. Let's rip up this contract and make a new one. I know what you've meant to the Yankees. I want you to be a Yankee for life." I guess there were adjustments made, but not enough, not nearly enough, and that ate at Thurman until the day he passed away.

I know I could have done it so much better with Thurman. If I knew when I signed with the Yankees what I know now, the first thing I would have done is picked up the phone and called him. When I joined the Angels, the first thing I did was place calls to Don Baylor, Rick Burleson, Fred Lynn and Rod Carew. No big deal. I basically said, "I'm glad to be on the ballclub, glad to be playing with you." I wanted them to know that I understood Anaheim was their stage, their town, the Angels their ballclub. We all lug our own insecurities around like carry-on bags. Mine, I think, came from childhood. Thurman's were different. It always bothered Thurman, for instance, that Carlton Fisk was the glamour catcher of their mutual catching era, not because Fisk was a better

player, but because he was taller and better-looking and more con-
versant with the press. Around the Yankees, Thurman knew he was
the leader, but he never felt he was completely treated that way by
Steinbrenner.

I should have called Thurman and said, "You're the captain,
and I know that. Let's just win the damn thing."

Shoulda.

Coulda.

Didn't. My insecurities ran dead into his. The only thing I
really knew about was Oakland. Baltimore was a pit stop. I was part
of a family in Oakland. I wanted to be part of the Yankee family
immediately, and when everyone didn't greet me with open arms,
I drew back, got more insecure, and started running my mouth a
little. I didn't realize soon enough that it was *their* home, *their*
womb, *their* village. The smart thing would have been to walk in
and say, "Thanks for having me. Great meal. Nice house."

Shoulda done it with Thurman. Shoulda done it with Billy.
Maybe George could have helped me there, given me a little shove
(Buzzie did it with me when I signed with the Angels). George
should have made sure Billy was at the press conference when I
signed. But Billy wasn't, and that always bothered Billy. George
should have sat the two of us down, and I should've said, "Glad
to be here. Glad to be playing for you." Maybe if there had been
just the slightest interaction, it all might have worked out better
with Billy, too.

Then again, maybe not.

20

THEY SAID IT
COULDN'T BE DONE.
AND IT COULDN'T.

It was a couple of weeks after the end of the 1979 season. Time to put the nightmare behind me. I'd played hard from August on and finished with a .297 batting average, twenty-nine dingers, eighty-nine RBI. But we finished fourth. The Orioles won the pennant, then ended up losing the World Series to the Pirates after being ahead three games to one.

I was in Carmel at my favorite home set back off all the beauty of Monterey Peninsula, just kicking back, enjoying the scenery and the solitude, tinkering with my cars, playing with my golden retrievers, not worrying about phones because I don't have one in Carmel, trying to get my mind clear and right after all the unhappiness, not even wondering what the next season would bring. This was not a baseball time. This was a peace-seeking time. I sometimes think the Carmel Reggie Jackson is the most relaxed of all.

I was driving through the little town of Carmel on my way to lunch, listening to some music on the radio, without any real plans for the day. Carmel is not a place for making plans. It is a place for getting up to another perfect day and just letting the day lead you around. A song ended. The on-the-hour news report came on. And suddenly I heard the announcer saying that Billy Martin, the Yankee manager, had gotten into a fistfight with some marshmallow salesman in a bar in Minnesota.

The announcer said that further details were sketchy.

I pulled the car over to the side of the road and pondered all that for a minute, then I just started to laugh. If anybody had pulled up to me, it would have been a curious sight. Me. Car stopped, but engine still running. Laughing and laughing.

"Damn," I said shaking my head. "Damn, damn, damn."

Billy and I *had* gotten along well through the end of the season, mostly because we stayed out of each other's way. Besides, August and September was such a sad, stunned time, there was no way any hostility could surface. In the back of my mind, though, I felt that things were never really going to change with us.

Now he'd popped another bar patron. Marshmallow salesman this time. Didn't know who started it. Didn't care. I knew he was gone again. Knew it was just a matter of time.

It was a week, to be exact. George fired him and named Dick Howser manager.

You know what they say.

Every cloud has a silver lining.

21

1980: STICKUPS, SHOOTOUTS, DINGERS GALORE, TANTRUMS FROM GEORGE AND A KANSAS CITY SWEEP . . .

By 1980, I felt at home in New York City and with the Yankees for the first time. My teammates had watched me go up and down, squirm and survive, saw emotional highs and lows, ballplaying highs and lows, saw me try to deal and cope. So had the city. The fans had accepted me. The team had accepted me. Thurman was gone, and just by the natural order of things, I seemed to be the fulcrum of the ballclub. They knew that if shit came down from George I would take the brunt of it, mostly because I *could* take it. I was the one with the bat in my hands, and because of what I could do with that bat, I could fight fairly with George. I could stand up to him. I was the lightning rod. If he tried to give the team a jolt, he had to go through me. I had trusted him, but now I was suspicious of him, and I was willing to fight him out in the open if it came to that. My teammates knew it. No one designated me as captain. I couldn't have been the captain. Thurman was the captain. But I was the buffer, and I had the feeling that most of the people in the clubhouse were grateful for that.

"We all know," Bucky said one time, "that if George wants to get to us, he's got to go through you."

I talked about that electrified fence that surrounds New York, the one no one tells you about when you're fixing to live there. I had scaled that fence. In many ways, there had been the same kind of fence surrounding the Yankees. I had scaled that fence, too. I felt like I had gotten a master's degree in two courses: the Big Apple and Big George's Yankees. Someone told me once that 90 percent of the human mind goes unused. Well, that may be true some places, but not in New York. Son, you better use *all* your brain there, or you ain't gonna survive.

You've heard of the movie *The Big Chill*? In 1980, I really felt like I was getting the Big Stroke from just about everyone except George. And with that kind of support from the town and the team, I knew I could handle him. Plus I had Dick Howser managing, and he was simply one of the best men I ever played for. No fuss. No big heart-to-heart chats. No nonsense. Howser treated me with respect, the way Earl had. He just put my name into the fourth slot in the batting order and left it there from April until October. The result was that I had my greatest regular season in the bigs since 1969 when I'd hit the forty-seven dingers in Oakland. We won 103 games, I hit forty-one dingers, had 111 RBI.

And I hit .300 for the first time in my major-league career, a milestone of which I was very proud. It's funny but that was a big deal for me. Even with all the other accomplishments it meant something—it was another barrier I was able to jump over.

The season would be marred at the end when we didn't make the World Series. I really wanted to go all the way for Dick Howser.

Howser was a quiet, dignified guy who'd left the Yankees' third-base coaching job to go coach at Florida State after the '78 season. He'd been a pretty fair little shortstop in the big leagues once, and after he stopped playing, he began to prepare for a career in managing. George had this idea of him being a company man through and through, and I'm not sure George ever recognized just how tough Dick was until he made him the manager to replace Billy. George was looking for someone who'd be 180 degrees away from Billy, someone who wouldn't make headlines, wouldn't make problems, would take all the garbage George would fling his way and keep his mouth shut about it.

George never saw Dick Howser coming.

Dick Howser was little big man.

Here's an example of the way Dick Howser handled things.

George had this big thing about beards. Hated them. That's how he got the derisive nickname "The Yankee Clipper." One of the first newsy things he'd done when he bought the Yankees was make sure everybody shaved their beards off and was really clean-cut. George had this idea of how a Yankee should look. Every once in a while, I'd start to grow my beard just to tweak him a little. Then the word would come down that I better shave or else. I'd tell you what that meant but I'm sure it didn't mean anything.

One time during the season, the growth got a little out of hand and George sent word through Dick that it was time for me to shave. Howser came over to me at my locker one day, grinning.

"George wants you to shave," he said.

I said, "Yeah, I figured."

Howser's grinning still. "I told him I'd pass the word along."

I said, "What do you think?"

Howser said, "Personally, I think it's a bunch of shit. I don't care if you wear a dress out there if you keep hitting for me the way you have. It'd probably be easier on all of us if you did, but I don't care one way or another."

I shaved to get George off Dick's back. I knew how much heat he had to be getting from upstairs, even over little things like the length of beard stubble, and I didn't want to turn the burner up higher. I liked Dick too much. None of us in the room ever knew just how bad George could make it for his manager privately, but we all had the sense that Dick Howser, with his unobtrusive demeanor, was doing things as manager exactly as *he* thought they should be done.

George was notorious for calling the manager's office before and after games. Writers used to tell me that sometimes the phone would ring and Howser would pick it up, say "I'm busy," and go back to talking to the writers. Never said who was calling.

All in all, it was a nice time for me, at least until the playoffs. Nice time to be a Yankee. Nice time to be in New York. I *belonged*. I could never be a city person full time, but I had formed a bond with the city that will remain with me as long as I live. I do have a personality that can split and split again. Oakland Reggie. Carmel

Reggie. New York Reggie. Things were never better on and off the field for the New York Reggie than they were in 1980.

But even in the best of times, you've got to stay on your toes in New York. Keep the hands held high.

It was in 1980 that I got shot at on the street.

And held up.

Street adventure number one.

It was after a home game, and I was driving my Mercedes west on Eighty-third Street, looking for a parking spot on my way to a restaurant called Oren and Aretsky's, a place a lot of the Yankees frequented. The food was good. They served late. And it was relatively safe and tame in the back room. The people who worked there made sure that you weren't bothered.

There was a car in front of me, and the driver was trying to park in a space that was clearly too small for his car. The result was that no one could pass, and traffic was held up in back. Horns were starting to blare impatiently.

I blew my horn a few times, just to let him know that time was a-wastin'. The guy rolled down his window and yelled, "Fuck you."

Oh, well. For some New Yorkers, that's just a way of saying, "Have a nice day." There's an old joke in New York about a tourist walking up to a New Yorker on the street and saying, "Can you tell me how to get to the Empire State Building, or should I just go fuck myself?" I got the joke.

Finally I passed the car.

As I went by, I heard someone yell, "You sonofabitch."

Variation on the "fuck you" theme.

Now I'm waiting at a red light at the corner of Eighty-third and Third. I've got my window down, and I hear the same voice —slight Latin accent—scream, "You stupid nigger. Stupid, stupid nigger."

Here I got slightly carried away. I pulled the Mercedes over to the side a little, jumped out, and started to chase the guy.

Every time you think you've been called a nigger for the very last time, you're wrong. And I just wasn't in the mood that particular night.

I started running after the guy, and he started running away, then all of a sudden he turns around and points this little handgun and . . .

Bam!

There is a first time for everything in your life.

This was my first bullet-dodge.

I screamed, "What are you, crazy?" Which was sort of a moot point, because I don't think the noncrazies go around shooting pedestrians.

At that point I said to myself, "Jack, let's get our ass *out* of here." *Because my friend was pointing the gun again.*

I was in a full gallop immediately. I heard another shot, which I assumed went over my head, but I wasn't looking back.

I got to Aretsky's intact. The police picked the guy up not long after, and the whole episode got a big play in the papers the next day.

It wasn't all that funny at the time, of course, but Jim McMullen had a funny line the next night when I showed up at *his* restaurant for dinner.

McMullen said, "Why can't you get shot on your way to my place? I could use the publicity."

McMullen inadvertently got his wish a couple of months later. It was the night I hit my 400th home run. I was elated about reaching that milestone, so I went to McMullen's joint to celebrate. I was with a friend I was dating named Gara. I was driving a silver-and-blue convertible Rolls I kept in New York. I had parked the car in front of the restaurant on Third Avenue.

It was a hot, humid night, so when Gara and I got into the car after dinner we both rolled our windows down right away. I was fumbling with my keys, trying to get the car and the air conditioner started.

I felt something against my neck.

Gun.

It was about one o'clock in the morning.

Voice said: "Get out and give me all your money."

As I said okay, I looked to my right real quick and saw that Gara hadn't shut her door yet; she was trying to let more air into the car. So as I started to open my own door, I pushed Gara out *her* door with my right hand. I wanted her to run. Or I at least wanted her protected by the car. If the guy with the gun made a move toward her, I figured I could do . . . something.

I don't want to make this sound overly dramatic, but I've got to level: Guns are dramatic.

Gara ran for help. The gun was still pointed at me.

Me: "Don't shoot."

The kid—by now I could see he was a kid—said, "Leave the keys in the car."

I did that. The rest seemed like it took an hour though it was really only a minute or so.

I got out of the car, slowly, not making any jittery moves, and then a funny thing happened: The kid recognized me. He'd had the gun pointed right between my eyes, but he dropped it to his side and said, "Reggie." I didn't say anything. Now there have been a lot of times in my life when it was no fun at all being recognized —on a date, on a plane, or having a hamburger at a truck stop on the road—and I just wanted to be left alone.

This wasn't one of them.

While he let the gun dangle at his side, I started to run. Full speed again. When I got to the corner, I could see that he was in the car, trying to start it.

He couldn't start the Rolls.

I just stood there on the corner, my heart up near my eyeballs, and watched. He still had the gun. He could have the car.

People were coming out of McMullen's by then. The kid gave up and ran.

I ate in for a few nights after that.

Maybe it was inevitable that the Royals would finally get us in the playoffs. In '76, the year before I got to New York, Chris Chambliss had beaten them with a home run in the ninth inning of the fifth game. In '77, the Royals took a lead into the ninth inning of the fifth game at home, and we came from behind and beat them again. In '78, Thurman turned things around with his monster home run in the third game, then Guidry slammed the door in the fourth. That sort of record makes a team hungry for vindication, revenge. It was get-even time.

The Royals were one hell of a team in 1980. Brett hit .390. As a team they made a mockery of the American League West, and they tuned us pretty good during the regular season, winning eight of twelve games and making our entire pitching staff look for an air-raid shelter.

Maybe it was just their time.

And maybe we all finally got so sick and tired of George Steinbrenner's badgering that we just died on the man a little. The Royals would sweep us three straight in the 1980 playoffs, and never in my professional life have I seen a team that I was playing on be so relieved to just get a season over with.

We'd played like supermen down the stretch, holding off a big rush by the Orioles in September. They ended up with 100 wins and we ended up with 103. That should have made Steinbrenner jump for joy, that kind of ball. For some reason it didn't. Perhaps it wasn't any more complicated than this: He didn't like Howser's attitude. I don't really know why, but George was never satisfied that year. Dick had been giving me indications during the last part of the regular season that George was being impossible.

"I don't know what more he wants us to do," Dick said one day.

The league championship series opened in Kansas City. Brett had a dinger and the Royals won 7–2.

George just snapped. Snapped. We'd barely gotten into the clubhouse when he came storming in. He must have broken his own seat-to-clubhouse record getting there, and as soon as I took a look at him, I knew it was trouble. Face red, screwed into this painful grimace. Big chest heaving. I've always thought that George, being as overweight as he is, just doesn't fit the image he wants to project. He wants to exude power; he wants to look like a military man, all spit and polish.

So now he walks to the middle of the clubhouse, ready to explode, and I just wanted to say, "Wrong time, George. Wrong day. This isn't the time. Don't do it, George. Pu-lease, don't do it now."

He went ahead and did it.

It was one of his pompous, what-the-hell-is-the-matter-with-you-jerks? speeches. We'd heard it before from time to time, usually during the regular season when he'd want to light a fire under us. It never worked. We could always tune him out, and he'd go away happy because he just assumed that he was doing what any great and powerful leader would do. This time, though, he had a special fury to him.

First words out of his mouth, loud: "This is . . . *stupid!*"

He went from there.

"You guys make me *sick!*" he said. "You guys are supposed to be so damn good, and I pay you all this money, and then you go out in the playoffs and perform like *that?* You're better than Kansas City. Hell, any fool can see *that.*"

I thought someone should point out that Kansas City had kicked the shit out of us during the regular season, but what the heck. George was on a roll.

George continued.

"This is sickening. I mean it! What's wrong with you? Well, I'll tell you one goddamned thing: You all better show me something or else."

Or else?

Or else what?

Were we going to pack up our bats and balls and go home, just forfeit?

Or else.

When he left, I looked around the room. No one said anything. The feeling in there wasn't anger or humiliation or disgust. It was more like we were all embarrassed for him. I was thinking, You're smarter than this, George. It was one loss. We *always* come back against this team. Why in the world are you trying to piss us off now?

I walked over to Bucky and said, "What the hell is he doing?"

Bucky grinned at me.

"Let me get this straight," he said. "*You* are asking *me* what's wrong with *him?*"

I had to admit that it was a valid point.

Then Bucky said, "You want to know something, Reg? I just want it to be over."

I thought about that one for a second, then said to Bucky Dent, "Sometimes I do, too."

We didn't try to lose the next night.

We lost.

We lost because of a crackerjack relay play by the Royals that merely cost:

The game.

The pennant, for all intents and purposes.

Mike Ferraro's job as third-base coach of the Yankees.

Dick Howser's job as manager of the Yankees.

It came in the eighth inning. Willie Randolph was on first. Bob Watson was at the plate. I was on-deck. Two outs.

Watson hit a shot into the left-field corner, which should have been a happy occurrence for us, except that as soon as the ball came off his bat, everything that could possibly go wrong for the New York Yankees did.

Randolph was supposed to be stealing, but he got a bad jump as the ball was being delivered and Watson was hitting it. With a better jump, he would have scored easily.

When the ball got into the corner, it didn't roll around the way marbles do in the bathtub, which is what balls usually do on the artificial surface in the Royals' park. It hit off the wall and came right to left fielder Willie Wilson. Like a dream.

Now the Royals had a shot because you could see that Ferraro was going to send Willie. In his mind, he had to. We needed the run, we only had four outs left in the game, and we sure as shooting didn't want to go back to New York down 0–2 in games.

So Randolph is running like hell and the crowd is on its feet —this was one of those wonderful baseball fire drills when everything seems to be happening at once—and Wilson is throwing the ball toward the infield.

Wilson throws the ball over the head of the cutoff man, shortstop U.L. Washington, who'd come out into short left to take the throw like a good soldier. As Washington jumps in vain, I think, Okay, Willie makes it.

Except that Brett is backing Washington up, and the ball comes right to him on the fly. You could see this play 100 times, and never in the 100 would you see the ball end up perfectly in the *second* cutoff man's glove. It did.

Now I thought, Uh-oh. Again, I was the next hitter. I had a front-row seat.

Brett wheeled and threw, and the ball got to the plate, and Willie slid.

Out.

By a mile.

Shit.

There'd be a great debate for some time about whether Ferraro should have sent Randolph. George screamed and hollered and jumped up and down. The only thing that bothered me was that I was the next hitter, and I was having the best all-around season I'd had at the plate in four or five years. But Mike had made the call he thought he had to make.

We lost.

None of us in the game knew it at the time, but George was being a bad boy up in the stands, live and on national television. If you remember the game, you remember the shot of George. We wouldn't see it until we saw the news next day back in New York, but George jumped up like somebody'd put a firecracker under his seat. As he grabbed for his coat, he looked like a man who'd just had a truck drive through his living room. He mouthed a curse.

Way to go, George.

Classy. The Yankee Way?

By the time we got to the clubhouse after the game, there was old George waiting for us again. Only he fooled us this time. Apparently this was George's idea of being a master psychologist. Or maybe he was as embarrassed about his performance twenty-four hours earlier as we had been for him. So there was no tantrum this time.

Instead, he gave us another one of his favorite bits, George being one of the guys.

No problem, guys. We'll get them tomorrow.

Don't worry, guys, we've been in worse spots than this.

No question we should have won tonight. But we'll get them in New York.

But we didn't much care. We were hardly listening to him. We didn't want any more of his silly psychological games. We were tired of them. I couldn't get out of my mind the spectacle George had made of himself the day before. George was acting like we were going to head back to New York and win three for the Gipper— he was the Gipper, of course. But it just wasn't going to happen. We were tired of all his frontrunning, having him tell us we were fabulous when we won and lousy when we lost. Maybe there was a sense in the room that if we did come back and win, he was going to take the credit again, just as he always had in the past.

It was like something had died in the room, like you could actually hear the balloon being deflated. The guys just wanted to go home. We didn't want to go through any of the formalities, didn't want to say goodbye, didn't want to say, "Have a nice winter."

We were tired of George's hot air. Just tired of it all.

That isn't supposed to happen in October, not to the Yankees. Not to me. The juices are supposed to be flowing as you chase the pot of gold. It had never happened in Oakland. It had never happened in New York in the other years when we'd have a chance. It went against my grain; I'm sure it went against everybody else's. But there it was. If George hadn't broken everybody's spirit, he sure had put a dent in it at a most inopportune time.

The next night in New York, George Brett hit a home run ten miles off Goose Gossage, and that was that. No pennant. No World Series.

It was over for everybody except Dick Howser.

George waited about a month before firing him.

22
I Was Just
Leaving . . .

I was in Florida in December, broadcasting a "Superstars" show for ABC, when Cedric Tallis got hold of me and said George wanted to have a meeting in New York. I asked Cedric what it was about, and he said George wanted to ask me about Dave Winfield, the big outfielder from the Padres who was the most glamorous free agent in that year's draft.

My own contract had one more year to run, and I figured that it would be a good time for me to gauge what thoughts George had about the future: mine, Winfield's, everybody's. So I told Cedric I'd fly up the next day. Cedric said that's what George was hoping and asked if I would meet George and some friends for dinner at Elaine's, the chic restaurant uptown on Second Avenue.

I went straight to Elaine's from the airport and walked in feeling a little out of place in my cowboy hat and sweater. George was at a big table in the back with Fugazy—he seemed to go everywhere George went, as though he were on twenty-four-hour call—Ed Broderick, the Yankee lawyer, and Dave Weidler, the comptroller. There was also an attractive lady whose name I never got but I think she was one of the guys' wife, Mike Forest, a furrier, and my friend Tony Rolfe.

George got right to it.

"I'm thinking of signing Winfield and I want to know what you think."

I said it was a good idea.

George: "Why?"

Me: "Because I know that you're looking for a big gun to hit in front of me, or behind me, and Winfield can be that gun. I'm not sure how he's going to perform power-wise, because he's going to be hitting a lot of his best shots into Death Valley (the largest part of Yankee Stadium). But basically I think he'll help us a lot. It's obvious to anyone that he can hit, run and throw, and he's a hell of an athlete. Plus, I'm not going to be around forever, and it's probably the right time for you to start looking for someone to groom as my replacement, someone who can be your horse when I'm gone. If Winfield is the guy you want, I'll do everything I can to help him."

The others were just listening. This was business.

George: "Can he play in New York?"

Me: "That I don't know, George, and that's something you have to consider, something that doesn't have anything to do with Winfield's skills as a ballplayer. This is a tough town to play in, a tough situation in which to perform up to your capabilities. It's no big secret that he's going to make a lot of money if he plays for you, more than me, more than anybody around. A lot of people—I'm talking players *and* fans—are going to be jealous of him. You've got to ask yourself two questions: Can he play in New York? *And* can he play for George Steinbrenner?

"Reggie Jackson is going to get old one of these days, George, so it's natural for you to be looking down the road. If you think Winfield *can* be the right guy, *can* play for you in New York, go get him and damn the cost because you can't play money. But remember that you're going to have to sign me after the season, and you're going to have to sign Guidry, and Winfield is going to throw even your salary structure out of whack the minute he signs on the dotted line. If you can sign him and me and Guidry down the road, then go ahead and do it."

George: "Don't worry."

I was wondering when he'd get to me.

Me: "I'd really like to get my new contract worked out before the end of the season, because I don't want it hanging over me, and I don't want to have to go through a lot of speculation about whether I'm going to go through the free agent draft again or not."

George: "I'm going to go talk to Winfield after I leave here."

Me: "Good luck. And I hope we can sit down together soon to work out my deal."

George: "Don't worry." He immediately got up and left.

Within the week he took care of Winfield, with an unbelievable contract of $23 million for ten years. Winfield got his.

I'm still waiting for George to get that new contract of mine worked out.

So you're wondering why I wanted to stay, aren't you?

Because I did. Because I was going to be thirty-five years old in May of the next season, and I was coming off a hell of a year personally, and I had gotten it into my head that I wanted to finish my career in New York. Just seemed to me that Reggie Jackson the baseball player should have always been in pinstripes. I didn't want to go through free agency again. I didn't want to uproot myself again. I had started to think of New York as my town. Even with all of George's nonsense in October, even with a new manager being moved in every hour or so, I was now happy in New York. I figured we could win two or three more World Series. I figured Winfield could come in and put us over the hump again the way I had in 1977, and with me showing him the ropes, he wouldn't have to go through what I'd gone through.

I was invited to the Winfield signing—the way Thurman had been invited to mine—and George, Dave and I all posed for pictures. Everything was fine. George invited me over to his suite at the Carlyle, just the two of us, and I figured he was going to tie up the Jackson-Winfield package right then and there. He offered me breakfast. I said that would be fine.

And then George began to dance.

"I know you're probably going to want a four- or five-year deal," he said.

I nodded sagely.

I'd never told him how long I wanted my new deal to be, by the way.

"Well, Reggie, I'm not sure I'm willing to give you that long a contract," he said. "You're going to be thirty-six next season, you know."

I told George I hadn't aged on my walk over to the Carlyle.

"Generally," he said, "I'm thinking more in terms of three years, but we don't need to get into that right now, there's plenty of time. But three years is what I've sort of got in my head."

He was racing through this all of a sudden, even though this meeting was supposed to be so leisurely, just the two of us and all that. He was looking everywhere in the room except at me, rambling on, not giving me a chance to say anything.

". . . but like I said, no reason to get concrete here, I've been so damn tied up with this Winfield thing, don't worry about the money, I'll get back to you, jeezus it's gotten late hasn't it, I gotta get going, this was nice, we should do it more often, we'll get together again soon, I'm glad you were able to make the press conference."

George made sure the door didn't hit me in the fanny on my way out.

I was very slowly catching on here. I was the rat, and it was George's maze. A new contract was the cheese.

Except there wasn't any cheese.

We met again in Fort Lauderdale in February before the start of spring training. I was again over in Key Biscayne announcing "Superstars" for ABC. George was staying at the Galt Ocean Mile, which is spring training headquarters for the Yankees. The dance became more elaborate now. George didn't want to talk about a baseball contract, which I assumed was the order of the day. He wanted to talk about the two of us doing business down the road, after I was done playing.

"I want you to be a Yankee forever," he said. "Broadcasting, of course, to start. That's a natural. But I want you to be a part of this organization as long as I'm a part of the organization. I'm talking about the whole corporate structure, Reggie."

I said, "Whole corporate structure. Right."

He said, "If the two of us can get together, I see unlimited financial potential."

"So a new baseball contract would just be the beginning," I said.

"Right," he said. "The beginning of a long-term association."

I know, I know. Why was I letting myself get mesmerized by a man who'd done so much to make me mistrust him over the previous four years?

Fair question.

Answer? Because first and foremost, I'd always thought of George Steinbrenner as a smart businessman. Whatever had transpired between us as owner and player, I always had the feeling that Steinbrenner knew in his heart that the George-Reggie Show had ultimately been good for both of us. I'd become famous as an athlete thanks to New York; I'd won for him; I'd helped him break attendance records all over the place; I'd kept the Yankees in the news without trying very hard. I'd hit the dingers when they counted most; I was Mr. October and all that B.S. Winfield had a chance to be a great player in New York, but Winfield wasn't Reggie yet, not in New York. George-Reggie was different. Never anything quite like it. The bottom line was this: George and I had made whole pots of money for each other. On that level, just thinking as a businessman myself, it made sense for me to be a "Yankee forever." I liked the idea because I would have been proud to have retired in a uniform of Yankee pinstripes. Then I thought I fit into New York and would not have minded being forever pinstriped.

I couldn't see that this was just another con from Steinbrenner, a power game with me as the pawn. What he was really doing was making me pay for all the times I stood up to him, all the times I wouldn't buckle under to him, all the times I wouldn't be his boy. He had no intention of signing me, but he was definitely going to get his licks in while he still had me under contract. I know it might sound counterproductive for George to mess with my mind this way—he needed me to play well if the Yankees were going to win —but George can occasionally lose sight of the big picture. If I was going to leave the Yankees after the 1981 season, and if that was his plan from the start, then he probably wanted me slinking out of town with my tail between my legs.

Anyway, I thought we were doing business, when in fact old Reggie was just being *given* the business.

When we shook hands at the Galt Ocean Mile, I thought we'd come to an understanding. A bunch of writers had gotten wind of the meeting, so after the "Superstars" taping in Key Biscayne later that day I sat down with them and told in general terms what George and I had talked about in Lauderdale. The writers called George.

And what George basically told them was that I had made up all the talk about the two of us being business associates. Imagined it. "There was no invitation for him to come into my business," was his response.

It did not make for pleasant reading over coffee the next morning. Bill Bertucio was with me at "Superstars," and he said, the man is setting you up. He's playing you for a sucker. He's never going to sign you. Forget about it. It's get even time for him, Reggie."

"But why go to all this trouble?" I said to Bill.

"Because it's get-even time for him."

That day I called George and wouldn't even give him the satisfaction of mentioning the newspaper stories. Screw him. I told him I'd have to be a couple of days late for spring training because I had to fly back to California to clear up some things. He said no way, that if I wasn't there on time, he'd fine me $5,000 a day.

"Do it," I said.

He did, and that was the way my last season with the Yankees began. It was even more bizarre than the rest. I'd get hurt in New Orleans before the regular season began. There'd be the strike by the Players Association. After the strike, I'd find myself in one of the worst slumps of my career. George ordered me to take a full physical in August, additional humiliation. He'd fire Gene Michael in September for insubordination and replace him with Bob Lemon (again). Rick Cerone would tell George to "fuck off" in the clubhouse after the fourth game of the mini-playoffs against the Brewers (the season was split because of the strike; we won the first half of the AL East and the Brewers won the second half). I'd hit a big dinger in the fifth game to help save us. I'd get into a fight with Nettles after we beat Billy and the Oakland A's to win the pennant. I'd be hurt for the first two games of the World Series against the Dodgers, then George wouldn't let me play in the third when I was healthy. George would break his hand in an alleged fight in a Los Angeles hotel elevator. The Dodgers would win the last four games of the Series to finally beat us. George would issue a public apology to the city of New York.

Bo*ring.*
But anyway . . . here we go.

The physical . . .

By August, I was a mess. Since the start of the season, I had told myself not to brood about George's lies about a new contract, but I had brooded nonetheless. In all my years with the Yankees, I had never once asked to renegotiate the original contract, even when salaries started going through the roof, concluding with Winfield's windfall. There were players all over baseball making more than I was at a time when I was still the number-one or number-two drawing card in the game. If you could play at all, and you became a free agent, it seemed you were a lock to make close to a million a year. I'd kept my mouth shut and waited for my day, and now my day wasn't going to come, at least not in New York.

I'd just go out every day, kneel in the on-deck circle, and hit behind a man, Winfield, who was making three times what I was making in yearly salary. I had nothing against Dave. Despite what everybody thought would happen, the two of us got along fine from the start. We'd talk a lot about how to handle the first year in New York, what to say to the press, what to say *about* George. I liked his attitude about George from the start. Winfield has a ten-year, no-trade, all-guaranteed contract. He isn't going anywhere. He gets his money as long as his lungs keep moving. Winfield doesn't make a big deal out of it, but his attitude toward George goes something like this: "Fuck me? Okay. But fuck you." What's George gonna do if he gets unhappy with Winfield? Have him bumped off? George was always able to play mind games with me because I let him, I was susceptible. Dave doesn't seem to be. Dave just laughs and goes to the bank.

The whole money thing began to cripple me slowly. It wasn't that I needed any more riches. It wasn't avarice. I just thought there was a principle of sorts involved. I was happy when I signed with the Yankees, and I'd never complained, but the free agent game had changed so much. Compared to what the market was from '76 to '81, George had gotten me at a bargain basement rate.

It shouldn't have bothered me as much as I let it. And I shouldn't have let George bother me the way he did. Considering my own economic state and all the things I'd done in the game, I should have handled the season more maturely. That's theory. The reality was that I brooded. The batting average kept dipping toward Cuba. You can hit 400 dingers and win five World Series, and that still doesn't mean that your insecurities can't grab you by the throat every so often.

The strike would last for fifty-two games. It got bogged down with the owners wanting compensation if they lost a free agent, and the players not wanting to give them compensation. The owners thought that if a team had to worry about losing a top player if it signed a Reggie Jackson, that team might give pause before signing a Reggie Jackson. What they really wanted was a rule to control themselves, and drive down salaries. Marvin Miller, the head of our Players Association—and arguably the most successful union leader this country has ever had—said, "Uh-uh." In the end, the compensation decided on was quite minor, and Marvin had beaten the owners again.

From spring training on, I kept saying there would definitely be a strike. It bothered me that it was part of the business, part of life, but it was inevitable. I couldn't let it upset me—I had enough things upsetting me—because I felt the players had no control over the avalanche of events. I felt the owners were bound and determined to force a strike.

I was on the players' side, but the strike wasn't going to affect me one way or another. The salary I lost was eventually just taken out of a deferred payment from the Yankees in 1982, after I'd left the team. I was thirty-five years old when we struck, I had had more than twelve years in the majors, I was about to become a two-time free agent. I qualified in all the areas where the eventual benefits of the strike weren't going to reach me at all. But I was responding to it with my support for the young players in the game. If I had to give up $50,000 or $60,000, whatever it was going to take, to help the players coming up, then I was glad to do it. If it wasn't for Marvin Miller and the forefathers of the Players Association, I never would have made the millions from baseball that I made. In that sense, I could step back from my personal fight with Steinbrenner and say, "Money doesn't matter." This was a bigger principle. I appreciated what the Players Association had done for me, so supporting the strike was something I felt morally bound to do.

I'm not patting myself on the back here. Quite the contrary.
It wasn't as tough for me as for some of the players who didn't have
options without their baseball jobs. I could broadcast for ABC. I
could do some things for Panasonic. I could do some things for
Nabisco. I could take care of myself financially off the field, so I was
fortunate.

And because of what was happening with the Yankees, I was
glad to get away from baseball at that particular time. When you're
doing something horribly, you're glad to get away from it. On a
strictly personal level, politics aside, I wanted the strike to last all
year.

So I traveled in California and Arizona. Every once in a while,
I would fly into New York for Players Association meetings, because Marvin valued my opinion. I worked for ABC on the Sports
Festival in Syracuse, "Summer Superstars," some drag races. It was
such an unusual summer. For the first time in my adult life, I had
a Fourth of July barbecue. Never got to do that before. I was always
playing ball.

When it ended in August, I was happy for the players and
happy for Marvin, because he'd won again. There is no way of
telling how much money Marvin Miller has made for every player,
but it's a ton. When he retires, he'll get something like $50,000 a
year for the rest of his life, and he's grossly underpaid. It's em-
barassing! He should get $200,000 a year for the rest of his life, an
office, a secretary. Anything he wants! He could be too stubborn at
times—I know about stubborn—but he was always honorable and
always sincere. As far as I could see, he never made a mistake. He
played every hand of poker and never lost one that counted. It was
sometimes difficult for him to be objective, because he was so letter
perfect in his negotiations. He was the glue of the Players Association from the beginning. He kept it together. And he was so persuasive with the players. If he were a vicious man, he could have
destroyed the game, because we basically did anything he said when
it came time to hammer out another Basic Agreement with the
owners. It's not that we were gullible or naive, but Marvin was so
intelligent and so analytical and had such cogent logic that we were
going to follow him wherever he took us. A trooper, Marvin Miller.
A real trooper.

When we came back, we found out we'd already won the
American League East, because the powers-that-be had decided to

split the season. The Yankees were in first place when the strike came. The Yankees were in the playoffs. Simple.

So there was no big incentive for us in the second half, and the result was that we played listless, .500 ball. I won all the listless awards. I could not get out of the funk no matter how hard I tried. I had to drag myself to the ballpark every day. I'd take extra batting practice with Charlie Lau, our batting coach. Didn't help. I didn't see that anything could help outside of perhaps a personality trans- plant. My average didn't get much higher than .200. I went three weeks without a dinger. Gene Michael, the manager, even pinchhit one of our utility infielders, Aurelio Rodriguez, for me one night at the Stadium.

The next day I showed up at the park early and found a typewritten message from Cedric Tallis, vice-president and Stein- brenner errand runner, informing me that the team was invoking its contractual rights for me to take a full physical.

I read it. I reread it. I went upstairs to talk to Cedric. I was so angry I couldn't see straight (which is sort of ironic since one of the things they wanted me to undergo the next day was an ophthalmological exam). It wasn't enough that Steinbrenner had jerked me around with the phony tease of a new contract. Now, in a free-agent season that had already gone so wrong for me, he wanted to have even more fun with me, planting seeds of doubt about my physical well-being. His game had gotten even dirtier than usual.

I went into Cedric's office. Lou Saban, who had the title of team president that season, was there with him. In a previous lifetime, Steinbrenner had been a football coach on Saban's staff at Northwestern. Saban had gone on to coach all over the pros and college after that. He pretty much had run out of decent coaching jobs finally, so George hired his old buddy to become president of a *baseball* team. In doing so, he showed the world just how mean- ingless the title of president of the Yankees was as long as George owned the Yankees.

I had the order for the physical in my hands as I said, "Cedric, what is this shit?"

I really had no quarrel with Cedric, but I had to get mad at somebody.

"Reggie," he said, embarrassed, "you know how it goes around here. I'm just following orders. I'm supposed to tell you that after the physical, George wants you to fly down to Tampa for a meeting."

Apparently the first part of the public chastising was the physical. Part two was going to be a verbal whipping in Tampa for the benefit of the press. Steinbrenner had, and as far as I can see, still has, this weird notion that the most public form of humiliation acts as a great spur to athletes, that it helps them to reach their top level of performance.

Saban, incidentally, wasn't saying a word. Never did. Just got real good seats for the games.

"Cedric," I said, "get this straight. I'm gonna take the physical because my contract says I have to. But there isn't a chance in the world I'm going to Tampa. I've got nothing more to say to him. You go ahead and tell him that. I'm going to take the physical, and I'm going to play out the string here, and then my ass is gone."

The next morning I went over to the New York University Medical Center and took the physical. And checked out fine, as I knew I would. I joked with the doctors and nurses. They joked with me. The eye doctor put me through my paces with the charts, and we discovered that my vision was 20/10, just as it had been for years (I just wear glasses to help correct a slight astigmatism). When I was done, I visited Tommy John's little son Travis, who the week before had nearly died in a fall at the Johns' New Jersey home. I played with Travis for a long time, salvaging some good from a bad day.

The only part of the physical I skipped was a dental exam, which was supposed to be in another office up on Madison Avenue. Maybe George was worried that my teeth were rotting because of all the shit he was making me eat.

Matt drove me back to my apartment to pack. The team was leaving later in the day for Chicago, and Matt was going to take me to the airport.

Cedric called.

"George is going to have his son pick you up at the Tampa Airport," Cedric said. "He just wants me to call with your flight information."

Flight information?

Tampa?

I was beginning to wonder why I hadn't taken a psychiatric examination when I'd been over at NYU.

"Cedric, what the hell are you talking about?" I said. "I *told* you I wasn't going to Tampa. I couldn't have said it any plainer than I did. What part didn't you get? If Steinbrenner's kid is going to pick me up at the airport, he better get his ass on the first flight to Chicago, 'cause that's where I'm going to be in a few hours."

And hung up.

I said to Matt, "How much crazier can this get?"

We got into the car, neither one of us saying much, and we had just about gotten to the Triboro Bridge on the way to LaGuardia when I said to Matt, "We're going to the Stadium."

Matt said, "What for? You're going to miss your flight."

"Screw the flight. I'll get another one," I said. "Turn the car around. We're going to get this settled once and for all."

Back we went to Cedric's office.

When Matt and I walked in, Cedric looked like he'd swallowed his car keys.

"You couldn't tell him, could you?" I said. "You didn't even have the guts to pass a message along, isn't that right, Cedric? Jeezus, what's happened to you? What the hell's going on around here?"

He just sat there with that whipped-dog look I'd come to expect from George's employees.

"Reggie," he said quietly, "if you don't go, you're going to cost me my job."

I was pacing around the room.

"I'm not going to cost anybody a job," I snapped. "Gimme George's number. I'll call him myself."

Cedric said in a smaller voice than before, "Reggie, don't do that." The words seemed to just fall out of the air and die.

But he got the number.

I called George. I wanted him to know that I wasn't flying all the way to Tampa for lip service. There was no point. The relationship was over and I knew it.

When he got on the line, he wanted to know what had happened with the physical.

"The hell with the physical, George." I spit the words into the phone. "I've got a plane to catch. To Chicago. So I don't have a lot of time. Maybe I had given up on the season before yesterday and today. Maybe the way I've been playing is my own fault. Maybe you don't think I can play anymore. Well, I am going to play my *ass* off the rest of the season, and I'm going to show you and everybody else that there isn't a player in the world further from being washed up than me. I'm not comin' to Tampa 'cause we don't have anything to talk about. I'm going to Chicago to play some ball and do my job. Then it's goodbye. 'Cause I'm gone!"

Conversation was over. Plane to catch.

I started playing my ass off the next night in Chicago. I went into Chicago hitting .217. From there, for the last seven weeks of the regular season, I hit .280 with nine dingers and twenty-six RBI, which was right there with any September I'd ever had in New York. For about the 900th time in New York, I was answering back with the best weapon I've ever had: my bat.

That wasn't so amazing. What was amazing was what happened when I got to Comisky Park that Friday night in Chicago.

Gene Michael basically told George Steinbrenner to take a flying leap.

Up until that time, I didn't really know anything about Michael. We'd had a couple of run-ins because he didn't think I was a good outfielder; he wanted me to DH. I'd taken to calling him Gene Michael Steinbrenner, because to me he was nothing more than an invention of George's. George had made him a coach with the Yankees. George had made him the Yankee general manager. George made him the manager. I think George thought Gene *looked* the way a Yankee should look. The way *George himself* wanted to look. Tall. Thin. Short gray hair. Military man. George's alter ego and one who did what he was told. But Gene was okay.

He always treated me fairly. Nothing special, but fairly. He treated me like a guy hitting .220, which is what I deserved. All of a sudden, though, I was his ally because, to everyone's amazement, here was Michael in his office before the White Sox game reading a prepared statement (the writers told me about it with varying levels of astonishment), saying he was tired of George's threats. Tired of the phone calls in the middle of the night. Saying that he'd informed his boss that if he wanted to fire him, then to go ahead and fire him.

I never thought for a minute that Michael had it in him. He didn't last long after that—George dragged his pout out for a week or so before bringing Lemon back—but in those days I felt a kinship with Michael that I'd never dreamt was possible. Hell, we had a bond. We'd both told Steinbrenner off in the space of forty-eight hours. From then until Michael went away, there was a running joke between us. The first thing I'd do when I got to the clubhouse was poke my head into the manager's office.

"Oh, still here, huh?" I'd say.

Gallows humor among the inmates.

Anyone who had a run-in with Steinbrenner would come to me for support or just to talk it out. They figured I was their ally, so they gravitated toward me like I was a magnet. I guess they figured I'd understand and be sympathetic. To be honest, I really wasn't. Most of their fights with George were temporary rifts or funny spats. Whoever it was on that particular day would tell me their tale of woe and I'd either nod sympathetically or laugh, depending on what was called for. But my fights with George weren't funny little skirmishes. It was sort of like the difference between Vietnam and a pillow fight.

There was a little more gallows humor, by the way, when Lem showed up in the manager's office on Labor Day. We were all filing in to say hello when Nettles poked his head around the corner.

Nettles pretty much spoke for all of us.

"Condolences, Meat," is what he said to our new manager.

It was not a dull postseason.

They never were.

We won the first two games of the AL East mini-series against the Brewers. In Milwaukee. And I began to think, Damn, we're going to pull ourselves together and win again. And I began to think that there had to be a special survival instinct in the Yankee clubhouse that came from playing for someone like George. I keep saying you have to be tough to survive in New York. Well, the players kept changing, but the toughness seemed to be a constant. Chambliss was long gone, but Bob Watson had taken his place at first. Dave Revering backed him up. Jerry Mumphrey, a teammate of Winfield's in San Diego, had come over in a trade before '81 to play center. A big kid named Ron Davis had joined Gossage in the bullpen. Cerone was behind the plate. Bobby Murcer and Oscar Gamble, who'd both come back to the Yankees in '79, gave us tough left-handed hitting. Dave Righetti, who'd come to the Yankees from the Texas organization in the Sparky Lyle deal, had shown all kinds of promise during the second half and looked like he would be a lefty pitching star for years and years.

Still the old soldiers from 1977 and 1978 formed the nucleus, except for Thurman. Jackson was still around. Guidry. Gossage. Piniella. Nettles. Randolph. Dent. It was October now. The strike was over. Our lousy second half was history. Lem was back. In the first two games of the Milwaukee series, it seemed like we all remembered how to get it done. I was coming off a hot September, even if my motives were a little more selfish than they'd been in the past.

I had decided that I wasn't going into the free-agent draft without my ID card.

Then a funny thing happened.

We lost the third game on Friday night at the Stadium.

And we lost the fourth game on Saturday afternoon.

Suddenly it was 1978 all over again. One game to decide the American League East. Yankee Stadium this time. A Sunday night this time, instead of a Monday afternoon in Boston. But the table stakes were the same.

It was after the fourth game that Steinbrenner and Cerone had their little tea-time chat.

We had played another sloppy game, losing 2–1 when we should have won about 5–2. Runners were left on base. Guys ran into silly outs (Winfield was thrown out trying to go from second to third on a grounder hit in front of him; a cardinal sin). I'd looked bad at the plate. It finally ended with Cerone striking out on a bad pitch with the tying and winning runs on base.

Guess who got pissed off the most?

Guess who was waiting for us in the clubhouse?

If you guessed Abner Doubleday, you're wrong.

General Von Steingrabber.

It was like an old sitcom rerun. George in his blue suit (I had this vision of closets and closets of the same suit, in Cleveland and Tampa and New York). George in his white shirt. George in that damn navy blue Yankee tie. George with the killer hair combed perfectly. George breathing fire.

He started while the guys from the bullpen were still filing in. It's a long way, and they're always last in. The door was open, the press was outside, and George was already into his standard presentation.

"I'm sick and tired of you guys embarrassing me this way!

Mental mistakes! I'm sick and tired of goddamn mental mistakes."

Sound familiar?

I yelled over to one of the clubhouse guys to shut the door. I don't know who I was trying to protect, but this seemed to be between George and the team.

"What's the matter with you goddamn guys?" George shouted, standing near a big long table in the middle of the room, waving an arm at all of us. "Do you *know* what it's like for me to have to look Bud Selig [the Milwaukee owner] in the face after you embarrass me like you did today?"

Now there was a twist on the old Rockne theme. We were supposed to go out there and win one for Bud Selig's face.

"We're gonna *blow* this thing!" he continued, voice rising. "I'm humiliated the way you've played the last two days. *Hu-mil-i-ated!* If we lose tomorrow, I'm telling you, it will be the worst and greatest disaster in Yankee history. In history! It's not just me you're embarrassing. You're embarrassing the fans. You're embarrassing *New . . . York . . . City!*"

Everytime you thought the man couldn't possibly do it again, he topped himself. I thought his performance the year before in the Kansas City series had been something for his personal Hall of Fame, but this was worse. I couldn't believe George hadn't learned his lesson. But he hadn't. One last time, he was being the epitome of someone who just did not understand professional sports. There are things fans—and George is a fan at heart, he really is—can learn. But there are things about the experience of being a professional athlete that they will never know. Because they never played the game. It sounds trite, but that's truly the way it is. And I always figured you can't really go around criticizing a man until you walk in his shoes for nine miles.

It was Jekyll and Hyde time again for George. It was as if he would go along and act normal, act like he understood athletes and games and victories and defeats. Dr. Jekyll. Then he'd just have to revert back to being Mr. Hyde and throw a bizarre tantrum like this one. Just kept topping himself. If you suspect that I couldn't understand him, you are *right.*

I sat there with eyes the size of, I don't know, baseballs. Thinking, This is *too* far out. What's wrong with you, man? What are you doing? Did they put something in your drink during the game?

George, what you been *smokin'*?

He stopped for a beat, and Bobby Murcer, sitting in front of his locker in his famous rocking chair, quietly said, "Now is not the time, George. Now is just not the time."

Murcer had always been a favorite of Steinbrenner's. When he'd been traded away to San Francisco in the early '70s, George had promised him he'd bring him back someday if he could. So Bobby wasn't afraid to say what he felt was needed.

"It is the time, goddamnit!" Steinbrenner screamed at Murcer. "You guys are playing like shit. Running into stupid goddamn outs! Striking out with men on base! Swinging at shitty pitches! I'm sick of it."

Another pause.

Then we heard Rick Cerone from the back of the room, behind George and to his right.

"Fuck it!" Cerone shouted. "And fuck *you,* George."

Now Cerone is a tough kid from New Jersey, and he'd played well for us in a tough situation—taking Thurman's place behind the plate—since coming over from Toronto. The kid didn't back down. And he'd had a bad day. He knew he'd looked bad at the plate. He understood full well that he'd made the last out with a chance to keep us in the game or maybe even win it. He didn't need to be told.

And he didn't need for The Man to throw it in his face.

Steinbrenner wheeled on Cerone like Cerone had slapped him from behind.

Myself, I wanted to start a standing ovation for the kid.

"You can't talk to me like that!" George was practically shrieking now.

Cerone wasn't backing down. He walked toward the trainer's room. "You think it's so easy to play this game?" he shouted over his shoulder. "*You* go out and play it. Ah, fuck it. Fuck *you.*"

And disappeared.

Silence.

George stared at the door to the trainer's room.

The rest of us stared at George.

It seemed to take the steam out of him. In a calmer way he reiterated how disaster was staring us in the face, how the city was counting on us—the city'd probably come to a standstill if we blew it, right?—and how a lot of us were going to be gone the next season if we didn't pull ourselves together and win the fifth game.

Now he started to make some sense. But why couldn't he have reached that point in some other way? Why did he have to yell and scream and make a fool of himself? I guess he just didn't know how to do it any other way. The intentions were probably good, but the execution was horrendous.

You know, as a result of writing this book, I've dredged up a lot of memories that have been submerged, hidden for a long time. Now that I've got some perspective, I've come to some fairly interesting realizations about George Steinbrenner.

Yes, he can be brutal. Yes, he can be malicious. But I really don't think that's his nature. I think he really does mean well. It just doesn't turn out that way. He's a perfectionist and he demands perfection from others. But I don't think he's earned the right to be such a perfectionist; at least he hasn't earned the right to demand such total perfection from his players. I can see it from a Bill Russell, a guy who did it on the court when it counted. Or a guy like Whitey Ford, who was so far above everyone else as a pitcher. But George? I don't understand it. What's he done?

Despite everything, and as hard as this might be to believe, I like George. I truly do. I think he's a fun guy to be around. He's powerful, interesting, a shaker and a mover; he makes things happen. But I don't trust him. You *can't*. It's a real pity. It's sad. He's not a guy I'd want to share a foxhole with, I'll tell you that.

When I signed with him, I clearly was looking for a paternal association, as I guess I have throughout much of my career. I was looking for the kind of relationship I now have with Buzzie. And with McNamara. And Gene Autry. Now there's a man with class —an American institution. I'd thought George and I had that kind of relationship. Obviously, we didn't. I suppose that's one of the reasons the break with the Yankees was as painful as it was when it finally came.

I called Cerone that night at his home just to tell him I admired him for standing up to George the way he had and that the team was on his side.

I said, "You okay?"

Cerone: "I'm fine, Reg. I'll be there tomorrow. Hey, you got to tell somebody to fuck off after you played the way I did. Don't worry about me."

Repeat: Tough act.

Before the fifth game, I went to the ballpark early and went up to talk to George. I'd called to ask if I could see him. When we met, I told him that regardless of what happened in the final game, "These guys on the team are busting their asses for you. They want to win, no matter what it looks like to you. They have not given up."

George said he knew what I was saying was true, that he'd just flown off the handle the day before. Then he asked me to carry a note to Cerone, which I did. I never read it and Rick never told me exactly what it said, but it was some form of apology. To tell you the truth, I think George respected Cerone for his outburst. I think he liked him for it. But Rick better watch out for the payback.

And the game? We won it, of course. The score was 7–3. Moose Haas pitched for the Brewers. And I hit a big dinger in the middle of a three-for-four night.

Beforehand, I was standing chatting with a writer for the *Washington Post,* Tom Boswell, at the batting cage. He was asking about the scene the day before in the clubhouse, the mood of the team, *my* mood. He wanted to know what was going to happen in Game Five, if we were going to bow our necks one more time or fold the tents.

I said something to Boswell that turned out to be fairly prophetic.

"You know," I said, "you guys have been writing for an awful long time about how I'm Mr. October. I guess tonight we're going to find out how much of that shit's true."

I found out.

I nearly hit one out in the first inning off Haas to dead center. When I came up in the fourth, the Brewers were leading 2–0. Man on for us. Haas was looking good for them, and I had the feeling that we couldn't go too long without putting the hit on him, or he might just blow us away and out of the season.

Haas threw me a forkball. I've kissed big dingers in big situations in the past, but this SOB was tattooed. It ended up in the third deck. Afterward, someone asked where it might have bounced back to if it had hit the facing, and I said, "Didn't matter."

I didn't move from the batter's box until it got into the seats.

Just *knew.*

Oscar Gamble was the next batter, and he hit one out, too. And later on Rick Cerone had a dinger himself, which I thought was sweet vindication. I didn't feel so bad myself. I'd been jerked around on the contract, I knew I was leaving, I'd spent my time in my stupid funk, I'd taken my physical, but I'd found something out again.

The Mr. October shit was true. Once more.

We beat the Oakland A's three straight for the pennant. Even though it was Yankees versus Billyball, George versus Billy, Reggie versus Billy, the Series turned out to be anticlimactic after the fifth game against the Brewers. The tabloids tried to have a field day with my rivalry with Billy, but I was having none of it. As far as I was concerned, the little fella was in my past, and I hoped he'd stay there forever.

Billyball had been all the rage when the A's got off to a great start, but the team hadn't been much during the second half. You could already see that Billy had "Martinized" another pitching staff. He'd worn out his kid starters during the season, never went to the bullpen, and by the time they got to October, they were done. We pounded them pretty good. Nettles had a great series with the bat.

We won the third game at Oakland, and that night what had been building between Graig Nettles and me for five years finally came to a head.

Steinbrenner threw a victory party for the entire Yankee entourage at an Oakland restaurant called Vince's, which had always been one of my favorites. Wives were there, and family and friends. George had rented us a private room.

My personal entourage was probably bigger than it should have been, but Oakland was home, and we had won, we had beaten Billy. Even though my leg was bothering me (I'd hurt it in the second game and was concerned about being 100 percent for the Series), I was riding high. I had my sister Tina with me and her husband Tony Jones. Everett Moss was there, my niece Wynoka, Bill Bertucio and his wife. Betsy, my girlfriend who lives in Oakland, was there also.

Betsy and I were at the buffet table, and when we came back, we saw that all our people were seated at one big table. And our people were very agitated.

Wynoka said, "She said her purse is missing."

"She" was Ginger Nettles, Graig's wife. Apparently what had happened was that Ginger had been seated at the same table and had left her jacket and purse draped over a chair when she went off to the buffet table. When Ginger came back, she saw all these people there and *didn't* see her purse, which had slipped to the floor.

And, according to Wynoka, Ginger had overreacted a little, shouting, "Where's my purse? My purse is *gone.*"

And Wynoka had overreacted, thinking that my people were being accused.

Words were exchanged before I got back to the table. I immediately assumed that Ginger might have jumped to conclusions.

I had also had a couple of beers.

I went looking for Nettles, who was in another part of the room, drinking a bottle of beer.

I said, "Hey, man. Why the hell did your wife think we stole her purse?"

Nettles looked surprised.

"What the hell are you talking about, Reggie?" Nettles said, gesturing to me with the beer in his hand.

And it all caught up with me, all the things I'd thought about him for so long, about the way he thought about people, about the things he'd said. The ethnic jokes. The cracks about my ability. Got me right there after a silly incident like a purse falling to the floor at a victory celebration.

I slapped the beer out of Nettles's hand, knocking it to the floor.

Nettles threw a left hook at me, grazing the side of my head. It wasn't much of a punch, but there was a chair behind me and another chair behind it. I fell back into the first chair and became the first domino in the row when I went down.

I was up by about the count of one, went for Nettles, and wrestled with him. I was thinking, Okay, let's get it on. Maybe the two of us should have done something like it a long time ago, just got it all out in the open and dealt with it.

But people began separating us, and by the time we got to our feet, it seemed there were 50,000 people in the vicinity.

Reggie and Graig are fighting!

The next voice you hear will be George Steinbrenner's.

He'd been down the hall, but when he heard the commotion and then found out it was Nettles and me, he tried the case very quickly. Steinbrenner's Court. Didn't even send it to the jury. Just issued a summary judgment.

"Goddamnit, Jackson! What the hell are you *doing?* You're disgracing me again. You're degrading the Yankees!"

I've mentioned that several times in my Yankee years I wanted to hold up a hand like a traffic cop and say, "Stop, George." This was one of them.

I said, "Not right now."

He looked at me.

"You should get out of here," he said.

I did that a few minutes later. Before we all left, I looked around for Nettles, but he was in another part of the room, surrounded by a lot of people. I felt foolish by then, but I figured we could get it worked out the next day.

We did, more or less. We sat together on the bus on the way to the airport, and I just told him, "Whatever we think about each other, fighting at cocktail parties isn't my style."

Nettles said it wasn't much his style either—he expressed embarrassment about it—and for the rest of the ride we talked about the Dodgers, since it was going to be one more Yankee-Dodger World Series.

It was to be the Series that the Dodgers turned the tables on us, and George Steinbrenner himself grabbed an end and helped.

The 1981 World Series was won by the Los Angeles Dodgers. I think it was probably lost by the New York Steinbrenner.

Here's how.

The calf muscle I'd hurt in the Oakland series got worse instead of better before the Series, and the decision was made to hold me out of the first two games. That would give me about five days of rest and therapy, and both Lemon and I assumed that I'd be ready when the Series moved back to Los Angeles for Game Three. I felt uncomfortable about that, but when we won the first two games rather handily, my leg felt a lot better and so did I.

After the second game, Lem came up to me and said, "Let me know when you're ready to go."

Me: "I'll be ready on Friday."

I didn't think anything more about it. Just assumed I'd be in there against Fernando Valenzuela, the kid screwballer for the Dodgers who'd been the sensation of baseball that year, the brightest, most exciting character in the strike season. I'd heard so much about Valenzuela, just like every other baseball fan in America. He was a lefty, of course, which meant that his screwball would be breaking *toward* me, like a right-hander's curveball. I couldn't wait to get into the Series, couldn't wait to get my licks against Valenzuela. The feeling on the team was that we were going to sweep the Dodgers—we *always* beat the Dodgers in the Series, right?—and I figured I could at least leave New York in style with a sixth Series ring to go with the three I'd won in Oakland and the two in '77 and '78.

I'd never played in a losing World Series, and I didn't think 1981 was going to be any different.

Wrong, Mr. October.

Dugout, Dodger Stadium, early Friday evening. Lem is sitting at the end of the dugout by himself. A lot of our guys are on the field. I hadn't looked at the lineup card. I never looked at the lineup card, right? But I figured I should touch bases with Lem, just out of courtesy.

I walked over to him.

"Just wanted you to know I'd ready to go, Meat," I said. "Man, I can't wait to get a shot at Valenzuela."

Lem just kept staring at the field. Wouldn't look at me.

"Ummm, I don't think you should play tonight, Reggie," he said. Not Meat. Reggie. For Lem, that was about as stiff and formal as he could get.

Trouble.

"What are you talking about?" I asked incredulously. I couldn't believe my ears. We had Dave Righetti going for us, and he'd been almost as spectacular as Valenzuela during the season; really, he'd been even better after the strike. Also Nettles, one of our big left-handed hitters, was on the bench; he'd wrecked his thumb in the second game. I thought there was no way Lem would want to have both Nettles and me on the bench, especially against a *screwballing left-hander* pitching in his first World Series game.

"Just to be on the safe side, I'm going to keep you out another day," Lem said.

"But I'm ready to go, Lem."

"One more day, Reggie."

End of conversation.

I went back to the other end of the dugout and sat down.

I couldn't lose my temper; you didn't do that with Lem. It was just going to be another time when I put the handcuffs on my emotions. So I sat there, and I kept my mouth shut, and I thought about what Lem had told me. He was holding me—*me*—out of a World Series game I was healthy enough to play in. I remembered what a nightmare it had been watching my first Series with the A's on crutches. I thought about all the numbers I had put into the books, numbers I thought no one would ever touch in October.

Then the light bulb went on.

Of course, it hadn't been Lemon talking to me at all.

It had been a different character, one the writers had already taken to calling "Lemonbrenner."

Goddamn George. He was going to show that the Yankees could damn well win the World Series without Reggie Jackson, and then he was going to send Jackson packing. He had messed with me, manipulated me, insulted me, tried to beat me down in every other month of the year. Now he was going to show Mr. October *in* October. He was going to put one last bullet into his ego gun and drill me right between the eyes. He must have been sure, so sure, that the Dodgers were going to curl up into the fetal position and die.

He wanted it to be the Series in which I was invisible.

The writers converged on me, and I tried to be as blasé about it as I could. Damned if I was going to give Steinbrenner the satisfaction of a public pout.

"I'm close to freedom now," was what I kept telling them. "No need to start anything now." Stuff along those lines. It was announced to the crowd before the game that I wasn't in the lineup because of an injury, and the crowd booed. They wanted to see me hit against Valenzuela as well.

I never got to hit against him.

The Dodgers didn't curl up into the fetal position.

We never won another game in the '81 World Series.

The tragedy—at least it's a tragedy if you're a Yankee fan—
is that we had Valenzuela on the ropes all during that third game.
He was in all kinds of trouble early, and when a great pitcher is in
trouble early, you've got to bury him. I've always been able to relate
to that. He was struggling, groping (he'd finish up allowing nine hits
and seven walks), and I would have had at least two at-bats in those
innings. I *know* I could have done *something.*

I sat. We ended up losing 5–4. Lemonbrenner wouldn't even
let me pinchhit. There were a couple of spots that cried out for me
in the late innings—in one of them Bobby Murcer *bunted* out into
a double play—but Lem never looked my way.

After the game I still wouldn't pout. Lemon joked with the
writers that he'd play me the next day because he didn't want me
to be mad at him. Of course I wasn't mad at him. He obviously
wasn't making out the whole lineup card. He was doing what he
was told.

Even if it meant blowing a World Series.

And I just kept thinking, This thing could be *over* now. I could
have won us this ballgame. Somehow. I could have put us up 3–0.

I joined the World Series the next afternoon. And I was
pumped. The adrenaline was rushing through my system so hard
I could hear alarms going off. The Dodgers couldn't have gotten me
out that day with a SWAT team. I went three-for-three with a
dinger, scored two runs, knocked in one and walked twice. I also
lost a ball in the sun in right, which helped the Dodgers to a run.
There was a lot of talk about it afterward, but most of the Dodgers
said that the field at that time of day is impossible, which was true.
It was the only bad fielding play I could remember making all year.

We finally lost 8–7. Now the Series was even. Afterward, I
couldn't get Friday night out of my mind. My brain held an "If"
festival. If I had gotten the chance against Valenzuela. If I had gone
three-for-three against him instead of the Saturday pitchers.

If we had gone ahead three games to none.

If George had not gone all the way over the edge, deciding he
could make out lineup cards in a World Series.

It became a blur of bad news and bad comedy after that. The
Dodgers beat Guidry on Sunday afternoon with a couple of late
home runs. George showed up with his hand in a cast—and a very
fat lip—Monday morning, saying he'd gotten into an elevator brawl
with a couple of drunk Dodger fans. He said they'd been bad-

mouthing New York and the Yankees. Said he had to uphold the honor of all of us by busting them up.

We all thought it was hilarious. On the flight back to New York, everybody wanted me to go up to George and interview him in my Howard Cosell voice—I happen to do one of the great Cosell imitations—but every time I walked near the front of the plane and looked at the cast, I started to get a laugh-attack, and I had a feeling George wouldn't be laughing along with me.

I figured one of two things had happened: Either George had been so frustrated he'd punched a wall, or else he'd *really* gotten into a fight. My one question about a fight, though: How come no lawsuit? 'Cause if I even *look* at somebody wrong, I get sued. He did have a fat lip, though, which you don't get punching a wall. But if this was a frantic attempt to motivate us, it wasn't going to work. The Series had gotten away from us. The Dodgers blew us out in Game Six—it was the one where Lem took Tommy John out for a pinchhitter, prompting that famous scene of Tommy walking up and down in the dugout, disbelief all over his face— and we were done. I didn't do much of anything the last game. Winfield, who in George's dreams was going to replace me as Mr. October, finished up a one-for-twenty-two Series. The Dodgers, who'd lost the last four games to us in '78, finally had their revenge.

The final irony had to do with Steinbrenner. Always he had screamed at us about embarrassing New York. Well, in those five October days in 1981, I think he had embarrassed himself most of all. Before we even left the clubhouse after the game, he had already issued his infamous statement apologizing to the city of New York for the Yankee loss.

When the writers asked me about the apology, I told them I didn't agree. I didn't care what George thought anymore. I now knew I had to leave to get away from him, even if I didn't want to leave the Yankees.

"I've got nothing to apologize for," I said. "You play hard, and you lose sometimes. I'm not apologizing to anyone. I've given my best since I've been here." Why not just be a pro and say the Dodgers beat us? Why make excuses? Be a man; stand up and say, "Hey, I did my best but someone else was better."

George Steinbrenner should have apologized for himself. No

one else. I had watched him play the fool for the last time, at least on my dime, anyway.

I rode to Yankee Stadium the next day to clear out my locker.

For all intents and purposes, it was the last time I would go there as a Yankee, and I knew it. And despite the fact that I knew it was time to go, there was a nostalgia about the day, a sadness. We had had ourselves a time.

It was a gray October day as I made the ride up Madison Avenue, the same ride I had made so many times over the five years, in good times and bad, sometimes driving faster than I should have because I couldn't wait to get to the park and get a bat in my hands, sometimes crying as I had that terrible day in 1977. I remembered all the summer days when there'd be groups of black kids on the corners as I got farther and farther uptown, into Harlem; they'd recognize the Rolls, and yell out my name, coming over and slapping me five through the open window when I stopped at a light on my way to the Madison Avenue Bridge. I remembered driving the same route the night I hit the three dingers against the Dodgers, hearing on the radio that Steinbrenner had sweetened Billy's contract and given him a raise. Lots of rides. To the House That Ruth built and that I'd helped keep filled.

I thought that day about having been a Yankee, and how even though we'd been the greatest show on earth, we'd made the image of the Yankees go wrong somehow. The Yankees are the most famous team in the world. Hell, the nickname for Americans is "Yankees." It's such a prestigious name, such an important name in its way because of the history attached to it. You can go anywhere in the world, and "New York Yankees" means something. You can talk about Red Auerbach and the Boston Celtics, and you can talk about the Dallas Cowboys, but they're not the Yankees. The Yankees were Ruth, DiMaggio, Mantle, Gehrig, Berra, Howard, Munson, Maris and Ford. I'm talking about *names.* You can make up an arbitrary list of the most famous athletes in the history of this country, and there'll be at least three Yankees near the top —Ruth, DiMaggio, Mantle—and probably four, because Gehrig belongs in there, too.

You can put my name on the list, but maybe with an asterisk.

I was grateful to have been a Yankee, will always feel that a part of me is a Yankee, but as I rode up Madison Avenue that day, I wished we all could have done it better.

I was grateful for the money, grateful for the fame, which then produced more money. I was black. I'd come from the most humble background possible, been born poor. I had climbed away from that and become wealthy beyond my wildest imagination, and the Yankees had had a lot to do with that. I will be making money from the Yankees for a long time. In that sense, it's difficult for me to paint Steinbrenner as a despicable person. The man hired me. The man paid me. We had a wild ride together.

I just wish he didn't have to negate what good he did all the time. He created money, he created jobs, he created interest, he brought the Yankees back from the grave. But he was always turning right around and destroying what he'd created. And it's a damn shame.

I don't think he's ever going to change, either. Too late for that. I was the least surprised person in the United States of America when he brought Billy back to manage for the 1983 season, and when he fired him after the 1983 season. The merry-go-round just keeps whirling. George keeps knocking people down as he grabs for the brass ring.

When I got to the clubhouse, I took my time packing. There were writers there, and I talked to them for a while. I shook hands with Pete Sheehy, the clubhouse man who was just a little bit younger than God. I chatted with some of the guys—Bucky, Cerone, Tommy John.

I told them I would see them down the road.

I walked out to the dugout and took one last look at the field. I knew I'd be back because I planned to stay in the American League, but I knew it wasn't going to be the same.

Dingers.

Dugout fights.

REG-gie.

Then I took the elevator upstairs to say goodbye to George M. Steinbrenner. It was business as usual in his office. He was flying off to somewhere or other. Bill Bergesch was there and Cedric Tallis, some of his p.r. people, secretaries. The frantic world of George. He asked me if I wanted to ride to the airport with him but I told him I was going to stay around New York for one more day.

One of the New York newspapers was on his desk. In it were stories about me *not* apologizing after George *had* apologized. George said. Reggie said. Et cetera. Et cetera.

George pointed to the paper.

Smiling.

"Same old stuff, right?" he said.

"Same old stuff," I said.

He asked me if I was all through downstairs. I said I sure was. He said, "Walk me down to my limo."

He said in the elevator that he'd be talking to me real soon about a new contract, that he'd be in touch with Gary Walker as soon as he got out from under all the end-of-season work he had. I just nodded. I knew he was bullshitting and so did he.

The limo was waiting near the big blue sign outside the Stadium that says, "Press." Long black stretch limo. First class for George always, from Reggie to cars.

We shook hands.

"I'll be in touch," he said, then he got into the car, and the car pulled away.

It's the last time I ever spoke to him.

23

AN ANGEL WITH A DIRTY BATTING AVERAGE . . .

So I was thirty-five years old going on thirty-six and between jobs. I was a free agent for the second time.

I went home to California and it was kind of sad. I'd been moving things back there really since July, 'cause that's about when I knew I was all through in New York. But the reality was hitting hard: The season was over. My New York ride had ground to a halt.

I was uncomfortable. Not positive I was going to be drafted by anyone. Concerned. Worried. I went to Carmel to try to relax, to get away from it all. I talked to Gary two or three times a day. He constantly badgered me about where I wanted to play and what kind of terms I wanted to play for.

I was tired. I was angry that I'd hit .237 in '81, that it had taken that physical for me to get with the program and start hitting the ball. I was angry about the way I'd been used in the World Series. I was hurt when I started hearing that Charlie Lau was going around saying I didn't even have one more good year left because I'd felt close to Lau.

Gary, much to my astonishment, kept telling me that not only should I continue to play, but I should continue to play for Steinbrenner in New York. We went round and round on that one after the season.

"You're too old to go through another sociological and psychological change," Gary said. "It's not worth it, you don't deserve it, it's a pain in the ass. Wherever you go, you're going to be on the spot. No matter how pretty a picture someone paints, you're Reggie Jackson, and you're going to get used a little and abused a little more wherever you play. Stay in New York. You proved over the last part of the season that you can handle the pressure if you set your mind to it. It's time for you to start thinking about maintaining some continuity in your personal life."

All I said was, "I don't want to go back there."

I said it more than once. It was time for me to move on. To grow somewhere else.

What Gary was really doing was cross-checking me. Before we went about the business of finding another team (the Yankees, Orioles, Angels, Braves, White Sox, Pirates, Rangers and Blue Jays had selected me in the November draft), he wanted to make absolutely sure that I wanted out of New York.

"And even if you don't want to play for the Yankees," Gary said, "I think we should keep George in the bidding because it will help. I'd like you to have just one meeting with him. Even with the bad times, it was an important relationship in your life, and there should be one more face-to-face confrontation, if only to sever the ties properly."

I told Gary, "George and I had our last face-to-face meeting in the parking lot at Yankee Stadium. I don't care if he does make an offer now, I don't care what he wants to do. I've been embarrassed by the man, been humiliated too many times. If I go back there, I'm turning my back on my principles. I think there's a part of George that thinks I will come crawling back, that he can dangle a few bucks in front of my nose and use the lure of the city and my off-the-field business associations to bring me back, just like he did five years ago. It won't work anymore. The only way I'd go back to the Yankees is if they're the only team that wants me."

I was thirty-five and I wanted to come home. I decided I wanted to play for the California Angels. If I'd been twenty-eight, still full of piss and vinegar, maybe I'd have gone to Baltimore. But I'd have gone for the wrong reasons. I would have done it to stick it to George and his Yankees.

Even though the Angels were clearly my first choice, I was glad that Ted Turner drafted me. I was glad the Yankees drafted me as well—they always throw the fear of God into the other owners financially. Turner doesn't throw that same fear into them because he doesn't really play the game. He's on a whole different level. If someone says, "Here's a nice new Chevy," Turner doesn't just say, "Here's a Rolls-Royce." He says, "Here's the entire dealership!"

But the action was starting and it was time to move on.

So Gary and I got out the Monopoly board, grabbed the dice, and started to play the baseball version of the game one last time.

I wasn't going to play in Chicago. I wasn't going to play in Pittsburgh, Texas or Toronto. I certainly wasn't going to play in New York.

In my mind, it was either going to be the Orioles or the Angels.

I talked to Ted Turner of the Braves, but I did that mostly for fun, because I was interested in getting to know him. A flamboyant millionaire, head of his own television empire, the first man to really understand the potential of cable. A yachtsman—unlike George, a sportsman, someone who played the game—he'd won the America's Cup. An owner who'd even managed a game with the Braves. I basically wanted to sit down with Ted Turner to see where the crazy ended and the genius began.

And there was always the chance that he might make me an offer I couldn't refuse. It was exciting to fantasize about what a colorful team the two of us would make.

We met once in Anaheim while I was there to meet with the Angels. Then we set up a dinner when both of us were going to be in New York about a week later. Turner asked where I liked to eat, and I said Jim McMullen's, of course.

It was about eight o'clock on a Wednesday night at McMullen's, a time when both the bar and the restaurant area of McMullen's look like they have more people than Yankee Stadium for a World Series game. I was about fifteen minutes late; Turner was waiting for me at a big round table in the middle of the room. McMullen's is not a dark place. It's quite bright and pleasant, all the better to see the Beautiful People I guess.

Anyway, Turner saw me before I saw him, as I was making my way through the bar crush.

Then I heard it.

"REG-gie! REG-gie!"

It was Turner.

"REG-gie! REG-gie!" Louder now. He was standing up, grinning a colorful grin under his mustache, clapping his hands rhythmically, and chanting my name.

That was Ted Turner's way of saying hi.

We sat there for the next four hours—Turner, me, Matt. And Turner was some piece of work from start to finish. He's a man of power, you can sense that, feel that, almost reach out and touch that, and you know that even when he's bullshitting you, he can back the bullshit up. He was animated that night as he rambled. He said outrageous things.

"I'd like to pay you a *billion* dollars, Reggie. I mean it. A billion goddamn dollars. I'd like to pay you a million dollars a year for a thousand years, or a thousand dollars a year for a million years, however you want it."

Sometimes he'd sprawl so far down into his chair only his face was visible above the table. Sometimes he'd lean all the way across the table when he was making a point, lay his head down, and look up at me. And he kept making these grandiose statements.

"Let's make history, Reggie. Let's make news! Damn, we'll make news every day. I'll give you a contract for $1.5 million for five years if you want. I'll give you your own television show on the Turner Network. I promise you, once you get to Atlanta, you'll never leave. You'll work for Ted Turner in one way or another for as long as you live. Turner and Jackson! Jackson and Turner! It will be unbelievable."

It was all fun watching this very wild, very crazy, very *rich* man give me his whole show at the middle table at Jim McMullen's.

He mussed his hair, he pulled his face, he took off his jacket, he drank some wine, he talked about ten subjects at once, he was hyper, he was hilarious, he was high-energy, he was wild. He was Ted Turner.

When we were done, I smiled at him and said, "I don't know if I'm going to come work for you or not, but we've got to get together and do this more often. You are not a dull date."

He was absolutely great.

I didn't need to be sold on the Baltimore organization because I'd been there, I'd seen it, I knew it was a high-class operation from top to bottom. Earl was still there. Hank Peters was still there. I had a soft spot in my heart for the Orioles because I'd had such an enjoyable season with them in 1976. And I knew they knew how to win. And they had Eddie Murray.

The only problem was geography. Baltimore wasn't in California, and the urge to go home was the fuel of that second free agency, that and the desire to prove to people that I was still Reggie Jackson.

With all that, Edward Bennett Williams damn near got me to sign with the Orioles. He was the owner then, having purchased the team from Jerry Hoffberger. Williams, one of the most famous legal minds this country has ever produced, is impressive. Very impressive.

To my mind, Edward Bennett Williams is a giant, a legal institution, a business institution, and possibly in the process of becoming a sports institution. He'd owned the Washington Redskins. Now he owned the Orioles. Even his name fits him: Edward . . . Bennett . . . Williams. EBW. He is a big man with great character lines in his face, and he has this way of focusing on you with an intensity, a sincerity, and a probing nature that keeps you on your toes at all times.

His law office in Washington, D.C., is something to see, an office that befits him. It's big, but it's warm. There is a bust of Vince Lombardi, who coached for him in Washington. There are pictures of him with John Kennedy and Bobby Kennedy and many famous people of this generation. There are plaques, and there are a ton of humanitarian awards. There are comfortable chairs and papers all over his desk at all times—the desk of a busy man, without affectation—and the whole picture just says that this is a solid individual. He's impeccably dressed. His secretary is a beautifully dressed woman, composed and adult. Everything just fits with this guy. But when he put his feet up on the desk the first time I was in his office, I noticed a hole in the bottom of his shoe and thought of Charlie Finley. I had to smile.

He did most of the talking over a couple of days. He talked about family and loyalty. He was sixty years old and he'd been in this extraordinary political and business environment his whole adult life, yet he wanted to talk about family. He told me he knew how interested I was in business and finance, and how when my baseball career was over, he'd like to get involved in that area of my life, help me reach the financial plateaus he assumed I was interested in, move in some of the economic circles he did. He told me he thought I could be a success in anything I tried; he said the only other sports figure he'd ever met about whom he felt the same way was Lombardi.

Ed Williams was mesmerizing me, not the way a hypnotist would, but with honesty and sincerity and the sheer force of his own personality.

"I want you to be a part of the Orioles world," he said at the end. "I want you to be a part of *my* world."

We shook hands.

I said, "I don't know what I'm going to do. I think you know how I feel about going home to California because I want to be close to Oakland, close to Carmel. You also know the warm feelings I have for Hank Peters and Earl. But whatever happens, I hope you and I can be friends for a long time."

It has worked out that way, and I am very proud to call Ed Williams a friend. I was thrilled when the Orioles won the World Series for him in 1983.

As much as I wanted to play for the Angels, the negotiations with Buzzie Bavasi, the Angels vice-president and general manager, dragged on for a couple of months. Buzzie kept telling Gary and me that he thought I really wanted to stay with the Yankees. I kept telling Buzzie that I didn't want to stay with the Yankees.

Buzzie: "That's not what I hear."

Me: "Where are you hearing that?" (He wasn't hearing it from G. Walker, and he wasn't hearing it from R. Jackson.)

Buzzie: "Here and there."

Here and there. Translation? George M. Steinbrenner.

Collusion is too strong a word for what was going on because that isn't Buzzie's nature. Buzzie is a big, amiable bear of a man who has been in baseball for forty years, much of that with the old Dodgers. He learned his front-office trade at Walter O'Malley's knee. And he was around in the Branch Rickey days. I like Buzzie enormously. I have also been called the fifth son of he and his wife Evit.

But he is a businessman, same as Charlie Finley was a businessman. He wanted to get me at a bargain basement price, and he also didn't want to make Steinbrenner mad if Steinbrenner still wanted me to come back to the Yankees with my tail between my legs.

See, they all have the same objective, all these people who either run baseball teams or own baseball teams. Ever since the inception of free agency, the powers-that-be have been trying to somehow drive the price of free agents down, and lately I think they've been succeeding. That's what the strike was about in 1981. The owners wanted to introduce heavy compensation into the system so teams might think twice about signing a Jackson or a Winfield or someone of that attractiveness and stature. They are all businessmen. They have to spend to stay competitive, but they don't want to spend a dime if they can get away with a nickel. They're all Finley at heart.

So Buzzie was nervous about competing with George, even though George no longer had any rights to me whatsoever. I was a two-time free agent, and there was no compensation whatsoever involved for the Yankees. (Later, though, Buzzie sold Butch Hobson to the Yankees. I'm sure that helped him stay on good terms with old George.)

I talked to Buzzie in California. I met him in Anaheim. I met with him in Phoenix and in Palm Springs. He kept going through his hem-and-haw number. Are you sure you're not still a Yankee at heart? Are you just using us as a negotiating ploy with George? Do you really want to come here?

Will you love me in May as you do in December?

Silly stuff like that. And all the while, he was telling writers that the Angels weren't really in the free-agent market. I wanted to tell Buzzie that if that was true, he was certainly beating the shit out of his phone bill for nothing.

Finally one day I called Buzzie from Hawaii, where I was doing the Hula Bowl for ABC. Buzzie said, "We're prepared to make an opening offer of $400,000 a year."

I didn't miss a beat.

"That's great!"

Buzzie was a little surprised because he knew what a ridiculously low offer he was making.

He said, "You mean it?"

And I said, "Absolutely. Buzzie, I've always wanted to just play home games."

Buzzie: "What do you mean, Reggie?"

Me: "That's a fine opening offer if you only want me to play home games. Of course, if you're going to want me to go on the road with the Angels, then we're going to have to make some adjustments."

"No, no, no," Buzzie started saying. "That's it, that's the whole offer."

I was having fun now.

"Oh, I see what you mean, Buzzie," I said. "You just want me to start playing in August, pick the Angels up, then go through the playoffs and the World Series. I've always wanted to do that, too. Hey, maybe that's why they call me Mr. October."

Gary and I had kidded for years about what fun it would be to just play ball at home and moonlight at another job. Now I was giving the joke to Buzzie, who was trying to be dead serious. He kept telling me to get serious, and I kept going on about home games and starting in August. I could just about see him shaking his head on the other end of the line. He just kept saying, "No, no, no."

I told him at the end of the conversation that if the Angels really wanted me, then he should come up with a real offer for real money and set up a meeting with Gene Autry, the Angels owner, the singing cowboy.

The meeting was set for Palm Springs, where Mr. Autry lives and where the Angels spend the second half of spring training after leaving Mesa, Arizona. Gary was there. Buzzie was there. Autry. Me. The four of us talked, then Gene and I went off by ourselves and effectively struck the deal.

He just wanted to know what kind of person I was and to see if I was worthy of the investment.

I have met successful men in baseball and in business. I have met loud geniuses like Finley and quiet geniuses like Hank Peters. I have sat across from high rollers like George Steinbrenner and true class like Edward Bennett Williams. Gene Autry is as important as any of them. His bank account is bigger than all the others put together. His name is important and has been since he was singing "Back in the Saddle Again." He is also one of the kindest, sweetest human beings I have ever met. He cares. He has made a fortune in real estate and radio stations and things like that. We even stay at the Gene Autry Hotel in Palm Springs during spring training. But he is still a cowboy at heart, with all those simple values.

We talked for an hour that day, about his philosophy of baseball and mine, about life, about the corporate world. I told him that if I signed with the Angels, this was going to be my last stop in baseball, and that I hoped someday I could move upstairs into the front office and work closely with him on building a successful team that would stay that way for years. In that famous, twangy voice, he told me that sounded fine to him.

"Gene," I said, "I'm at the point in my life where I no longer care if I'm the highest-paid member of a team. I know you've got Fred Lynn and Rod Carew. I'm not here to put your salary structure through hoops."

"Reggie," the cowboy said, "that is music to these old ears."

"What I would like," I said, "is to have the opportunity to be the highest-paid player if this team wins. If we get into the playoffs, if we get into the World Series, if we draw a lot of fans and you make money, then I'd like to have a piece of the pie. But if the team doesn't do well, if for one reason or another we have a bad season, then I don't want to have to justify to you—or to me—a contract that is guaranteed at a million and a half, something like that."

"That is as fair as I've ever heard an athlete be," Autry said.

By the end of the day, we had a four-year base contract of about $900,000 (options for two more). There was an attendance clause where I'd be paid fifty cents for every fan the Angels drew at home after they'd drawn 2.4 million. There were some playoff perks and home run perks, some tricks and bonuses (these were done with a handshake, by the way, because that's the way Buzzie wanted to do it).

The attendance clause got a lot of publicity that first year with the Angels because we drew over 2.8 million and I picked up an extra two hundred grand. It was Gary Walker's idea, by the way. His mind has never stopped working overtime.

I have to say publicly that Jackie Autry, Gene's wife, also helped convince me to sign with the Angels. When we met, she told me she thought I could help turn the image of the Angels around and that I was worth the money they were going to pay me. That made me feel awfully good. I was impressed as hell with what good people Gene Autry and his wife seemed to be. They seemed to care about their players the way parents care about their children.

After all the years and all the storms, after all the headlines and controversy, I had finally become an angel.

Capital "a," of course.

And there are now two things that motivate me while I'm playing baseball: my dad—and wanting to see Gene Autry in a World Series.

I called Gene Mauch, the Angel manager, as soon as I signed my contract. It was the phone call I'd never made to Billy Martin.

I wasn't sure how I was going to get along with Mauch. I knew he was very intense, very tightly wound, a tough man with cold, hard eyes and white hair who'd been manager of the Phillies and several other teams. He had a terrific reputation among baseball people and he'd managed twenty years in the big leagues. He had a reputation for having his team play a brand of ball—"Little Ball," he called it—that revolved around a lot of sacrifice bunting and playing for one run at a time. Earl Weaver had a romance with the home run; Mauch had a romance with the bunt. He had it in Montreal, in Minnesota, and with the Angels. It was not exactly Reggie Jackson's idea of textbook baseball.

I didn't care about any of that. I was thirty-five years old, I was delighted to be coming to California, I liked the makeup of the team (veterans and winners like Don Baylor, Bob Boone, Bobby Grich, Brian Downing, Fred Lynn, Rick Burleson, Doug DeCinces and Rod Carew). I didn't want any trouble. I just wanted to play well and make a third World Series with a third different team.

When I called Mauch, I said, "I don't want you to worry about what you may have heard about my attitude or my personality. I'm willing to do whatever you want me to do. I'll play right. I'll DH. It's your call, your team. You just point me in the right direction."

Mauch waited until I finished and said, "I don't need to hear anything like that."

I said, "Well, I've had some problems in the past, which you may have heard of . . ."

Mauch cut me off.

"Don't get me wrong, Reggie," he said. "I appreciate you calling me like this. But all I want you to do is play for me the way you did against me."

I thought that was a hell of a thing for him to say, and I didn't forget it. I respected him all season long. We had only one disagreement the entire year. Mauch liked to take me out of games in the seventh, eighth and ninth innings if we had the lead, putting young legs out in right in the form of Bobby Clark or Juan Beniquez, for defensive purposes. Most of the time it worked fine, and we'd go on to win. But sometimes the game would get tied up and there I'd be, folding and unfolding my hands on the bench, my evening's work over with the game still going on.

It went against my nature. One way or another, I've always wanted to be the bull in the ring.

After one game, I was in the middle of the clubhouse, and as Gene Mauch walked by, he shook my hand and said, "Nice game." Then he started to head for his office.

I held onto his hand.

"Gene," I said, "you've got to know I want to play. I want to be involved in the party when the game is over. I want to be out there when we win."

He gave me a *look*. Steely gray eyes that could bore a hole in you.

He said, "Look, this is my way of doing things. It's my way of giving you a rest and keeping you strong. You've got to trust me on this. I want you to be right there for me in September and October because this team is going all the way and I'm going to need you. Really. Trust me."

Maybe once this would have provoked a confrontation. Maybe in New York this would have built into something else, and then the something else would have built, and Gene and I would have been plastered all over the back pages of the tabloids for days. But this was a new time in my life, a more placid time, a more mature time. I respected Mauch. I wanted to get along with him. I was an Angel, and he was the Angels' manager.

I said, "I'll hold my opinion until the end of the year."

Of course, we won the American League West and came within a game of winning the pennant before blowing a 2–0 lead against the Brewers in the playoffs. After I hit the home run off Guidry in my return to the Stadium, I started to bash dingers all over the place; even though I had some tendonitis in my left hand in September, I was strong for Mauch throughout and wound up with thirty-nine homers, which tied me for the American League lead with Gorman Thomas. I also finished with a .275 batting average and 101 RBI. If I hadn't gotten off to such a coyote-ugly start, I believe I could have hit fifty home runs for Mauch, knocked in 120, maybe even hit .300. I also played in 153 games, the most since I played 157 in my last year at Oakland.

On the last day of the regular season, after we'd locked things up, I walked over to Mauch and said, "You were right. I was wrong. You handled me perfectly. Thank you."

Mauch grinned around a cigarette. A rare grin.

"I told you to trust me." Gene Mauch—good guy, good man, a baseball pro.

Baylor had a big year, leading the league in game-winning RBI. Burleson went down in April with a rotator cuff, but Tim Foli was there to step in and have a fine year. Downing, a Muscle Beach specimen who'd been converted from a catcher to a left fielder, batted leadoff for the first time in his life, hit twenty-eight homers and scored 109 runs. Carew hit his usual .319. Doug DeCinces had the kind of year they'd always predicted for him in Baltimore after he replaced Brooks Robinson: thirty homers, ninety-seven RBI, .301 batting average. DeCinces got some well-deserved MVP votes. Geoff Zahn pitched well all year long. Much to my delight, Tommy John came over from the Yankees in September and won four important games for us. Bob Boone, who'd come over from the Phillies, played 143 games at catcher, led the league in putouts and assists, and was a great team leader.

It was a calm, professional team filled with people who had won in other cities. That's why I was so surprised and disappointed when we could not slam the door on Milwaukee after winning the first two games of the playoffs at home. I really thought we were the best team in baseball. There is no doubt in my mind that we would have beaten the Cardinals in the World Series. I had always played for teams that just put the boot on the neck when they had you down. We did it in Oakland. We did it in New York. I thought we would do it in Anaheim, but there was something lacking after that 2–0 lead, an inability to get with the task at hand.

After we won the second game, I started hearing players saying things like:

"How soon will the party be when we get back?"

"Where will it be?"

"Will it just be for family, or for friends, too?"

A lot of family members made the trip east to Milwaukee. A lot of front-office people. I thought it was the wrong way for a supposedly hungry team to go about things. No one was putting enough emphasis on closing the Brewers out. There was a lot of World Series talk. It was "after" we win. Not "if" we win. We didn't read the "Beware of Dog" signs that were all around us. The dog was the Brewers, and the dog bit. At that point in the Series, we hadn't heard from Robin Yount. We hadn't heard from Cecil Cooper. We hadn't heard from Paul Molitor. I kept saying to some of the writers that we had to guard against getting overconfident because those Younts and Coopers and Molitors were due to stand up and be heard when they got back home to County Stadium, but no team had ever lost a playoff series after being up two games.

No one listened.

We lost the Series after being up two games.

When we got to Milwaukee, I stopped hitting. Just about everyone else on the team except Baylor and Lynn stopped hitting. The pitching fell apart. We went oh-for-the-weekend, and the Brewers went to the World Series instead of us. Gene Mauch got some heat for the way he used our pitching—he brought back Tommy John, who'd pitched the first game of the series, to pitch in Game Four, and Tommy didn't have it. But it was just one of those things where if it worked out, he was a hero, and if it didn't, he was a bum.

It was very frustrating for me. I had been excited about going to the Series with my new team. I wanted to win for Mr. Autry, I wanted to win for Buzzie, I wanted to see Gene Mauch win so he could get the monkey of never having won off his back. Maybe I wanted Steinbrenner to see Tommy John and me in the World Series wearing Angels uniforms. It had been such a storybook season for me personally after I hit the home run off Guidry and got my mind right and started swinging the bat.

It never occurred to me that it would end with three straight losses in Milwaukee. I was happy living in Newport Beach, I had made new friends, I could walk on the beach in the mornings. There hadn't been any fireworks, any headlines, any hard feelings in the clubhouse. I was at peace for the first time in years. Smiles were not forced; smiles just happened.

There was only one reminder of the way some people liked to perceive Reggie Jackson, and it came after the last game of the playoffs. I didn't know it at the time, but when I slid into third during that game, a piece of dirt had lodged itself underneath my eyelid. It didn't bother me over the rest of the game, in the clubhouse afterward, or at dinner that night. But I woke up in the middle of the night, and I couldn't see out of the eye. I felt like someone was sticking a needle into it. I had to go to the doctor in Milwaukee and have the dirt taken out, and he put a patch on it and said to check with my doctor in California. When I got back to California, I found out there was a slight scratch on the cornea.

When we arrived back at the Ontario Airport the next day, I had the eye covered with a patch, and Joe Ferguson, a teammate and a buddy, had to all but help me off the plane like a blind man.

The next thing I knew, people were calling me about some fight I'd allegedly had in a Milwaukee bar. Which of my teammates had popped me? That was the big question. Had it been Baylor? Did Baylor and I get into an argument?

I explained about the slide and the cornea, but they thought I was covering up.

The best story of all, I heard, was in New York. I had run into Ken Norton and tried to pick up his date, and Norton had drilled me. Ken Norton, as in the former heavyweight champ.

I finally just laughed and thought, Perfect. I was still fun for people, still created excitement even when there was no real excitement to be had, perhaps especially then. I still sold papers. There hadn't been any controversy all year, but they thought I was reverting back to what they wanted to perceive at the very end.

Well, I've got news for everyone. I'm out of fighting shape. I've retired from the ring.

.   .   .

Gene Mauch left after the '82 season, but he was replaced by old friend John McNamara. I was definitely excited about being reunited with John, who'd meant so much to me in Birmingham. He'd also managed the A's for a time while I was there, but Charlie got rid of him before we started winning, so I figured that this was going to be the year John McNamara got all the rewards he deserved. In my mind, I was going to hit fifty dingers for him, and we were going to win the World Series.

I hit fourteen dingers.

I knocked in forty-nine runs.

I hit .194.

Just about everyone on the Angels was hurt at one time or another, and we finished with a 70–92 record, tied with the Twins for fifth place, a cool twenty-nine games behind the Chicago White Sox at the end. I got to the World Series only because I was in the ABC broadcasting booth with Al Michaels, Howard Cosell and Earl Weaver.

Personally, collectively, any way you wanted to slice it, it was the worst season of my athletic career, at age thirty-seven. It stung. It hurt. It was frustrating. I didn't like it one damn bit.

But you know what?

I survived. And I'm looking forward to the next season, and the one after that. I'm entering this last phase of my baseball career with more perspective than I've ever had.

Maybe in another period of my life I would have blamed the season on a back injury, or pulled muscles, or the ribs I nearly wrecked running into a railing in Texas. I could say that every time I felt like I was starting to swing the bat well, I got hurt again. I could talk about the way the team fell apart and how it was difficult to find the motivation to pull myself up in a setting like that. I thought about all those thing during the first three or four months of the season, during which it became obvious that I just wasn't going to pull out of the dive this time the way I had so many times in New York. I spent a lot of sleepless nights trying to cope with the sort of failure that was totally out of my realm of experience as an athlete, amateur or professional. I couldn't eat. I had a mysterious fever in the middle of the season that lasted a month. I'd wake up sweating in the middle of the night. I had trouble communicating, even with people like Gary, Matt and Everett, all of whom were like brothers to me.

For the first time in my life, I felt like I wasn't earning my money. For the first time in my life, I went to the ballpark expecting *not* to play and being numb to that. I couldn't hit. Just could not hit.

Everywhere we went, I'd talk to other players about hitting, about hands, stance, striding, and pitchers. I talked to Carl Yastrzemski and George Brett. I talked to Hal McRae. I interrogated just about everyone on the Angels at one time or another. Burleson one day. Carew the next. Lynn the next. Boone the next. They all gave good advice, advice that sounded right, but my *mind* wasn't right. I'd try to fire the engine and simply couldn't do it. I came to the ballpark early and stayed late, and after a time it became almost comical because I was really thinking how difficult it was just to hit .200.

I was sometimes asking for advice from players who'd never come close to accomplishing what I've accomplished in baseball, and I was listening and nodding like a school kid, like it was algebra class and the teacher was going over this tough equation that I couldn't quite get.

I was embarrassed. Reggie Jackson couldn't even hit .200.

I kept telling myself, Well, Jack, you've had fifteen good years, and you had some bad times, but most of it was damn good. You've gotten a chance to see the top, Jack. All in all, let's face it: Baseball has given you a wonderful life.

But I never was very convincing. It's not my nature to succumb to anything so passively.

Then finally, as the season dragged on into August and September, I just stopped feeling sorry for myself. I was going to be a man, a pro, a Christian, a good human being. In the years when I was riding high, when I was hitting dingers at will and making the World Series every year like it was a clause in the Constitution of the United States of America, I'd never felt the urge to look up into the sky, beat my chest and scream, "Why me, God? Why are you being so good to Reggie Jackson?" I had survived a lot worse than this in my personal life. I had survived a lot worse when I was having a good statistical year with the Yankees in 1977. I could survive .194. This was no great tragedy. I would make it.

John McNamara, who was kind and considerate and supportive all year, even though he had other things to worry about, pulled me aside one day in September and said, "I'm taking you out of the lineup. Get ready for the winter and next season. I don't want you to hit under .200."

I said, "John, I'm gonna keep swinging until the last day. Maybe the last day of the season I'll have two good swings and find out something that I haven't been able to find out all year long."

At one time or another, almost every player on the team made a point of coming up to me in private and saying, "I respect the way you're handling this." Writers in all the cities said the same things. So did broadcaster friends like Frank Gifford, Don Meredith and Howard Cosell. It meant a lot to me. Maybe all the years of being Reggie Jackson had caught up with me.

Maybe I was emotionally whipped. But maybe I had finally grown up.

I've seen both sides of the coin now. I've hit three home runs in a World Series game, and I've hit .194, and maybe I'm a better person for having done both those things.

People are always asking me whether I think I'll make the Hall of Fame. I tell them, "I honestly don't know." I'd like to make it for what I've accomplished on baseball fields over the last sixteen years. I'm going to end up with 500 home runs. I've got the five World Series rings. I hold or share ten World Series individual records. I'd like to be remembered as a Hall of Famer, but ego-wise I really don't need to make it. I've lived the life of a king, and I feel fortunate and appreciative for what God has given me. If He doesn't intend for me to make the Hall, then I won't make it.

Still, I wouldn't have changed any of it, even the bad parts. If there's a Hall of Fame for living, baseball has given that to me.

I am grateful, is what I'm trying to say. I am closer to my mother now than I have been at any other time in my life. I've just bought her a home outside Oakland, and I'm going to be seeing a lot more of her. There is still time for us. Martinez is happy and healthy, with a new wife, Resurrecion, and a ten-year-old son named Marty. He has a tailor shop in North Philadelphia and another in Center City; he's become a celebrity in those places because he is Reggie's dad. I always thought he was a celebrity, from Wyncote on. My brother Joe is still in the Philippines, but his hitch there will be up soon, and I think he'll be coming back to the States. My sister Tina and her husband Tony Jones live in Oakland, and I see a lot of them because Tony manages some of my real estate holdings. Another sister, Beverly, is moving to Oakland soon. It's a family spread out, but family nonetheless.

I have Gary, Matt, Steven and Everett. I have a great affinity for women. They truly make the beauty of the earth. No man is complete without a girlfriend or wife. I have my beloved cars.

The future? After baseball? I'm not sure. I'm undecided as to which way I want to go in television, having become disillusioned over the past few years with the way I've been used by ABC—I don't think they've even begun to take advantage of my ability. I want to be careful which business opportunities I lend my name to. But those things will take care of themselves. They always have.

At the moment, I'm dealing with Marvin Davis and 20th Century Fox. They want me to become a member of the Fox family. It's very attractive to me because they are such a huge entertainment complex—they're into movies, TV, licensing, and Aspen real estate, and I hope that in the future I can get them involved in owning a few sports franchises. It's a one-man show—Marvin Davis is the show—which appeals to me.

I mentioned earlier that I thought there was a real gap between the rich and the poor. That's one of the things I'd like to become a lot more involved with. I think, for certain corporations, I can help bridge that gap. I can communicate with and relate to the man on the auto assemblyline, and I can just as easily deal with Jim MacDonald, the president of General Motors, or Ross Johnson, C.O.O. of Nabisco. I think there's a real corporate need for someone who can go both ways like that. It's a role that, though it clearly needs more definition, I'd like to explore further.

Right now I'm just thinking about having a good season in 1984. See, it's one more Reggie Situation now. Maybe the last big Reggie Situation. I've been knocked down, but I've gotten myself up, dusted the uniform off, and stepped back into the box. The pitcher thinks he's got me, and the crowd is cheering and wondering if I can produce one more time. And I'm trying to get my mind right, just like always.

I'm thinking about hittin' a rocket.

I can't wait to get it on.

During this past World Series between the Orioles and the Phillies, a friend of mine was talking with Bill Veeck, the old maverick who owned the Indians, the St. Louis Browns, and the

White Sox a couple of times, and who has been like a colorful history of the game across this century. I have always been an admirer of his. He's been an admirer of mine. He's past seventy now, still grinning, still loving the game, still limping around on his wooden leg. And he has seen it all.

My friend asked Veeck, "If you could have one last perfect day in baseball, if you could have anything you want, what would it be?"

Veeck said, "I'd like to see Reggie Jackson have one more great game in a World Series."

So would I.

So would I.

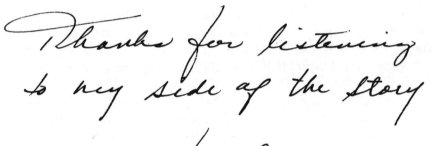

Thanks for listening to my side of the story

Live, happy &

laugh a lot

Reggie Jackson

About the Authors

REGINALD MARTINEZ JACKSON has houses in Oakland, Newport Beach and New York City. Between the months of April and October he can be found traveling around the country with the number 44 on his back. He has hit more home runs than any active player. In his fifteen-year career, he has been on three division winners, five world championship teams and one pennant winner. In addition to his baseball career, Reggie Jackson is the automotive editor for *Penthouse,* an announcer for ABC-TV, and spokesperson for Standard Brands and Panavision among many other companies.

MIKE LUPICA is the youngest writer ever to have his own column in a New York newspaper. His column now runs in the New York *Daily News* four times a week and on Sunday. Mr. Lupica is also writing a mystery novel for Villard—the first of a projected series.